D1414048

SHOW-
STOPPER!

G. PASCAL ZACHARY

SHOW-STOPPER!

The Breakneck

Race to Create

Windows NT

and the

Next Generation

at Microsoft

LITTLE, BROWN
AND COMPANY

A *Little, Brown* Book

First published in the United States of America by The Free Press, 1994

This edition first published in Great Britain by Little, Brown and Company 1994

Copyright © G. Pascal Zachary 1994

The moral right of the author has been asserted.

All rights reserved.
No part of this publication may be reproduced, stored in a retrieval system, or transmitted, in any form or by any means without the prior permission in writing of the publisher, nor be otherwise circulated in any form of binding or cover other than that in which it is published and without a similar condition including this condition being imposed on the subsequent purchaser.

Excerpt from "I Want a Little Sugar in My Bowl" by Nina Simone, copyright © 1962 and 1990 by Sam Fox Publishing Co., Inc., Santa Barbara, CA. All rights reserved. Used by permission.

A CIP catalogue record for this book
is available from the British Library.

ISBN 0 316 91113 5

Printed and bound in Great Britain by Mackays of Chatham, PLC, Chatham, Kent

Little, Brown and Company (UK)
Brettenham House
Lancaster Place
London WC2E 7EN

TO

HONORAH CURRAN

CONTENTS

INTRODUCTION

David N. Cutler, wearing white Reeboks, white pants and a T-shirt bearing the legend OVER THE LINE, bursts into the Build Lab and takes stock of the largest, most complex program ever created for a personal computer.

It is 10:20 in the morning, and the latest "build" of the program, called Windows NT, is hours late. Cutler, the leader of the team making NT, is angry about the delay, angry about a botched test the day before, angry at the world. He knows that nothing slows progress more than a steady accumulation of small lapses, and he is bent on pushing ahead.

Cutler insists on frequent builds, or samples, of NT so that his 250 programmers can "eat their own dog food." It is a frustrating experience, not unlike building a house from scratch while living in it. The sooner a build arrives, the sooner his team will test their latest creation, discover its imperfections and improve it.

Scowling, Cutler now slumps into a swivel chair and glares at the computer screen before him. He hits a few keys and groans.

Cutler's unhappiness is contagious. Three builders, who stitch together NT with the aid of computers, hover behind Cutler, busying themselves while Cutler churns. One, a shoeless and jittery young man, juggles three rubber balls. He is surrounded by dozens of computers. The voice of Aretha Franklin, romping through

"Dr. Feelgood," fills the room from the stereo speakers mounted on the wall.

No fan of juggling or Aretha, Cutler growls. He jumps to his feet, flinging the chair behind him, and storms out of the lab. The shoeless juggler and the chief builder dip into a big jar of Rolaids, popping one each. The day has soured early.

Minutes later, Cutler returns to the Build Lab even more upset. His bowlegged gait and burly arms remind people of Popeye. "You're wasting the whole goddamn morning not having this goddamn thing ready," he snaps. Then, sounding dejected, he tells the juggler, "Call me if you ever get this [build] out today."

His face reddening even more, Cutler leaves again, steaming. His rough creed forbids him from containing his emotions. "The way you let off stress is to let it out," he says. He isn't too particular about how he does it. A circle drawn on the wall near the door marks the spot where he once unleashed a violent kick, cracking his toe. Just the other day, he smashed a wall with his fist, which ordinarily would not have caused a stir except that this time he hit a stud and broke a finger.

Cutler's impatience is ill mannered but understandable. Time means everything to him now. He is a year behind schedule, and after years of work his team is tired and frustrated. Only the enormity of their goal sustains them now. The 250 members of the team aim to produce a computer program so powerful and versatile that someday everyone will need it. Standing in their way are thousands of bugs, or coding errors, and persistent doubts about the basic design of NT, which stands for "New Technology."

Rather than a single entity, NT consists of scores of intertwined programs that together comprise an *operating system*. This software turns a personal computer into a precise tool of thought, helping a person or an organization control its most valuable asset: information. NT exerts its power through a dizzying succession of ordinary actions. Seemingly at once, it may open a computer file, move text or graphics from one place to another on a screen, print a letter, calculate a row of numbers and keep several word processors, spreadsheets and other applications from getting in each other's way. NT's most profound benefits are hidden. Its invisible acts sustain a computer much as unconscious acts—taking a breath, blinking an eye, hearing a sound—sustain a human life.

NT is alarmingly complex. Consisting of six million lines of code, the program is among humanity's most intricate handiworks. "No one mind can comprehend it all," Cutler says.

A system as complicated as NT requires a rich patron. In William H. Gates, NT has one of the richest. Gates is cofounder and chief executive of Microsoft Corp., the world's largest software maker. With NT, Gates seeks to extend his software dominion from desktop software, which he monopolizes, to the network. In the 1980s, Microsoft's DOS and Windows system software defined the way most people worked with computers. In the 1990s, the company aims to define the software that electronically ties together workers and businesses, consumers and homes. The making of NT, Gates hopes, will be the first step toward realizing this grand dream.

Gates also intends to bring full circle the computer revolution of the past half century. NT marks the latest chapter in the decades-long push to free software from the clutches of hardware. Until now, the structure of a computer determined the shape of its software. If a certain type of computer died, the software died with it. NT puts software at the center of computing, lending programs some universality by letting them take advantage of the best computers available—and to survive even after their chosen hardware dies.

The making of NT is at once a primer on software, a portrait of a community of programmers and a gritty melodrama about the perilous task of managing complexity in an age of information. As people and machines come to depend wholly and unreservedly on computers for everything from air traffic control to medical diagnostics, good code is crucial to the smooth running of a society. And writing good code is increasingly the work of large teams. Yet such teams often sink into mediocrity because their size alone can breed bureaucracy and sterility. The challenge for every large team is to organize its diverse talents while encouraging leadership and flexibility.

Cutler excels at this balancing act; he is uniquely suited to bring Gates's dream to fruition. A star player and a star coach rolled into one, he sets priorities, writes crucial pieces of code and reviews the work of others. But the price of his leadership is stark. Most of his followers live one-dimensional lives: Work pervades their existence. Friends fade into the background. The ties of marriage fray or rip apart. Children are neglected or deferred. Hobbies wither. Computer code comes to mean everything. If private dreams are nursed at all, it is only to ease the pain of creating NT.

Those who fight against immersion in Cutler's world—and some stubbornly do—risk incurring their leader's wrath or, worse, losing his respect. Those who succumb to his will are amply rewarded, earning millions of dollars in Microsoft stock bonuses. Yet even these workers are not exempt from the insecurity of the workplace. The pace of technical change and the pressure of competition lend a do-or-die quality to their jobs. They pour their entire spirit into work because there is no alternative.

Cutler embodies the sobering side of today's workplace. He rejects the distinction between work and leisure, job and family, home and office. The very harshness of his ethic strangely intoxicates his acolytes. He presents a world in which great deeds occur against a bleak backdrop. The enemies are laziness, confusion and incompetence. Each member of the team hungers to transcend his own frailties. "Our work is really, really hard," Cutler says. "Years from now people on the team are going to look back with pride. They will say, 'Never before did I accomplish so much or was my life so simple. I didn't have to worry about my career or my happiness or whether I got along with my boss or my friends. I had only one concern—to ship this product. And to make it as good as I could.'"

When he first conceived of Windows NT, Cutler only dimly saw the path ahead. Building this most complicated of all PC software programs took him and his loyalists deep into the digital wilderness. For a time, it seemed as if they might never emerge whole from their adventure. Some lost pieces of themselves along the way. Others saw the arc of their lives cross the blurry border that marks the known from the unknown. And in the end, they grasped that every worthwhile creation is at once an act of love and an act of violence.

This is their story.

1. CODE WARRIOR

Dave Cutler was reared on adversity. He learned at a young age to care for himself, to keep his own counsel, to find a way around or through the obstacles in his path.

He was born on March 13, 1942, in Lansing, the state capital of Michigan. Lansing was auto country, home to a slew of car and car-parts makers. His father, Neil, worked in Lansing's Oldsmobile plant for nearly his entire life, first in the plant's shipping department and then as a janitor.

Neil Cutler was an intelligent and exacting man, but he was quiet and lacked ambition. He had been stricken with rheumatic fever as a boy, and it had left him too frail to play sports. Poor eyesight made it difficult for him to enjoy the outdoors. A certain bitterness crept into him. He was not sociable; he struck some as almost a hermit. At home, he could be unpredictable, angry and gruff. He drank.

Arleta, Neil's wife, raised her son Dave and his older sister, Bonnie, in an apartment above the home of Neil's parents in DeWitt, a town of some one thousand people about eight miles north of Lansing. DeWitt was surrounded by farmland and consisted mainly of retired farmers who had moved off their farms and into the town. When Dave was eight the Cutlers moved out of town to a forty-acre spread. The land wasn't suitable for farming and did not contain a dwelling. Neil built a small home, one side of which was literally carved out of the earth. By then Arleta had given birth to two more children. The family seemed to spend all its time together in one large room. Arleta kept a large garden, and the family planted pine trees on the land. In time thousands of trees took root and grew.

From the age of ten David Cutler earned money whenever he could. He mainly worked during the summertime for the many farmers in the area, building barns or doing odd jobs. One summer, he worked in a fertilizer plant. Another year he collected old newspapers with a friend, filling an entire trailer for sale to a recycler.

As a teenager, Cutler was drawn to sports. With a graduating class of thirty-four students, his tiny high school pressed him into service. He ran track and played baseball, basketball and football. He was co-captain of the basketball team and the quarterback of the football team. In one game, he ran for two touchdowns, running almost the entire length of the field for one score. He was very fast.

The local newspaper treated Cutler as a star, chronicling his exploits. Neil skipped nearly all of his son's games; it took a personal invitation from the football coach for him even to consider attending the one game during his son's senior year in which every player's father was introduced. Neil (who went) said he disliked sports, but Arleta suspected that jealousy had kept her husband from the sidelines.

Father and son were distant. While still in high school, Cutler moved out of his parents' home for a time, living first with the family of a baseball coach and then with Bonnie. At school, meanwhile, Cutler did well enough without studying hard. Graduating in June 1960, Cutler seemed serene about his prospects. Somewhere inside him sprang a confidence bordering on arrogance and a belief that he could be the best at anything he tackled. Others shared Cutler's buoyant sense of himself. In his high school yearbook, classmates captured his specialness in a line beneath his photograph:

"None but himself could be his parallel."

A small Michigan college called Olivet cobbled together several athletic and academic scholarships, offering them as a package to Cutler. He signed on. His freshman year, he started at quarterback, calling and directing his own plays just like a pro. He threw the ball well and ran one hundred yards fast—in less than eleven seconds. He was about five feet nine inches tall, weighed about 175 pounds and had thick, strong legs. His coach, Stu Parsell, called him "a one-in-a-million player" and marveled at his elusiveness. Cutler was a wily player who confessed he "loved to run over people."

In the huddle, Cutler smartly dished out assignments in between plays. He brooked no dissent, berating teammates for their lapses and telling them: "This huddle is my territory. When you're in it, shut up." When players "screwed up," he said, "I'd really ride them, telling them what to do . . . to get out there and do their job."

Coach Parsell realized that Cutler relied on more than athletic skills. "He was smart enough to know he couldn't win alone," Parsell said. "He brought the other players up with him. They rose to him." The team responded to his brash assertions because Cutler led by example and "knew what he wanted."

Cutler's game peaked in his sophomore season. The long-suffering Olivet Comets, who had lost twenty-one games in a row in the late fifties, suddenly went white-hot in the fall of 1961. With Cutler at the helm, the team won its first eight games. Then, in its final game, disaster struck. Midway through the game, Cutler took the snap from the center and rolled right, preparing one of his quarterback rushes. He had already scored that season on just such a gambit. This time, he was in the clear, running full tilt along the sideline, right along his team's bench, so close that Coach Parsell could have grabbed him. Then a defender charged toward him, hurling his body in Cutler's way. Cutler tried to jump over him, but the defender smacked him squarely. He crumpled to the ground, his leg broken, his season over.

Cutler tried to return the next season, but on the eve of the opening game a doctor told him he risked permanent injuries if he played on. Cutler reluctantly withdrew.

With the end of his football days, Cutler concentrated on his studies. He excelled in math, dabbled in the sciences but finally decided to pursue engineering. When he graduated in January 1965, he was offered a job programming computers for General Motors. Along with other big companies, GM had begun shifting its business records from paper to computer in the 1950s. But Cutler was not eager to join GM. He knew nothing about computers, which seemed vaguely threatening—even sinister—to him. In the mid-1960s, many people shared this dystopian view of computers. These machines, which were designed to crunch numbers, were treated with skepticism and sometimes hostility because they symbolized regimentation. Computers seemed to bend humans to their will, forcing men and women to do little more than tend smart machines.

This gave a bad reputation to computers and the task of writing programs for them. Hardly anyone wished to call himself a programmer, and people who did were considered odd. Just a few years before Cutler graduated from Olivet, the top programmer in the Netherlands, an erstwhile physicist, described himself as a programmer on his marriage license. To his dismay, authorities rejected the license on the grounds that there was no such job.

Alert to signs of esteem and status, Cutler held a "very stereotyped view of programmers." To a young man, raised in relative penury and intent on making his way up the economic ladder without kowtowing to authority, programming "seemed a very uncreative job"; and those who did it followers of "this fixed bunch of rules," not leaders who called their own plays.

He wanted no part of software and turned General Motors down flat. Instead he took a post with DuPont. He adapted easily to the conservative and prosperous chemical giant. He kept his hair short and maintained a military bearing. He thought first of earning his keep; he had married a woman he'd met in college, and had already fathered a child.

DuPont assigned Cutler to a unit that helped customers find uses for its materials. One of his first jobs was to model a new way that Scott Paper intended to make foam insulation for use in jackets and other garments. The model was so complicated that it required a computer to create. Off Cutler went to a school run by IBM, where he learned how to program an IBM computer.

Cutler spent a week at the school. He felt humbled. Programming "was just the most bizarre situation, because you're used to doing something and thinking you've done it right," he later said. "But it isn't right. You just don't notice it isn't right. On a computer there is no consolation in discovering you're almost right. Almost means you're still just wrong."

Even veteran programmers often found their jobs excruciatingly tedious. In those days, no one had his own computer, of course. Dozens of programmers would share a single mainframe computer. The mainframe, large enough to fill a room, handled many jobs at once in batches. In batch jobs, a programmer punched instructions onto perforated cards, added a stack to the queue and waited for results. Since the mainframe was so expensive, the batch schedule was strict. It often took hours or longer to learn the fate of a program. If it failed, a programmer could spend an entire day just correcting keypunch errors.

Cutler returned to DuPont determined to excel at programming. The activity intrigued him because, in a program, he was master of his environment. He also found he had a rare ability to hold in his mind at once the various and far-flung pieces of a program. He began to crave programming. Impatient with the long lines in DuPont's computer facility, he worked in the middle of the night, when computer time was much cheaper and he could assemble and revise his cards in peace. "There was hardly anybody there," he recalled. "I could make twice as many mistakes, and get on and off the computer when I wanted to."

Foam making, by contrast, did not keep Cutler awake at night. In less than a year, he had succumbed to the attraction of computing. Having found in the computer the ideal means to answer a question, he promptly lost interest in the question and fell blindly in love with the tool. Indeed, Cutler had found a calling in life. "What I really wanted to do was work on computers, not apply them to problems."

So Cutler, looking for a new job that involved programming, found one with another DuPont division that needed help in maintaining its central computer, which was made by Univac. In the 1950s Univac made the best computers for data processing, but by the late 1960s the company was in decline. DuPont asked Cutler to improve the reliability of its aging Univac, which meant fiddling with the machine's operating system. Until then Cutler had never even thought about operating systems. But the company's computer experts seemed not to know much either, and he jumped in.

Computer programs fall into two rough classes. Applications, or "apps" for short, are the visible world of software. They comprise the programs used by ordinary people. Applications track orders or inventory, retrieve names and phone numbers, prepare a document for printing or control the design of a newsletter.

Operating systems, on the other hand, are part of the invisible world of software. They are the computer's heartbeat, throbbing in the background. Applications may appear to do all the work, but in reality operating systems open and close files, create directories of the stored information and direct the traffic to and from the computer's input, output, storage and networking devices.

In the formative years of digital computing, following World War II, both the operating system and applications were considered afterthoughts by designers. The "hardware" of electronics, as distinct from the "software" of programs, was so difficult that engineers could hardly see past it. The most important type of hardware was the circuitry or processors that actually carried out the instructions given the computer. A second set of devices made it possible to get data into and out of a computer. A third class stored information. A fourth class allowed one computer to send information to another, over special cable or telephone lines.

The question of software generally arose only after the hardware pieces fell into place. Computers were not designed with specific software in mind; rather, the programmer worked with what the hardware gave him. E. W. Dijkstra, a leading theorist of programming, once summarized the prevalent attitudes toward code writing in the formative period of computing. He declared:

What about the poor programmer? Well, to tell the honest truth, he was hardly noticed. For one thing, the first machines were so bulky that you could hardly move them and besides that, they required such extensive maintenance that it was quite natural that the place where people tried to use the machine was the same laboratory where the machine had been developed. Secondly, the programmer's somewhat invisible work was without any glamour: You could show the machine to visitors and that was several orders of magnitude more spectacular than some sheets of coding. But most important of all, the programmer himself had a very modest view of his own work: his work derived all its significance from the existence of that wonderful machine. Because the machine was unique, he knew his programs had only local significance. And since the machine would live for a short time . . . he knew that little or none of his code held lasting value.

The essence of programming seemed deceptively simple. A person wrote a request to a computer. This request was stated in a way the computer could understand. It also was stated, ultimately, in terms that only a specific computer could understand. The same request, written exactly the same way, fed to a computer with a different design or circuitry, would be unintelligible.

Besides being handmaidens of a specific computer, the first computer programs were crude. Before World War II, when computers were largely mechanical, a program often amounted to nothing more than a person flipping switches, rerouting wires or shifting gears. In the 1930s, it took many days to prepare the Differential Analyzer, the decade's most powerful mechanical computer, to attack a fresh problem. A decade later, it still could take a few days to set up an early digital computer to answer a tough question.

More flexible machines read requests contained on punch cards or paper tape, but these were fed by hand into a machine. The primitive state of programming cried out for an advance.

The breakthrough came in 1944 when John von Neumann, a Hungarian-born mathematician living in the United States, advanced the concept of a stored program. The idea was familiar to others in the field, but von Neumann saw its significance most clearly. With a stored program, the instructions for the computer could be kept in the machine's own memory and treated in the same way as data. This would make it far quicker to launch a program and easier to modify it or switch from one program to another.

As the stored-program concept spread throughout the nascent computer culture, programming exploded, quickly gaining adherents. It was hard going. Digital computers have either two states, on or off, and so respond only to binary messages, which consist of ones (on) and zeros (off). Every term in a program ultimately must be expressed through these two numbers, ensuring that ordinary mathematical statements quickly grow dizzyingly complex. In the late 1940s, programming a computer was, as one observer put it, "maddeningly difficult."

Before long programmers found ways to produce binary strings more easily. They first devised special typewriters that automatically spit out the desired binary code. Then they shifted to more expansive "assembly" languages, in which letters and symbols stood for ones and zeros. Writing in assembly was an advance, but it still required fidelity to a computer's rigid instruction set. The programmer had to know the instruction set cold in order to write assembly code effectively. Moreover, the instruction set differed from computer model to computer model, depending on its microprocessor design. This meant that a programmer's knowledge of an assembly language, so painfully acquired, could be rendered worthless whenever a certain computer fell out of use.

By the early 1950s, organizations that relied heavily on computers, most notably the three branches of the U.S. military, began to realize that software was a headache, and an expensive one. Leading-edge programmers searched for ways to make it easier to write effective programs. In 1951, Grace Murray Hopper, a mathematician with the U.S. Navy's Bureau of Ordnance Naval Reserve, conceived of a program called a compiler, which translated a programmer's instructions into the strings of ones and zeroes, or machine language, that ultimately controlled the computer. In principle, compilers seemed just the thing to free programmers from the tyranny of hardware and the mind-numbing binary code.

Hopper's insight spawned countless efforts at simplifying code writing. Probably the most important came from IBM which built a compiler called Formula Translation, or Fortran. It contained thirty-two instructions, such as PUNCH, READ DRUM and IF DIVIDE CHECK, which referred to the precise binary terms required by the computer. By the late 1950s, Fortran was hugely influential. "Now anyone with a logical mind and the desire could learn to program a computer," one historian of computing has written. "You didn't have to be a specialist, familiar with the inner workings of a computer and its demanding assembly language. By using Fortran's simple repertoire of commands, you could make a computer do your bidding, and the compiler would automatically translate your instructions into efficient machine code."

While Fortran enabled a programmer to use the same set of instructions to program any number of computers, the resulting programs often required changes to run on different machines. Moreover, Fortran was geared toward scientific and engineering problems. Other languages, such as Common Business-Oriented Language (Cobol, for short), sprang up for other purposes. Before long, programmers confronted a jungle of computer languages, and the course of their careers was often decided by the one they chose to learn best.

Hopper was convinced that overcoming the difficulties posed by proliferating computer languages would rank among the greatest technical challenges of the future. "To me programming is more than an important practical art," she said in a lecture in 1961. "It is also a gigantic undertaking in the foundations of knowledge." Ironically, she fretted that the greatest barrier to progress might come from programmers themselves. Like converts to a new religion, they often displayed a destructive closed-mindedness bordering on zealotry. "Programmers are a very curious group," she observed.

They arose very quickly, became a profession very rapidly, and were all too soon infected with a certain amount of resistance to change. The very programmers whom I have heard almost castigate a customer because he would not change his system of doing business are the same people who at times walk into my office and say, "But we have always done it this way." It is for this reason that I now have a counterclockwise clock hanging in my office.

In the early 1960s, IBM attempted to revolutionize the field of software by making it possible to run the same program on any number of computers. IBM proposed a family of machines, covering most of the market and controlled by one operating system. The System/360 line, developed at a cost of five hundred million dollars, was a huge success. But its birth was painful, mainly because the cost and difficulty of creating the software was grossly underestimated. It wasn't until five years after the first 360 hardware was introduced in 1964 that all of its software ran well. By then, IBM had spent nearly as much writing the software as designing the hardware. This astonished the company's managers and vividly highlighted "the greatest impediment to advances in computer technology," the problem of managing large software projects.

At DuPont, Dave Cutler found himself on the front lines of the effort by big business to tame the computer. The growing standardization of operating systems greatly improved the usefulness of computers. But much of the burden for writing applications still fell to the purchasers of computers themselves. This had the unintended effect of turning large companies into breeding grounds for programmers. DuPont asked Cutler to create a program to analyze experimental data from its labs. The job was tricky because it required two computers working in tandem. One would receive data, put it in a file and then ship it to the second computer, which would analyze the data and send results out to researchers.

The desired program was called a "real-time" system, which enabled a computer to receive information and respond immediately rather than within hours or days. The first real-time system had been created for the Whirlwind computer the Air Force and Navy used to track enemy aircraft and direct U.S. attack planes to their targets.

Real-time programs were a valuable innovation. To a company such as DuPont, trying to find new materials and uses for them, fresh answers were far more helpful than delayed ones. DuPont wanted Cutler's programs to run on small, fast computers from Digital Equipment Corporation. Formed a decade earlier by a Whirlwind engineer, Digital was a rising star among minicomputer suppliers, who broke sharply with tradition. In the past, computer designers had promoted large mainframes that shared their power between many jobs. Minicomputers, often priced well below a hundred thousand dollars, made it practical for the first time to dedicate a computer to a single job, such as keeping track of parts, the data for an experiment or the operation of a machine tool.

Though useful, minicomputers such as Digital's PDPs typically arrived with little software. Buyers usually had to create their own. Over the next few years, Cutler wrote his real-time program and other PDP software, becoming an expert in Digital code.

But Cutler grew tired of DuPont. He wanted to work for a computer company, and he chose Digital. The company, by exploiting a hole in IBM's product line, was not only growing rapidly but eschewing conventional business practices. It avoided acquisitions and housed Digital's employees in an abandoned mill outside Boston, in Maynard, Massachusetts. Rather than enforce the top-down style of management embraced by IBM, Digital allowed engineers to run with their own ideas, even at the risk of duplication.

Cutler was eager to write software for Digital's computers—so eager that a casual meeting with a Digital salesman led to a job interview with the company. Digital, its hardware proliferating, needed strong code writers. Cutler fitted the bill. In 1971, at the age of twenty-nine, he took a job with Digital and moved to Massachusetts.

Cutler took Digital by storm. Before long, he was ranked among the company's software stars and given his own team of code writers. He was completely absorbed in his work. By then, his first marriage had broken up and his second was headed toward the shoals. He was, by his own admission, no family man. When he finally split up with his second wife, he vowed never to marry again. "Marriage is a mistake you only make twice," he said.

Cutler was the classic programmer. He was single-minded, obsessive and competitive. He had great stamina and confidence. He paid tremendous attention to details. And he kept getting better at designing and writing code. "Most people learn one neat thing and spend the rest of their life doing it," a colleague observed. "Not Cutler. He learns from his successes. He does the next one better. And every time he gets to another level. That's just astonishing, because so many people who succeed in technology never repeat it." Moreover, his very single-mindedness—beyond his software assignment at hand, he displayed no other intellectual passions—was a boon: "He not only ignores anyone and anything that might interfere, he denigrates them."

Cutler turned insults into an art form. Volatile and stubborn, he could be all brass and bravado, unconcerned with even the most mundane courtesies. He lost his temper, issuing a stream of profanities at the slightest provocation. Each new outburst burnished his legend. Strangers suffered most. A woman engineer once first met

Cutler in a room full of printers, where he was fumbling with crumpled and twisted sheets of paper. She looked at him expectantly as he glanced her way. Then Cutler shouted: "Are you the fuckhead that screwed up the printer?"

Though he impressed no one with his manners, Cutler won praise for his role in building a series of real-time operating systems for Digital's PDP-11 computer. He excelled at the tricky task of squeezing a program into a smaller space. This was crucial, since the smaller the program, the faster it would run and the less computer memory it would consume. Cutler made plain his desire for compact code by keeping a rubber stamp on his desk that bore the motto: Size Is The Goal. When he thought a programmer wanted to add a feature that too greatly increased the demands on memory, he would use the stamp on his rejection memo. The stamp made programmers more careful about adding to their code and provided a source of jokes. Soon, the phrase "Thighs Is The Goal" was prominently displayed in the men's room.

To his crew, Cutler was a hero, a superman exempt from the ordinary rules. "He makes you feel you're one of his partners in greatness and that you will never have a better, more trustworthy ally," one said. Cutler expected everyone to perform flawlessly. To convey an urgent message, he'd call a huddle. He enjoyed teasing his mates but went to any lengths to improve the quality of their code. Sometimes, he even retrieved code thrown in the trash, corrected it with his red pen and returned the code to its author.

Not only could Cutler be stern and unfeeling, he expected absolute candor from his team. "If you try to snow him, if you try to deceive him, he'll be ruthless," one colleague said. "He won't just let you hang yourself, he'll attack. And he doesn't forget."

He was tight with praise too. Roger Heinen, one of Cutler's favorite programmers, often ached for a kind word from his mentor. "When you're out there and drop the ball, he is quick with criticism," Heinen said. After weathering such an attack, Heinen wondered if Cutler still valued him. Too afraid to ask, he would reach inside his desk for a note that Cutler had written him sometime before. The note said simply: "Roger, you really did a good job. Thanks, Dave."

A powerful patron made it possible for Cutler to flourish at Digital. Early on, his careful coding and driven leadership caught the notice of Gordon Bell, Digital's top engineering executive and the designer of its most important computers. A rare combination of technical genius and strategic savvy, Bell joined Digital in 1960 at the age of twenty-six after studying at MIT. He spent the next fifteen years "guiding, arguing, fidgeting and creating the computer strategies that [turned Digital into] IBM's strongest challenger."

Engineers were drawn to Bell, a warm and animated man. His short attention span was both endearing and aggravating. His mind would wander so much that those who really needed to speak with him tried to isolate him from distractions. "To talk to Gordon you had to take him in the car, drive and not let him turn on the radio," one said.

By early 1975, Bell saw Digital losing steam, despite its impressive financial results. The PDP-11 computer was then five years old, and IBM was on the verge of introducing its first true minicomputer. Bell felt Digital needed a much-improved machine to retain its lead over IBM. Over the winter, he conceived of a new line of computers that he felt would keep Digital ahead of its rivals in minicomputers while at the same time satisfying those customers who had invested heavily in the PDP-11. The new computer line, called the Vax, would run a new operating system, known as VMS, which would make it possible to run both new programs and old ones written for the PDP-11. "Backward compatibility" meant that many existing programs would work on the Vax computer from its inception, rather than waiting for programmers to write new applications as often happened in the past. The Vax design, meanwhile, was "scalable," which meant that the same software would run on Vaxes of varying sizes. Customers could switch to a larger Vax while retaining their familiar software.

All this suggested that the Vax marked a watershed in the history of computing. In assembling a team, Bell had his pick of Digital's brightest engineers. He asked Cutler, who he felt was Digital's top programmer, to lead the effort to create the VMS operating system.

Calling together Cutler and four other senior engineers, Bell launched the Vax project on April 1, 1975. For months the group hashed out design concepts in fiery meetings. "They started out quietly, with fifteen minute overviews of the agenda, but inevitably dissolved into shouting matches of apparent chaos and animosity. Somehow they always ended on a high note, engineers streaming out of the conference room smiling."

Bell helped Cutler by protecting him from meddlesome outsiders. "I wouldn't tolerate anyone getting in Dave's way on anything," he said. Even so, the VMS project put Cutler under great pressure. It showed. When he got out of bed some mornings, he was too dizzy to stand straight. An examination showed him to have sky-high blood pressure. He immediately went on medication to lower it. As a precaution Digital examined the other managers on the VMS team. The nurse who performed the tests said Cutler's blood pressure was the highest she'd ever seen.

Colleagues, often bloodied by Cutler's verbal jousts, couldn't resist taunting him about his health problem. During a heated debate one coworker jokingly said the suspense was killing him. Couldn't Cutler have his heart attack now, so they could stop worrying about it? "Can't you just get it over with?" he pleaded.

It was clear by then that Cutler needed help creating the VMS software. The team was small—ten people at its height—and Cutler was the senior programmer. But he wouldn't ask for help. He didn't do that kind of thing. He had a favorite saying: "When all is said and done, much more is said than done."

While Cutler was busy doing, the project's general manager, a man Cutler jokingly called "the boss," planned to hire a senior programmer to help Cutler whip the VMS software into shape. When Cutler left for a week's vacation, the boss interviewed his prime candidate and hired him, after Cutler returned. Cutler didn't think he needed a codesigner, but the newcomer proved to be his technical equal. If Cutler was grateful for the help, he did not say.

The first Vax computer was produced in October 1977. Its wild success vaulted Cutler into the front ranks of software designers. Bell, for one, didn't hesitate to call him the best writer of operating programs in the world. Wealth and recognition—the hallmarks of achievement—came Cutler's way. None of this altered his temperament. Digital's burgeoning bureaucracy annoyed him. "I'm a doer, and things became harder and harder to do," he said. To his distress, he could no longer direct the VMS project with his customary authority. The program was now so important to the company's future that a bevy of managers wished to improve it. Cutler fumed: "This was an opportunity for every Tom, Dick and Harry to come and poke holes in whatever you wanted to do, and hold up the project. Sure, there has to be a certain amount of review. That's healthy. But people who had no business with anything were popping up saying, why are you doing this, why are you doing that?"

Seeking less interference, Cutler left the VMS team. He wanted out of Digital's stultifying atmosphere. One day, he threatened to quit, telling Bell he wished to form his own company. Bell countered with an offer Cutler couldn't refuse: "Take anybody you want. Go anywhere you want to go. Do anything you want to do. And Digital will pay for it. Tell me how much money you need, and we'll fund you."

Cutler jumped at the chance. In the spring of 1981 he gathered his faithful flock and, wishing to move as far from Digital's Massachusetts office as possible, toured the West Coast in search of a new home. After spending a day in Seattle, Cutler made his decision. He was swayed by its proximity to mountains (he enjoyed skiing), the wilds (he still hunted) and the Pacific Ocean. A fine seafood dinner at a restaurant overlooking Shilshole Bay burnished his mood. The lack of a direct flight from Boston to Seattle, making it more time consuming for his corporate overseers to reach him, added to the location's appeal.

Cutler was happy at the helm of his own lab. "We knew what we wanted to build, and we could make all the decisions right there," he said. Bell stood ready to promote his ideas. At the lab, Cutler dressed casually, wearing his familiar sweat suits and sneakers, only now he didn't even don what one cohort called the "higher-quality T-shirts" he used to wear back east. A couple of nights a week, he invited everyone to join him at a pub, where he wasn't bashful about drinking large amounts of Red Hook, a local brew that he treated as a divine fluid. During the winter, he led his gang on ski trips, often outskiing people ten years younger. "He's not fun to ski with," said one coworker. "I just eat his snow."

Cutler was ambitious, but his plans met with mixed reactions. Along with software, he wished to design entire computers. Digital agreed to bring one of his machines to market, but his support withered after Bell, his patron, left Digital in 1983. "When Gordon left, our support network [at Digital] started to disappear," said Heinen. Suddenly, Cutler lacked clout. "It was clear the move to Seattle was a mistake," one colleague said. "From so far away, he lost his ability to champion his ideas effectively."

But he still had his freedom. On his business card he unabashedly identified himself as "Supreme Commander." In a lab "yearbook," compiled for the amusement of his crew, Cutler mocked the button-down etiquette of corporate life by posing for a photograph attired in a sleeveless white undershirt with a cheap striped tie hanging sloppily around his neck. Another photo, purportedly of his desktop, revealed three prominent items: an aerosol spray can inscribed with the words Bull Shit Repellent; a sign, issued by the "British Chicken Authority," that asked: Is your cock plump enough? and a drinking glass bearing the slogan: Joy Is A Tight Pussy.

Cutler balanced his ribaldry by espousing a stark and appealing philosophy of excellence. Mediocrity was for the weak, and greatness could be achieved only through a willingness to break irrational or outmoded conventions (and damn the consequences). "First of all, quality is something that has to be believed in by everybody," Cutler wrote in the yearbook. "This means management on down to the lowest peon. There is no room for a wishy washy manager that always leans the way the wind is blowing in the front office nor is there room for an engineer that tries to make it look like he did more work than he really did by short changing the quality aspects. It takes balls to stand up for quality at times and everyone on my projects gets that license. If some jerk somewhere wants to ship before we're ready, we tell him to pound sand."

In 1985, Cutler narrowly won approval from Digital to design a new family of computers called Prism. The hardware was based on a chip created in-house. The operating program, called Mica, would be a fresh design, though it would be able to run Vax applications. Cutler assembled nearly two hundred people for the project, which had all the trappings of a stand-alone company. He designed the first Prism computer for scientists who wanted specialized calculations known as vectors performed at blinding speeds. These calculations helped scientists simulate everything from the weather to a nuclear explosion to the composition of the ocean floor. Typically, so-called supercomputers, costing millions of dollars, were needed for such mathematically intensive simulations. Because of its innovative hardware and software, the first Prism computer could be priced at a tenth of the cost of a supercomputer.

Even as Cutler's team pushed ahead with Prism, rivals elsewhere at Digital skewered his plans. By June 1988, Cutler had been asked to revise or discard so many projects that he wasn't shocked when he was flown to Digital's headquarters and told of Prism's cancellation. Digital wished to disband Cutler's hardware group, forcing almost one hundred engineers to find work elsewhere at the company. This, Cutler felt, was "the last straw." On the plane back to Seattle he drank heavily. The following morning, June 18, 1988, he still seemed tipsy when he entered a room packed with his staff. He was furious at Digital for letting his people down. He could afford to walk away; he had a two-hundred-thousand-dollar annual salary and a two-million-dollar home on Puget Sound. But he worried about the future of his people.

He looked at them before speaking. Some people started to cry; others went numb. A few veterans couldn't even face a defeated Cutler and rode out the meeting in a bar.

"You all look so sad," Cutler said.

Then he told them: Prism was dead. There was nothing he could do to stop it. He cried.

Gathering himself, Cutler gave everyone at the lab a month off—with pay.

2. THE KING OF CODE

No matter how rich and powerful Bill Gates became, his mother still enjoyed telling of her failure to impress upon him the virtue of neatness.

Gates was the only son of a wealthy and successful Seattle family. His mother, Mary, was the scion of a Northwest banking titan and a politically connected regent of the University of Washington. His father, William II, was a prominent downtown lawyer.

Bright and willful, Gates often defied his parents as a child. Born on October 28, 1955, he shared with the rest of the baby boom generation a taste for sloppiness. His boyhood room was, in a word, messy. This worried his parents, who repeatedly insisted he tidy up. He refused.

Mary punished Gates for his messiness, removing the items she found strewn around his room. He seemed not to care about the loss of his things even when Mary began taking away the clothes she found on the floor.

Gates appeared stubbornly serene at the prospect of his impending nudity.

Mary then felt it was time for more professional measures. She called in a counselor to assay the standoff. The counselor interviewed Gates, his two sisters and his parents before delivering a verdict: *Leave Bill alone.*

So Mary did. She let her son wreck his room and asked only that he close the door. To her slight irritation, he wouldn't always do even that.

A skinny kid with pale skin, freckles, brown hair and light blue eyes, Gates had a lopsided grin and a nose somewhat too large for his face. His eyeglasses never seemed to fit right, tilting sideways and making him look silly.

With a fervor most young men reserve for girls or sports, Gates embraced computers. His posh private high school had an impressive computer for students to hack away on. The crisp impartiality of programming appealed to Gates. Hard logic, not opinions, settled coding debates and settled them surely. "Running your program is the absolute test," Gates once observed, recalling his first efforts. "You write a program, try it and it either works or it doesn't."

Gates's awkwardness, however, was only skin deep, covering an innate grasp of commerce. Almost as soon as he learned to write programs, he tried to sell them. He was drawn to the crucible of the marketplace. This was unusual for a teenage programmer in the early seventies. Most of his peers styled themselves as socially rebellious hackers, who saw in computing a means to tweak the establishment. Not Gates. He devised a gadget that compiled traffic data, selling his Traf-O-Data system to several towns in the area. He hoped to land the city of Seattle as a customer too. But when a city official came to Gates's home for a demonstration, the traffic program failed. A distraught Gates, trying to hold the official's interest, pleaded: "Tell him, Mom—tell him it really works!"

Gates, a math whiz, became a freshman at Harvard University in the fall of 1973. At school he gambled at poker, incessantly played computer games and generally seemed in a hurry. Sitting in his room, he often considered his future, "being a philosophical, depressed guy, trying to figure out what I was doing with my life." In December 1974, he received a clue from Paul Allen, a high school pal three years his senior. Allen, who had helped Gates build the traffic device, arrived at Harvard one day with the latest issue of *Popular Electronics*. On the cover of its January 1975 issue the magazine touted a computer named the Altair. It was a hobbyist's dream. For less than two thousand dollars the Altair packed the power of a computer costing anywhere from ten to one hundred times as much. The secret? The Altair was powered by a microprocessor. Invented a few years before by Intel Corporation of Santa Clara, California, the microprocessor crammed the essential elements of a computer onto a silicon wafer, or chip, no bigger than a fingernail. This silicon chip provided the Altair's heartbeat.

The harbinger of a revolution, the Altair was the first mass-marketed personal computer. For the first time a computer was dedicated not just to a single task but to one person. The old guard of computing entirely missed the significance of this. Fans of mainframe computers boasted of the benefits of handling many jobs in large batches. But the mainframe was as efficient as mass transit— wonderful as long as everyone wanted to travel to the same place at the same time. The PC was like an automobile; it would go anywhere its driver wanted. Instead of organizing work around the mainframe's schedule, a person with a PC could do computing anytime.

The PC's promoters saw its radical appeal. It turned the blandly efficient computer into a consumer product. As the editors of *Popular Electronics* declared when introducing the Altair, "The era of the computer in every home . . . has arrived!"

These words intoxicated Gates and Allen, who saw a gaping hole in the Altair: It came without software. Buyers had to write their own, or they were stuck, essentially, with a useless machine. This was something Gates and Allen could fix.

To start with the Altair needed a language out of which to create programs. Gates and Allen called the small Albuquerque, New Mexico, company that made the Altair and promised to supply a language. They chose Basic, originally designed in the 1960s for the sorts of minicomputers made by Digital. Basic (Beginners All-purpose Symbolic Instruction Code) was ideal for short programs and easier to learn than Fortran because its instructions were simpler. The language caught on widely, and its authors, two Dartmouth College professors, asserted no ownership rights over the program, allowing anyone to use or modify it free of charge.

Within six weeks, Gates and Allen had written a version of Basic for the Altair and formed a partnership called Microsoft to peddle the program. Allen flew to New Mexico to strike a deal. Soon Microsoft's Basic sold so well, even at its five-hundred-dollar price, that Gates left Harvard. He never returned.

The Altair passed from the scene, but Microsoft's Basic remained an essential programming tool. This was because Gates and Allen had tailored it to Intel's popular chip line, which powered the Altair and many of its PC successors. The price of Basic, which amounted to a hefty percentage of the entire cost of a small computer, irked many enthusiasts. They began copying the program and freely passing it around, arguing that software was a public resource. Gates violently disagreed with the notion that software was the electronic equivalent of air or water. He openly denounced the bootleggers as thieves. "As the majority of hobbyists must be aware, most of you steal your software," he wrote in a computer newsletter. Deriding their communal ethic, he observed acidly, "Hardware must be paid for, but software is something to share. Who cares if the people who worked on it get paid?"

Who cared? Bill Gates did.

The personal computer vastly changed the way individuals worked and played. Beginning in the late 1970s, legions of people began trading in their typewriters for desktop computers. Everything from design to word processing to bookkeeping could be done faster and easier electronically. By 1980 IBM, the world's biggest computer maker, decided to offer PCs. IBM had a tradition of making everything itself, but in this situation it was faster and easier for IBM to rely on outsiders for the PC's two most important parts.

The first was the microprocessor, or chip, which made a PC possible. The power of a chip was determined by the number of switches crammed on to a sliver of silicon and the connections between those switches. At the time, the best chips had hundreds of thousands of switches, but designers already imagined chips with millions of switches. Each switch was a shred of intelligence not unlike an individual neuron in the brain. The switch on a microprocessor was always either on or off, zero or one. The chip's very structure made it ideal for carrying out the instructions contained in computer programs, which were ultimately converted into strings of zeroes and ones. The more switches working in concert, the faster a program computed. Each species of microprocessor, however, had a distinct profile, or way of receiving instructions. As a result, chips that had different instruction sets were incompatible, meaning that the software written for one such chip could not work on another.

The operating system was the other part of the PC that IBM bought from the outside. It canvassed the infant PC software community in search of a supplier. Microsoft's chief rival treated IBM dismissively, but Gates jumped to attention, instantly grasping the importance of such a deal. He didn't even own an operating system, but he knew where to find one. Seattle was also home to the author of the Disk Operating System (DOS), which controlled the basic functions of an Intel-type personal computer. This was just the sort of machine IBM planned for its original PC. DOS was crude, but it would do. For fifty thousand dollars, Gates bought the program, without telling the author of IBM's interest. Later, some called the purchase "the deal of the century," but *steal* of the century was more accurate. Gates always denied that a great crime lay behind his fortune, but if one did it was his purchase of DOS.

Of course, DOS would have been worth relatively little had Gates not retained the right to license its use to IBM's rivals. This arrangement—the source of Gates's wealth and power—became clearer as IBM set the standard for the burgeoning PC market. By the mid-1980s, every rival except Apple Computer felt that the only way to compete against IBM was to sell a clone of IBM's PC. Making a clone required, among other things, licensing DOS from Microsoft. Over time DOS became a kind of annuity for Microsoft: Buying DOS was the price of admission for entering the PC business.

Gates was after more than just DOS. He wanted dominion over every aspect of PC software, from the home to the office. Besides DOS, Microsoft sold Basic, other programming tools, and such applications as word processing and an electronic ledger called a spreadsheet. Gates also had high hopes for a program Microsoft was building called Windows. DOS forced the user to memorize combinations of seemingly nonsensical commands in order to open a file, copy a document, or do any number of commonplace acts. To make controlling a PC easier, Windows presented a visual menu of frequent commands and pictures of files, programs, and other things stored on disk. The user selected commands by directing an on-screen arrow (usually with a mouse, a palm-size pointing device attached to the keyboard).

By the summer of 1988, Bill Gates was the leading representative of a new breed of tycoon: the software superrich. Just as oil created a kind of royalty in the last century, "wildcat" programmers had emerged among the wealthiest self-made men in America. Paul Allen, who had left Microsoft because of illness, was worth megamillions. So were the founders of other leading software companies. At the age of thirty-three, Gates was the youngest billionaire in the United States. Yet money wasn't his motivation. "For me it's more fun to work with smart engineers and create products that you can actually go out there and see people using," he said. "I'd certainly rather do that for free than make money in some way unrelated" to software. He bristled when he was labeled an entrepreneur, declaring, "If you look inside my brain, it is filled with thoughts about technology."

His actions, however, were all business. He had not written a line of code in five years but still reviewed much Microsoft code. These reviews resembled a court proceeding, with Gates as prosecuting attorney. He often began by asking simple questions but then might turn the screw by insisting that he grasped a technical question better than those paid to answer it. He didn't mind when engineers defended themselves or even screamed at him, so long as he could do the same to them. In reviews he spared no one's feelings, launching a typical tirade with the observation, "This is the stupidest piece of code ever written."

Despite his harsh criticisms Gates admired programmers and invariably put them in charge of projects, where they could both manage and program. While this double duty was stressful, Gates wanted to avoid a situation in which professional managers, with either no programming experience or out-of-date knowledge, held sway. It was destructive to rely on management pros to run software teams—or the company. They could not distinguish a promising program from a bust or evaluate schedules or product designs. At companies run by professionals, managers almost always came to mistrust their programmers, whom they could neither understand nor control.

Gates's hallmark was flexibility: He had a knack for shifting course at the right time. In a world in which people too often clung to absolutes, Gates would rather be right than consistent. However, he could be moody and anxious and sometimes succumbed to paranoia. Haunted by visions of failure, he saw himself encircled by enemies. These thoughts helped to keep Gates "running scared," which he considered a beneficial condition. Complacency "would be the road to ruin," he said. "You always have to be thinking about who is coming to get you."

His parents and friends worried that Gates drove himself too hard. After all, Microsoft was among the most successful young businesses in the world. Yet this offered scant comfort to Gates, who seemed irritated by his reknown. When things seemed to go badly, his money and celebrity meant nothing to him. As his father put it, his attitude was: "Everything is going to hell in a handbasket."

The summer of 1988 was one of those hell-in-a-handbasket times. Gates's absorption in work had just cost him a love affair, and a few months earlier Apple Computer had filed suit against Microsoft, alleging that Windows illegally copied the Macintosh's operating program. The case turned on ill-defined concepts of software copyright and intellectual property law, and the outcome was far from clear. Still, the case enraged Gates because it fueled the claim that his facility as an imitator accounted for his success.

Then there was IBM, his great ally. Ever since Microsoft's DOS emerged as the standard PC operating system, IBM had sought ways to distinguish its PCs from clones through software. In April 1987 the two companies publicly agreed to create a replacement for DOS called OS/2. Besides giving the program perhaps the worst name in merchandising history, IBM and Microsoft erred by failing to offer DOS fans an immediate means of running their old programs on the new operating system. At the outset, Gates had been so bullish about OS/2 that he vowed it would supplant DOS in less than three years. By the summer of 1988, barely eighteen months later, OS/2 was beginning to look to him like a disaster. The first release was unwieldy, wouldn't run Windows programs, and lacked a graphical user interface that made controlling the software a matter of pointing at pictures and making choices from on-screen menus. Despite the strains, Gates did not want a rupture with IBM, which was Microsoft's largest customer and zealous in its promotion of OS/2. He didn't dare deviate from IBM's path, but he wasn't the computer maker's prisoner either. Even as he pledged continued support for OS/2, he charted an alternate course. In this he resembled an ambitious son who daydreamed about how he would run the family business should his father suddenly die.

Gates had a simple approach to management: Surround yourself with people of great intelligence. "Smart people," he said, "ought to be able to figure anything out if they get enough facts." Defining the species of the smart was hard, but Gates knew a member when he met one. Invariably these people were male, so gatherings had the air of a boys' club. One of the newer members that summer was a twenty-seven-year-old refugee from the field of theoretical physics.

Nathan Myrhvold had been a protégé of the celebrated physicist Stephen Hawking before forming a software company in Berkeley, California, with some fellow Princeton University Ph.D's. What drew Myrhvold, or any physicist, to programming? The outer reaches of science increasingly relied on computers; the days of a genius scribbling formulas on the back of an envelope had almost vanished. Physicists usually saw programming as a means to an end. Myrhvold found that his attachment to software superseded his fascination with physical science. His company gained wide notice when he and his friends wrote a faster, smaller clone of IBM's TopView graphics program. IBM briefly considered making TopView the software interface—the piece seen by customers—for PCs. Trying to keep pace with IBM, Gates wanted a clone of TopView, so he bought Myrhvold's company.

Since IBM junked TopView shortly afterward, the acquisition's sole benefit was that it brought smart people to Microsoft. Myhrvold hit it off with Gates, and before long the physicist was stimulating Gates's curiosity with a succession of lively memos on software trends. In one Myhrvold argued that Microsoft's cash cow, DOS, faced two related threats that would loom larger over time.

The first threat was a new type of chip, potentially far faster than Intel's chips, which powered DOS and all its applications. The source of the new chip's extraordinary speed lay in a design technique called RISC (Reduced Instruction Set Computing), which made it possible for the chip to concentrate on performing common operations. Should a RISC chip replace the Intel chip at the heart of a PC, Microsoft's empire might collapse.

The second threat was an operating system called Unix, which had been created a decade earlier at AT&T's Bell Labs and had gradually won a strong following among scientists, engineers and even a few businesses. Unix had two main attractions. One was technical: The system handled several computing tasks at once, connected easily with other computers and worked on any kind of hardware without sweeping code changes. Unix also was attractive for economic reasons: It was essentially available free of charge. AT&T owned the core of Unix, but it allowed others to adapt and expand it for a nominal fee. This encouraged scholars and engineers to improve Unix. Numerous companies began shipping computers outfitted with a variant of the operating system.

But Unix had a serious shortcoming: No common version existed. Over the years different versions of Unix had proliferated like weeds, so that an application written for one would not run unmodified on another. While DOS presented a single target to consumers, applications writers and computer makers, Unix did not. The fragmentation of Unix was a boon to Microsoft. However, the prospect of Unix on computers powered by RISC chips convinced Gates that he needed a "Unix killer." He asked Myrhvold to experiment with writing an operating system that was "portable," meaning that it could run on any of the competing RISC chips under development.

Myhrvold, whose frizzy beard and hair made him look like some forgotten Russian revolutionary, polled experts in academia for their advice and then formed a small team, which he called Psycho because many of his colleagues saw the attempt to write a portable program as "a crazy idea."

Only a few miles from Gates's office at Microsoft, David Cutler stewed in his Digital lab over the killing of Prism. Afraid that he might poison the plummeting morale at the lab, Digital planned to move Cutler to another building in a few days. Even though they would keep him on salary, Cutler felt he was being quarantined, and he intended to leave Digital. He wanted to resign immediately, but his boss in Massachusetts insisted that he hold off, dangling the promise of another post elsewhere in the company. Cutler was suspicious: Digital was only trying "to keep me happy for awhile, so I didn't piss all over the company in the press."

Word of Cutler's estrangement leaked out. On August 4, 1988, one of Myrhvold's staff burst into his office at Microsoft. The staffer, who had worked with Cutler at Digital, gave Myrhvold some juicy gossip: Cutler's latest project had been canceled, and he wished to leave Digital.

Myrhvold called Gates with the news. "It was like an amazing coincidence," Gates said. He had never met Cutler but knew enough about his career to consider hiring him. "I very much wanted a portable [operating system]," Gates said. "It was not a question of if, but when we could get the team together to do it."

Gates felt Cutler would be the ideal leader for such a team, but he restrained his enthusiasm. Cutler was reputedly headstrong and disagreeable. Gates assumed the odds were against Cutler choosing to join Microsoft. He wanted to try to recruit him anyway, and through an intermediary he arranged a meeting.

The contrast between Cutler and Gates was sharp. Cutler, stocky and strong-willed, came from blue-collar roots. His language was peppered with profanities; he lifted weights, drank beer and hunted animals for pleasure. On the other hand, Gates came from a privileged background: rich parents, prep school, Harvard, a fast ascent into the corporate pantheon. Life had hardly left a scar on him. He dressed like a college sophomore, spent his vacations reading books and held a summer contest called "MicroGames," in which friends formed teams and competed to see which ones could, say, build the best sand castle.

The day they met, Gates greeted Cutler warmly and began feeling him out. "I'd heard about him, but it was one of these funny things where everything I knew was indirect," Gates said. "And I didn't know how much [of his reputation] was bullshit."

Gates quickly decided that Cutler was the real thing. He relaxed, talking about his desire for a portable operating system and where it fitted into Microsoft's future. Outwardly unimpressed by Gates's wealth and power, Cutler didn't disguise his scorn for Microsoft and its products. He thought the company's code was poorly written and that DOS, its crown jewel, was a "toy." He wanted to create a "real" operating program for powerful computers—a program that was reliable, managed networks and handled huge amounts of information—in short, everything DOS was not and never would be.

Gates was glad to hear this from Cutler. This was roughly his own vision of Microsoft's future. Although they had reached a common view, there was still a hurdle to clear: Cutler refused to join Microsoft unless he could come with a dozen or more engineers from Digital, including a group of computer designers. Gates was happy to have the software people, but since Microsoft didn't build computers he wanted to pass on the computer designers. Cutler refused to leave them out of the deal. "I enjoy building hardware," he insisted, pointedly noting that he would sooner form his own company than part with his hardware group.

After the meeting, Myhrvold argued in favor of hiring Cutler's computer designers, saying they could build the hardware that would make it easier to test and refine a new operating system as well as advise customers on how to design PCs that took full advantage of the software. Gates needed little convincing. He was sold on Cutler, considering him "the man for the mission." And "the cost of paying for those hardware guys wasn't prohibitive."

Indeed, money wasn't an issue. Microsoft was hugely profitable, earning a stunning twenty-five cents on every dollar of revenue. Besides, it wouldn't even match the current salaries of the Digital people (Cutler, for instance, expected to earn about half his old salary). As an inducement the company would grant each newcomer many options to purchase Microsoft's stock at a 15 percent discount from the prevailing price. These could potentially make the Digital defectors multimillionaires if they stayed with Microsoft for even four or five years, time enough to complete their portable software program. Cutler himself was promised so much stock that he felt, "Gates really wants [me] to do this."

For Cutler, the entire package—the stock options, the ability to handpick his core team and the chance to create another seminal operating system—testified to his reputation and experience as a software designer and leader of programming teams. At the age of forty-six, Cutler was old by software standards, making Gates's confidence in him all the more extraordinary. Only a handful of companies in the world could serve as Cutler's patron. At Digital, Gordon Bell had nourished his ambitions; now Gates would do the same for him at Microsoft. Cutler didn't expect to forge a special bond with Gates, but he was grateful for a fresh start. He felt he had another big program in him and worried only that Gates might prove fickle or vindictive, canceling his project or burying him under endless demands.

Gates could not think far enough ahead to know for sure if in Cutler he had the architect of Microsoft's next generation of software. He simply was "excited beyond belief," said Steve Ballmer, Microsoft's second-in-command. "We were jazzed: Cutler joining Microsoft. This was incredible—a match made in heaven."

Cutler arrived at Microsoft on October 31, 1988. A few days later, Rob Short, Cutler's chief computer designer, resigned from Digital to become the first to join Cutler's new team. A native of Cork, Ireland, Short was Cutler's closest friend. His was an atypical trajectory to the top rank of his field. After finishing a course in electronics, he had joined Digital's plant in Galway, Ireland. In the early 1970s, he moved to the United States, working by day in a series of jobs for Digital and taking at night courses in engineering and computers. One night, he finished his homework, a program in assembly language, and he printed it out. When he searched for the printout, he could not find it so he printed it again. Returning to the printer, he found Cutler correcting his homework. Short broke into laughter. "That *he* would actually play with my homework," Short said, "was hilarious."

Short went to work for Cutler in 1982, moving to the Seattle lab. After two years, Cutler put Short in charge of computer design.

When it came to solving technical problems, Short had a bulldog attitude, but he handled Cutler deftly, reading his moods expertly and often defusing an angry outburst with a wisecrack. Although intensely loyal to Cutler, Short realized that the journey he was about to begin at Microsoft might well strain him and others to the breaking point. "Dave leads by doing vast amounts of work and by pushing other people to do vast amounts of work," he said. "And the funny thing about Dave is that really complex technical things don't slow him down a bit. It doesn't matter how complicated it is, he just goes through it at the same speed."

After being escorted from Digital's premises by a security guard, Short drove to Microsoft's corporate campus, which was located on a piece of land large enough to fit two dozen buildings (the company then had fewer than ten), several playing fields and jogging paths, a library and many parking lots and cafeterias. The buildings were low and dark and modest, but everyone had his own office, which he could decorate as he saw fit. In every wing of each building, a wall-size refrigerator chilled juices and soft drinks. Employees could drink as much as they wanted without charge. Myrhvold, for instance, drank at least a six-pack a day of Diet Pepsi. He was, friends joked, "living proof there's no lethal dose for NutraSweet."

Navigating his way through the curving roads of the campus, Short found Building Two, entered and blanched at the unfamiliar surroundings. He was suddenly nostalgic for Digital, where "we had had this big fancy place and our own goals and we knew what we were doing." He found Cutler sitting alone in an upstairs office. Cutler didn't have a computer or a chair for a guest, and he looked uneasy. Short sat on the floor. The two men eyed each other and laughed. Then Short said, "Maybe this is going to be a disaster."

3. TRIBES

Cutler's arrival at Microsoft triggered an exodus of his most trusted colleagues from Digital. He didn't raid his former employer but was simply the beneficiary of the loyalty felt by people who viewed him as a high-tech Moses. Within a week, Microsoft hired seven of the top code writers from Cutler's old lab.

Everyone on the core team had worked under Cutler for years. All were men, and only one was younger than thirty, making the group far older than the average at Microsoft. On their first day Microsoft's personnel staff gathered the newcomers together for a perfunctory review of company policy and practices. A film recounted Microsoft's rise. It included sentimental interviews with Gates and his mother, Mary, which "was okay as long as you didn't gag," one of Cutler's guys joked later.

At the end of the morning the newcomers were asked to sign employment contracts, whose text bound workers to keep sensitive matters secret and gave the company ownership of a worker's ideas and output. It also had a provision, known as paragraph 10, that barred an employee from joining a competitor for at least a year after leaving Microsoft. This was an onerous covenant, and Cutler's people, who had been warned about it, objected. They refused to sign the contract. If Digital had imposed such a restriction, they insisted, Microsoft wouldn't have been able to hire them without a legal fight, so why should they sign? The company wouldn't budge: Without a signed contract, they could not work. Since it was nearly noon, Cutler's people filed out of the room. Though they were hungry for lunch, it looked like a walkout. Then somebody called Cutler to inform him of the hitch. Maybe his guys wouldn't join Microsoft after all.

Cutler quickly solved the dispute. With the approval of Microsoft's lawyers, paragraph 10 was deleted. Cutler's people signed the modified contract.

The standoff, while brief, sent a message to the rest of Microsoft: Cutler's tribe was different. They all considered themselves more talented, mature and, yes indeed, superior to their new colleagues. On the surface this judgment seemed reasonable. To start with, they were a good deal older and more experienced than the ordinary Microsoft employee (called a "Microsoftie" around campus) who was in his twenties and probably hadn't worked anywhere else. The Digital defectors also were more methodical about their jobs, hewing to textbook engineering practices in contrast to the Microsofties, who often approached a problem helter-skelter. Cutler's people took work seriously, while Microsofties sometimes tossed nerf balls in the hallways or strummed guitars in their offices.

The differences in style were apparent to Cutler's people, who derisively referred to Microsoft as "Microslop." By the same token, Microsofties were put off by the clannishness of Cutler's gang. "Cutler and his boys came in as a very tight clique," one programmer said. "They presented that view outwardly, and it tended to get people's hackles up."

Cutler, who disliked thinking about the murky, psychological side of life, got a laugh out of that. He also sensed that his adjustment would be more difficult than he first expected. Though seen as a monolith by outsiders and rivals, Microsoft more closely resembled a patchwork of feudal baronies than it did a united nation. Gates ruled, but he relied heavily on a collection of programming lords and managers who had grown wealthy from their connection with Microsoft. At Digital, Cutler had been a star, and he expected star treatment at Microsoft. Yet here few people knew anything about him; he felt anonymous. "My credibility just wasn't there," he said.

Cutler instinctively turned inward, finding comfort in his tribe, which consisted of a half dozen hardware engineers along with the code writers. They occupied a single hallway in Building Two, and their offices contained whatever furniture could be scraped together in a hurry. The team's first few days were oddly calm. "There was zero direction," one member said. "We didn't know what was in store for us or how it would turn out." They had little to do except to learn the ins and outs of a personal computer. Despite their experience, none had ever programmed a PC. They felt lost. Views like "it was . . . total culture shock" and "not love at first sight" summed up their reactions.

A dark mood descended on Cutler's gang. "It was depressing," one teammate said. "For the first few weeks we all felt that way, even Dave." Still traumatized by the cancellation of Prism, they wondered whether Microsoft would in the end treat them as badly as Digital had. "Just finishing a product was the foremost thing in our minds," said another. "Even if we hated it here, we wouldn't let that get in the way. We'd finish, then quit the next day."

Gates was immensely pleased to have gained Cutler's services. Long criticized for the company's limited programs, he now had a software designer who could bring the utility of big computers to PCs. Cutler's arrival lent credibility to Microsoft's claims that its software would someday handle any and every job. Gates wasn't sure when Microsoft would actually need Cutler's operating system, so he maintained a public silence about his software star. On November 10, 1988, the company confirmed that Cutler had been hired, saying only that he had joined to direct work on an advanced version of OS/2. In a statement, Cutler was described as "someone who can manage large projects and bring them in on time with the highest quality." Cutler offered no comment. At Digital, he had given no interviews, and he insisted that Microsoft never ask him to speak with the press. He even warned Gates: "If you bring the press in to see me, I'll do something that will make you never bring them in again."

To celebrate the arrival of Cutler and his crew, Gates threw a beer-and-pizza party in an unfinished building on the Microsoft campus. Before a small crowd, Gates introduced the newcomers, talking excitedly about the "great stuff" to come from them. Gates rarely doted publicly on his programmers, but for the moment Cutler was his favorite. Gates even seemed in awe of Cutler and was reluctant to interfere with him. "He's a guy who is serious about his job . . . the ultimate professional," Gates said. "That doesn't make him easy to talk to. Before you go to see Dave you think, 'Jeez, am I going to say something stupid?'"

Gates worried that Cutler, surrounded by familiar faces, might be too isolated from the rest of Microsoft. He asked Steve Ballmer, nominally Cutler's boss, to teach him the company's ways.

Ballmer was a sound choice to serve as Cutler's tutor. He was the yin to Gates's yang. A Detroit native and the son of an automobile executive, he had met Gates at Harvard, and the two were close friends. After stints at business school and Procter & Gamble, Ballmer, who had never written a program, joined Microsoft in 1980 as the company's first general manager. Warm and jocular, he tended to shout rather than speak. In contrast to the standoffish Gates, Ballmer prowled the hallways carrying a yellow legal pad on which he jotted down "action items." He greeted people with a high-five. During visits with staff, he often lay on the floor hugging a basketball, or he tossed a tennis ball against a wall, nervously moving back and forth.

Cutler, who thought Gates was overrated, was happy to report to Ballmer, whom he considered to be the key to Microsoft's success. "Steve is my kind of guy," Cutler said. "A real go-getter with lots of energy."

Ballmer helped his standing with Cutler by giving him free rein, at least within a certain realm. "Dave came on with the assumption the insides of [the operating system] were his, but we would specify the outside design [what the customer sees]," Ballmer said. "This [division] made sense because he could innovate inside, while the outside design is where marketing meets the technical."

The arrangement left ample room for disputes. Ballmer repeatedly reminded Cutler of the need for existing OS/2 programs to run on the team's portable operating system. Cutler, wishing to limit his commitments in order to speed the completion of his program, felt that Ballmer "always wanted more than we could deliver." He refused, for instance, to promise an operating system that would run existing DOS and Windows programs. "DOS compatibility? Windows compatibility? No one will ever want that," Cutler said. "Why should we even think about that?"

These debates sometimes grew heated. Cutler once underscored a point to Ballmer by pounding on his desk and screaming that he would not "pollute [NT] with crap." Ballmer ambled over to the door and smacked it a few times. "Don't pound," Ballmer brayed. "It's not constructive. I can pound too, and just as loud."

Nathan Myhrvold also sought to expose Cutler and crew to Microsoft's ways. He wanted to see the project start strong and make some use of his Psycho experiment into portable code. Cutler, however, only promised to look at Psycho, which he found to his dismay had almost no documentation and unimpressive design. Rather than reform Psycho, Cutler preferred to discard it.

Regarding the selection of a RISC chip, which would serve as the target for Cutler's software, Myrhvold held sway. He chose a still-unfinished chip from Intel, which also made the chip for standard PCs. Intel was pushing its own RISC chip, called the i860, as a hedge against the same kind of sea change in computing that prompted Microsoft to start work on a portable operating system. Both companies shared a common desire: to stay on top.

Cutler thought the i860, which he had examined at Digital, had "serious problems," but he acceded to Myrhvold's decision. After all, Myrhvold was one of his few allies. Many people at Microsoft believed the company should write software only for existing PC hardware and not waste time and money on portable software, whose following was unproved. "While Bill [Gates], Steve [Ballmer] and I support your project, a lot of other people don't," Myrhvold explained. "They don't understand it or think it's too far out or crazy. Don't let this [criticism] bother you or slow you down."

When it came to forging a link between Cutler's crew and the Microsofties, Gates had one more hand to play, assigning a veteran Microsoft programmer named Steven Wood to Cutler's all-Digital team. The move was crucial because "I had to see if they would accept a foreign body" on the team. If Cutler failed to embrace one of Microsoft's best and brightest, perhaps these newcomers would not fit, Gates reasoned.

If anyone could impress Cutler's crew, it was Wood. A prodigious code writer, he had joined Microsoft in 1983 after completing all his requirements for a doctorate in computer science from Yale University save for the dissertation. He was equally at home with the two great software traditions: the highbrow, detached, anticommercial and formal style fostered by university computer science departments and the pragmatic, just-get-it-done outlook of the self-taught programmer. His formal training made it hard to dismiss his ideas, while his resourcefulness as a programmer was undeniable.

Wood was unusual. He had a shuffling, phlegmatic walk and a furtive look that made it seem as if he didn't like the daylight. By choice he had a windowless office, even though an office with a window was the only outward sign of status at Microsoft (a company without reserved parking spaces, executive cafeterias, chauffeured limousines or corporate jets). In a company of iconoclasts, Wood rebelled against the rebels, taking an irreverent view of the irreverent people about him.

The son of a dentist, he was born in the Seattle suburb of Bellevue in 1951. As a boy, he liked to build go-carts and model planes and ships. When bored with an old ship model, he and his younger brother would set it on fire and float it out on a nearby pond. Old model planes were dispatched more spectacularly, by sending them down a long wire and, it was hoped, landing them on a fake aircraft carrier. For special effects, the boys would set the plane alight before sending it on its way.

By the age of fourteen, Wood stood six feet tall, his full adult height, but weighed just one hundred pounds. He was a clumsy beanpole, and shy. When his father realized that public school didn't challenge Wood, he sent him to Lakeside, the same elite private high school Gates would attend a few years later.

Wood hated Lakeside. He felt like an outcast among the children of Seattle's wealthiest families. Some of his classmates had cars, a few even flew planes, and the easy money left Wood, the child of independent-minded Quakers, feeling out of place. He floundered at school, earning B grades. His one "distinction," he later ruefully recalled, "was I once got caught with a master key to the school, and somebody saw us using it to get into a storage room." Apprehended, Wood and a friend were dragged before the student body and "humiliated" by the headmaster.

After enrolling in college in 1969 to avoid the Vietnam draft, Wood drifted. After changing schools and a stint as a postal worker, he enrolled in a physics course. "All of a sudden school was fun," he said. But he could not imagine a career in physics. "I could see twenty years of study in a field where you only do important stuff if you're a genius," he said. "If you weren't a genius, you'd be a lackey to a genius."

Wood turned to computer courses and took a job programming for the regional phone company in Seattle after graduation. Four years later, he enrolled in Yale to study computer science. After a year, Wood was skeptical about the benefits of his Ivy League education. When his mother celebrated the arrival of his master's diploma, Wood told her, "Mom, it's toilet paper. I got it for not flunking out."

Wood spent six years at Yale, and while he did solid work he never got swept up in the self-congratulatory fervor that generally infects university research. Wood felt his professors were out of touch with reality and, while "very smart people in their limited field, . . . they had no business judging whether I did something good or bad."

The only benefit of Yale was that Wood met his wife there. It was November 1982, he was thirty-one years old and he had never dated a woman before. An administrative aide for the department took his fancy. She had a seven-year-old son and didn't recognize Wood when he phoned to ask for a date. Improbably they fell in love and soon talked of marriage. Wood, now with a reason to leave Yale, inquired about jobs. One of his Yale classmates now worked as a programmer for Microsoft, and he arranged for a job interview. Wood flew to Seattle to meet Gates, who rocked himself furiously in his chair during the meeting and doodled on his hands with a pen. The ink ran onto the sleeve of Gates's shirt. Wood, who was sold on the company's prospects, pretended not to notice.

Wood first worked on the original version of Windows, which put him in the limelight because Gates saw Windows as the main way for Microsoft to achieve independence from IBM. Next Wood took another high-profile, tough assignment, working on OS/2, which at IBM's behest had become the putative successor to DOS. In November 1988, he had just finished a "fun and insane" year on the project, including a total of twelve weeks at IBM labs in England and Boca Raton, Florida. The experience left him disillusioned with OS/2, which—while capable of running multiple applications (impossible for DOS)—halted entirely when any application crashed. Wood dismissed OS/2 as "a bag of dirt," citing the program as proof that good designs don't come from committees.

Having alienated his OS/2 colleagues, Wood needed a place to land. While intolerant of "inept people," he was a natural underdog whose prospects early in life seemed dim. Even when he discovered computers, he found neither a home nor success. Then he put it all together. His experience at Microsoft was at once singular and yet utterly typical. Unquestionably a star, he would make a good addition to Cutler's team. He was a fast, first-rate programmer, a feisty veteran who could hold his own with hotshots while carrying the Microsoft flag. Gates approved.

Wood was thrilled to joint NT, where he found "some smart people." Yet it struck him as strange when Cutler's crew looked to him for clues on adapting to their new home, since "I wasn't a big fan of the Microsoft way myself."

Cutler's team talked for hours about the operating system they hoped would become the most advanced ever built for the PC. "It was like being in a new sandbox," Wood said. "We didn't have a product. We had no schedules. We were all having fun."

They were in no rush either. Ballmer expected the team to spend from six to nine months hashing out technical ideas, learning about the PC's terrain and compiling a list of "deliverables." This pace suited Cutler, who "wanted to be right the first time." Many code writers worked incrementally, strengthening a piece of code over the course of several versions. Each version acted as a bulwark for their imagination and reasoning. Cutler, by contrast, created a map of his code before beginning and then wrote it with an uncommon exactness. "I'm not one of those guys who believes you write code as fast as you can and then revise and revise until it works," he said. "On the other hand, I'm not afraid to rewrite anything. If it didn't turn out the way I wanted it to, I'm not afraid to scrap it."

Cutler took a pragmatic approach to coding. He believed form preceded function, but he wasn't a prisoner to structure. He usually didn't have false starts, and when finished, his code contained few flaws. As usual, he intended to write the most abstract piece of the team's code. He envisioned an operating system with dozens of pieces, each piece preceded by a specification. Writing specs was itself a craft. Engineers learned early in their careers that a poorly written spec might result in the death of a project. A good spec was a beacon; when a programmer lost his way, the spec might help him back on course. But a spec helped more than its author; it helped everyone contributing a piece of the program. The pieces existed symbiotically; the program was a kind of delicate ecosystem, where flaws in one piece, even when not directly connected to another, might wreak havoc over the totality.

Reliance on specs had two drawbacks. It could take months to write one. And once coding began, the spec needed constant revision or it would quickly fall out of date. Old specs might mislead; usually they sowed confusion. So as specs were living plans, they needed a keeper. The job fell to Lou Perazzoli, who had been Cutler's software chief at his Digital lab.

Perazzoli, a tall, thin man, rarely stood erect or raised his voice. "Dave's a doer," he said. "I like working for doers." A talented programmer, Perazzoli was another player-coach. His management philosophy consisted of a single rule: Keep your people happy. He assumed his programmers would sooner or later do the right thing. Still, he was practical. If someone was so overworked or angry that he felt he couldn't go on, Perazzoli asked what would ease the pain. Sometimes, a programmer gave a straightforward answer, asking for a larger computer monitor or a bigger hard-disk drive to store data. Perazzoli kept a slush fund to handle these requests and often granted them. Other times, the frustration was more profound and the cure grander. A programmer wanted a month off to visit Italy or scuba dive off the coast of Costa Rica. Perazzoli often met such requests by saying: Do this, this, and this, and then the trip will follow.

The cool and caring Perazzoli was the perfect foil for Cutler. "Lou's the sugar to Dave's salt," Wood said. When people were afraid to speak with Cutler, they confessed their sins and anxieties to Perazzoli. When Cutler was so angry he couldn't bear to chastise a person, he instead chewed out Perazzoli, who quietly conveyed the bad news or kept it to himself, depending on the situation. Many teammates felt immense gratitude toward Perazzoli. "Lou keeps a bunch of people with big egos and severe tempers from murdering one another," said one. "He keeps people from quitting when they've had their fill of Cutler." Wood, however, complained about Cutler and Perazzoli's good-cop, bad-cop routine. "The trouble with the team is that Dave is too rude and Lou is too nice," he once wrote.

There was little to be done about it, though. "Lou's just much easier-going than I am," Cutler allowed. "He's the kind of guy who'll say, 'This is a problem, but I'm not going to do anything to fix it because I know it will fix itself. Eventually, everyone will discover it's wrong. So I'm not going to spend the mental energy on it.'"

Perazzoli's Zen-like attitude toward life was in keeping with his own circuitous route into the software elite. Ten years Cutler's junior, he first worked as a programmer for NASA in the early 1970s. The space agency, which relied heavily on computers for everything from controlling missions to analyzing celestial data, assigned Perazzoli to write code for the PDP-11, the Digital computer that ran Cutler's early operating systems. Perazzoli tired of his ten-thousand-dollar federal salary after a few years and joined Digital as a roving programmer who helped hardware customers with their software. During a Digital training course, Perazzoli met Cutler, who stopped in to teach the class one day. The two hit it off and spent an evening talking about Cutler's favorite programs.

Over the years, they kept in touch. In 1981, Perazzoli moved to Lynchburg, Virginia, to help Digital customers in the area. He bought an eighty-acre farm with his girlfriend, a high school teacher from Alabama, and went "back to the earth." He rarely worked later than 5:00 p.m. and spent plenty of time on the farm with his girlfriend, who taught school in a town nearby. The couple lived an idyllic life they knew from the start could not last very long. They raised turkeys and chickens, baked bread and gathered firewood in the summer and burned it in the winter. They let local farmers graze cattle on the land in exchange for chicken feed and had a tobacco barn that they sometimes loaned out to neighbors.

In August 1985 Cutler offered Perazzoli a programming job at his lab outside Seattle. Perazzoli accepted and soon impressed Cutler with his poise and diligence. He then put Perazzoli in charge of Mica, the software that would control Prism. Prism's cancellation hit Perazzoli hard. He had never shipped a commercial program (all his code had been consumed internally by his employers or clients). Shipping was perhaps the only true measure of a programmer's craft. "If you don't finish," Cutler said, "all the bright ideas don't mean anything."

Digital had robbed Perazzoli of the experience of finishing. He vowed not to let a company do that to him again. In his last e-mail to friends at Digital, he expressed glee at joining Microsoft and wrote, "Hopefully we'll ship a product before my hair turns gray."

Perazzoli thought Microsoft had given him a second chance at making a splash in software, and he was determined to make the most of it. His bittersweet experience at Digital would help in this regard, because the Mica software had been essentially "a dry run" for NT. For Perazzoli, the past was prologue. He was eager to get on with the main act.

What is an operating system, really? What did Cutler's team wish to create?

Picture a wealthy English household in the early 1900s. Think of a computer—the hardware—as a big house, the family's residence. The house consists of plumbing and lighting, bricks and mortar, windows and doors—all manner of physical things and processes.

Next, imagine computer software as the people in the house. The household staff, living downstairs, provide a whole range of services at once. The butler stands by the door, the driver washes the car, the housekeeper presses the linen, the cook provides meals and bakes cakes, the gardener rakes the leaves from the lawn. And this activity, which seemingly happens of its own accord, is coordinated by the head of the household staff. Such is the life of the downstairs dwellers, who in a certain sense exist in the background.

Then consider the people upstairs. They are the whole reason for the toil of the people downstairs. The husband desires a driver not simply for peace of mind but because he wishes to travel. The wife employs a cook, so her family can eat well. The children benefit from the work of the gardener, who clears the yard of debris, enabling them to play outdoors safely.

The picture of the family upstairs and their faithful downstairs servants neatly illustrates the great divide in the world of software. The people upstairs are the applications: the word-processing, electronic ledger, database, publishing and numerous other programs that satisfy human needs and wants. The people downstairs collectively perform the functions of an operating system. Theirs is a realm of services, some automatic, some requiring a special request. These services lay the basis for the good stuff of life.

Cutler had three main aims for his operating system:

Portability: This was the Holy Grail of software—making a single operating system that could fit every species of hardware. At the time every commercial operating system was tailored to a specific family of microchips and thus worked only in computers powered by those chips. Programmers wrote a substantial amount of code in assembly, the language closest to their target hardware. This chained software to hardware. When hardware costs dwarfed software costs, no one minded. But as the investment in applications programs outstripped hardware investment, customers grew reluctant to render obsolete their installed software. NT was a chance to create a universal program whose advent would mark a new era in computing.

Reliability: In the Macintosh, OS/2 and DOS operating systems, the failure of an application often halted, or crashed, the entire system, wiping out data and forcing a user to restart the machine. If many applications were running at once—a feature planned for NT—the failure of one halted the others. Cutler hoped to put an end to unwanted crashes by making an operating system that was "bullet proof." This would give PCs more value by making them reliable enough to run what businesses call "mission-critical" services, such as maintaining airline reservations or bank automatic teller machines. Cutler and his team knew how to ensure reliability; their Digital operating systems sprang from an era when computers were so expensive and scarce that "if you brought down a system for an hour, it was terrible," Cutler explained. "Compared to nowadays, you couldn't do that much with a computer in the first place, so every lost minute was a big deal."

Personality: NT should be flexible enough to host more than one user interface, or "personality." Current PC operating systems were limited to only one personality, which meant that applications written for DOS could only run on DOS. NT would support the Presentation Manager interface of OS/2, but it was designed so that it could—if Microsoft chose to do so—support other personalities such as DOS or Windows or even ones not yet even invented.

In creating NT's design, Cutler and his team first wrestled with the problems of portability.

Portable code was easy to write but inherently inefficient. By definition, writing in a high-level language produced code that would run, after a routine compilation, on different microprocessors. A high-level language produced relatively slow and large programs. Microsoft's DOS, Digital's VMS and Apple's Macintosh operating systems, for instance, relied on assembly language because it produced small, tight code that fully exploited specific hardware. Compact code was inherently good since it consumed less internal memory. Consisting of slivers of silicon chips called DRAM ("dynamic-random-access-memories"), internal memory was like a gas tank. The larger the tank, the farther the car would go. The smaller the operating program, the more gas was left for all other programs.

Because NT was portable, Cutler knew it would be big. The question was, how big? This depended on the cleverness of his programmers, the features sought and the design of NT itself. Much time would pass before Cutler knew precisely how big a memory tank NT really required. But he knew enough now to realize that NT would consume more memory—perhaps far more memory—than any existing PC operating system.

This made Bill Gates nervous. At a minimum, NT might require a PC with eight megabytes of memory, or eight times the amount then standard with a new machine. Gates worried that customers might forgo NT if it meant spending hundreds of dollars on extra memory for their machines. Even though the prices of memory chips were expected to decline sharply, NT's memory requirement was a significant uncertainty.

It fell to Perazzoli to design and code the mechanism within NT that managed internal memory (he had written such a memory manager at Cutler's lab). Continuously active, the memory manager made sure that every part of the operating system and every active application had as much internal memory as was needed to perform an action. This was a complex task, which required the precise tracking of available memory when an application demanded memory and there wasn't enough. The job was made all the more difficult because "everybody needs memory, and they want it now," Perazzoli said.

Better to appreciate the role of the memory manager, imagine five restaurants that share a single parking lot with a fixed number of spaces, say one hundred. The only practical way to eat at any of these restaurants is to park in the lot. A lone valet controls the flow of cars coming and going and parks each car. The restaurants stand for the applications, the parking lot stands for the computer's internal memory and the valet stands for the memory manager piece of the operating system. In the morning, only one restaurant is open, there are plenty of spaces free and managing the lot is easy. Lunch is stressful. All five restaurants are open, and the demand for parking spaces is high.

Then the valet's life is a grueling one. He must not only keep track of every space; he must also unerringly park cars when they arrive and find them when guests wish to leave. Since the parking lot occupies physical space, it can always expand: Adding more spaces is expensive, but it will ease the parking bottleneck. A better alternative, though, is for the valet to work smarter and faster. When the lot fills, the valet must hold cars at the entrance until a space frees. Sophisticated valets are able to occupy the drivers of these cars, so that no one causes such a ruckus that the lot stops operating. Less able valets often manage the unparked cars so badly that chaos consumes the lot. Then every guest must leave his or her meal, find his or her car and have it parked all over again.

As the image of the valet shows, it was easy to go awry. Perazzoli intended to produce a sophisticated valet but to stick to well-worn paths in doing so.

The need for reliability greatly influenced the design of the operating system. What was the best way to isolate applications, so that their failure would not bring down NT too? Cutler's answer was to split the operating system into two major pieces. One piece was the "kernel," which never interacted directly with applications and thus couldn't be contaminated by them. The other piece was the graphical, visible portion of the operating system.

To grasp the benefits of a kernel, return to the upstairs-downstairs analogy. Imagine a chief of household staff who was so diligent that he served the family upstairs at any moment, night or day. He was on call, handling every request. If a meal needed cooking, he cooked it. If clothes needed washing, he washed them. In his absence, he arranged for a substitute. He kept the house running no matter what. The unexpected actions of someone upstairs should not bring the life downstairs to a halt—ever.

This was roughly the kind of operating system that Cutler wanted. Just like the family upstairs, applications could act in unexpected or irrational ways. In programming terms the piece of the operating system that sustained activity when all else failed was the kernel. It protected itself by imposing certain restrictions on applications, the most important being that only it, and never the applications, directed the hardware.

The structure of the kernel was itself complex, consisting of many pieces, which called each other or the hardware directly. Often pieces of the kernel called a bedrock layer of code, the "microkernel," which was the ultimate chief of staff within NT. Cutler, who had written a microkernel while at Digital, planned to write the one for NT. This seemed fitting to one teammate, who saw eerie parallels between Cutler's role on the team and the microkernel's authority over the operating system.

A kernel design had two main benefits. First, the kernel ensured reliability by allowing a user to keep other applications active or launch new ones even if one program accidentally halted. Second, the kernel made it possible for an operating system to display multiple personalities. Each operating-system personality called the kernel in order to issue commands to the computer. OS/2 would be one of these personalities, per Gates's orders. But NT could host other personalities, making it potentially a universal software platform.

The compelling virtues of Cutler's kernel design—reliability and multiple personalities—came at a price, however: speed, or rather the lack of it. The reason was strictly logical. Placing the personality into a module meant at least doubling the number of calls made by the system. An application had to call, say, the OS/2 module, which in turn called the kernel. In Cutler's parlance the personality became a "client" of the kernel, which "served" it.

When Gates first heard about this client-server model, he balked, thinking, "It creates a huge overhead to do it this way." He felt the evidence buttressed his opinion. "I have a pretty clear model in my head as to what the overhead is, so my view is that we shouldn't do it this way," he insisted. But Cutler vigorously defended client-server, saying it would not degrade performance. He provided mathematical data supporting his model, and one member of his crew wrote a twelve-page paper that ruled out other design alternatives as being unreliable.

Even after this debate, Gates still had doubts about NT's basic design. He knew better than Cutler how much customers cared about the speed of their programs. They would judge NT against DOS and OS/2, assembly-language programs designed for high performance. To be sure, microchips would be so fast someday that they would offset NT's sluggishness. But five or even ten years might pass before blazing-fast chips were so cheap that software sizzled no matter what. He worried that critics might crucify NT on a cross of speed.

Cutler stood his ground. He impatiently vowed that his team could work its "magic"; coding "tricks" would offset the limitations of the client-server design. Gates was unconvinced, but acquiesced, thinking, "Hey, it's their project, it's their project. And they think it's Okay."

As the blueprint for NT took shape in early 1989, Cutler shed the polite demeanor of his first months at Microsoft, exposing his real nature. Always impatient, he sent brief, blunt and unmistakable messages. He didn't like to repeat himself either. "If he explains something to you once, he expects you never to ask about it again," one teammate said. Cutler demanded that people keep pace with him. When asked to repeat an explanation, he'd do so, "only this time a little louder," said a Microsoftie who joined the team that summer. "Then, if you asked him to clarify what he meant by something, by this point he's starting to turn red. Like he's getting mad because you don't understand what he's saying. So I learned to listen very carefully to what he said and sometimes nod yes even when I didn't understand him. Then in my office I'd think about what he had said. Or I'd ask Lou [Perazzoli], 'What did Dave mean by this?'"

Cutler never apologized for his impatience or his tantrums. "I thrive on stress," he boasted. He viewed his team as a community built on common joys, sacrifices, and secrets. He was a stern but caring patriarch; he never asked more of anyone else than of himself. In a society in which excuses were the currency of toleration, he accepted none. "I expect everybody to do their best—all the time," he said.

To intimates, Cutler seemed like a force of nature, but over time his outbursts grew to seem routine. Those unfamiliar with Cutler, however, were warned to protect themselves. "When you see Cutler start to steam, get out of the way," a Cutler friend told a Microsoftie, who thought this was exaggerated advice until one day she heard a terrifying shout from Cutler's direction. "What was that noise?" she asked. It was the sound of Cutler's temper.

Though it didn't take much to set him off, sometimes his bluster was an act. "I can shout at people without being mad," he said. "They might think I'm mad, but I might not really be mad." Still, it was hard to tell the act from the real thing. When Cutler began referring to Microsoft as "this scumbag company," most people figured he meant it.

Myrhvold tried to relieve tensions by inviting some of the company's top designers, dubbed "architects," to meet Cutler's gang. This backfired badly in the case of Gordon Letwin, the veteran OS/2 architect. Letwin felt snubbed that Cutler had been asked to run the advanced OS/2 project. Moreover, he felt Myrhvold and Cutler had overblown both the prospects for RISC chips and the importance of a portable program. In his talk to Cutler's team, Letwin seemed patronizing. This upset Cutler himself, who already objected to OS/2's "crummy design," unreliability and inability to carry large loads. After examining OS/2 Cutler felt "sore" because he had promised that NT would run OS/2 programs. "Here we were trying to produce this state-of-the-art [portable system] that is compatible with this junk OS/2," he said.

Letwin felt Cutler had no appreciation for the compromises Microsoft had to make in order to ally with IBM—compromises Cutler would not have to make since IBM wasn't assisting in the development of NT. Letwin found that in designing OS/2 good ideas were rejected or endlessly debated. Fuming over Cutler's hubris, Letwin felt Cutler saw himself as a Prometheus, "bringing fire from the gods to illuminate the poor pathetic lives [of Microsofties]. We didn't exactly see it that way."

On March 9, 1989, Arleta Cutler telephoned her son to say his father had died of a heart attack at the age of seventy-seven. Cutler seemed unmoved, which didn't surprise her. Her son took "with a grain of salt" the gulf between him and his father, she said. "He isn't emotional about it." Yet some suspected that Neil's aloofness was the source of Cutler's own abiding anger. No matter how close he felt with his tribe of code writers or how much wealth he accrued from his achievements, anger sat on Cutler's shoulder. It accompanied him like a perverse but familiar friend. While he might blame an outburst on the frustration of the moment, Cutler acted according to a script written long ago, when his father stubbornly refused to show pride in his achievements. "What Dave missed as a young man was a dad who could tell him: 'Dave, you've done well. Relax,'" said Cutler's high school football coach, Larry Churches.

Neil Cutler endowed his son with a desire to win the respect and admiration of others through competition. "Whatever Dave was doing, he had to prove he did it better than anyone," Churches said. Even idle pleasures fell prey to Cutler's need to outdo others. "If you have a father who says you've done well, you don't have to keep proving it, but Dave was always proving it to his dad."

Cutler said little of his father's death: "It didn't affect me very much. We were never very close." As usual he let his actions say what his words could not.

He skipped his father's funeral.

Cutler's society was not for those who preferred PG movies. The women vying for a new job as Cutler's secretary were asked in their interviews, "What do you think of the word 'fuck'?"

"It's my favorite word," answered Callie Wilson, who got the job. Formerly an aide in Microsoft's sales department, Wilson shrugged off Cutler's outbursts and quickly came to enjoy the power of being his emissary. The mere mention of his name usually prompted a speedy response to any request. "Cutler's like having your own Rott-weiler," Wilson said. "He seems vicious to others, but he doesn't act like that with me. He backs me up."

A few months after she joined the team, Wilson turned thirty, and to celebrate she was brought into Short's hardware lab for a party at which a male stripper entertained. Miffed, she got her revenge by asking a girlfriend to strip at the next birthday party, for a man on the team. Her friend arrived with a boom box, flipped on the music and danced, moving closer and closer to the birthday boy. Then the woman froze and, looking at him, said, "They didn't pay me enough to strip for you." She walked off, taking her boom box with her, shocking the guy and leaving Cutler laughing.

At work, Cutler could swing from laughter to anger in an instant. He shunned levity, advising against playing in the office. He never worried about people's feelings. His purpose wasn't to make anyone feel bad; he just wished feelings weren't a concern at all. "We're all here to do a job," he said. A leader should not "walk around on eggshells, saying, 'Geez, how are you today? Isn't it nice you could make it to work today? It's so great that you can come.' Hey, we're getting paid for this, right? So I expect everybody to do their best all the time. I expect them to do their job: If they do their job, and they do their best all the time, they don't have any problem with me at all. But if they don't do their best, then they do have a problem with me."

Technical disputes are the bane and boon of a lab. Yet engineering and invention often allow many ways to achieve the same result. Honest disagreements, then, are endemic in every technical enterprise. Some disputes, however, involve what programmers call "religious differences." The points at stake seem important only to zealots; a neutral party might say that both sides are right. But zealots—unable to silence their opponents with logical arguments—hurl insults.

One of the oddest disputes, which brought out the worst in zealots, involved the notational system used to write instructions in C, one of the most popular computer languages. Over the years Microsoft had adopted its own convention, called Hungarian, after its creator, Budapest-born Charles Simonyi, perhaps the most influential code writer at Microsoft. Hungarian conveyed much information in a compact form, but it lacked the ready familiarity of conventional notation, which relied largely on English words rather than opaque abbreviations.

The differences between the two styles spawned many arguments, whose merits were lost on outsiders. The following two lines contain identical instructions; the top is Hungarian and the bottom is not:

```
pfi->pbufCur->ibCur = ibFile;
File->CurrentBuffer->Offset = File Offset;
```

Cutler and his team rejected Hungarian. This pleased Wood, who called Hungarian "the stupidest thing I'd ever seen." He added, "Coding style wars are a waste of valuable resources, although the confusion caused by Hungarian probably wastes more time. But then so do a lot of religions."

Even though he came down on the "right" side of the Hungarian "religious" question, Wood showed no signs of becoming a true believer in the Cutler cult. He found it odd that the ex-Digital men "walked on eggshells around Cutler, straining not to offend him." Some on the team were afraid of Cutler, while others adored him. Their affection was so blatant that a Microsoftie once asked, "Is [Cutler] the Messiah?"

In a way, the answer was yes. Cutler gave purpose to the lives of his crew members, lifting their spirits in a way that natural leaders can. He exuded a self-confidence that made his followers feel things were right and good.

Wood, however, saw Cutler less affectionately but more clearly. "Steve stood up to Dave," said one code writer close to Cutler. "He didn't treat Dave as a cult hero. He questioned Dave's directives."

Wood could afford independence of mind. His work at Microsoft had brought him millions of dollars in company stock—and financial security—so that he was not beholden in any way to Cutler. If he didn't want to work, he never had to again.

Among the crew, only he realized that Cutler's career was at a crossroads—and that his moment might have passed. Many engineers had posted a string of successes only to come up short. Ultimately this was the fate of almost every great engineer or inventor. Wood felt Cutler had a lot to prove. Moreover, he sensed that the story of Cutler rising from the ashes of Digital to lead NT was meant more to inspire than to inform. Cutler, the story went, was only there because Digital had stabbed him in the back and ungraciously driven him out. Cutler probably had been so provocative that the killing of Prism, Wood felt, was "as much Cutler's fault as Digital's."

Wood's irreverence toward Cutler spilled out in small ways. Cutler was fanatical about supplying reams of comments with his code. These "coding comments," as programmers call them, are buried inside a program, visible to those who wish to learn more about the intent of the original code writer. It is frustrating but useful to read these comments. Code often persists long after the original code writer leaves the scene; comments suggest the motivations and reasoning behind the code. Well-written comments help those who wish to modify or improve a program. Cutler's comments were beautiful yet overdone. Practically every line of his code spawned a comment. Wood's objection partly reflected the reality that he wrote much more code than Cutler and had less time for writing comments. "The problem [with commenting] is that the code evolves," Wood said. "I'm working on five things, and the code is changing every day," requiring parallel changes in the comments too. Cutler, of course, had a simple solution to Wood's problem: As the code changed, change the comments.

Wood's reluctance to document his work made Cutler "uptight. Steve's a very hard guy to manage, extremely hard," Cutler said. "He could retire at any moment. So his attitude is like: 'I'm going to do what I want to do.'" Cutler complained about Wood to Perazzoli, but it went no further. Perazzoli thought it made no sense to hassle Wood about habits he'd never break, and that an unreformed Wood was better than no Wood at all.

Tensions simmered. "I don't take anything lightly," said Cutler. Once he confronted Wood about some failing. Enraged, he sounded to Wood like someone gulping down water. He stood nose to nose with Wood, who wondered: "Is he gonna hit me?"

Cutler didn't.

While Cutler's clashes with Wood stayed within bounds, his run-ins with Darryl Rubin did not. Microsoft's chief for networking software, Rubin was both smart and comical: a Woody Allen of coding. He had been excited by Cutler's arrival, considering him "one of the giants of the industry." He had used Cutler's programs in college and knew him by being "intimately familiar" with Cutler's designs. But when he first met Cutler, Rubin was taken aback. Cutler strode into the room "like an Air Force colonel . . . with his superclose shave and short hair and this hard-driving, serious, tough attitude." Rubin didn't "think of a software guy as being a down-to-business kind of guy."

Networking was already a sore subject at Microsoft. A standard feature of minicomputers and workstations, networking had been slow to arrive in the world of PCs. Aside from Apple, whose Macintosh contained a simple and effective means of sharing files and printers between machines, customers had yet to find a standard way of linking together different brands of PCs. A Utah company named Novell had grabbed the lead with a program called Netware, which made it possible for many PCs to both share a single printer and handle a set of files located on one PC. Print and file services, though mundane, were the lifeblood of PC networking. Novell's lead stemmed largely from its fast delivery of these services: Microsoft was unable to better or even match Novell's products. At the moment Rubin led a large group that was building a networking attachment to OS/2 called Lan Man, which was Microsoft's latest hope in the attempt to overtake Novell.

Cutler brought his own religious ideas to networking. He thought Novell's Netware crashed too often and lacked the means to keep intruders from commandeering files and printers. He thought people would flock to an operating system that made networks reliable and secure, even if they were slower.

Rubin felt Cutler was mistaken. Customers were concerned about the speed of their software above all else. Microsoft had no alternative but to offer the fastest code possible, he insisted. And the best way to accomplish this was to let Rubin do it, "since I was highly concerned about performance issues and Cutler far less so." His demand, Rubin said, "created the inevitable clash" with Cutler, who asserted his rights to networking with rising stridency. A Rubin ally neatly dissected the dispute: "We were saying: 'Don't go learn those lessons over again.' They were saying: 'We're smart enough so we won't make those mistakes.'"

Neither Rubin nor Cutler would budge. Rubin told Cutler to keep his hands off networking. Cutler responded icily: "I basically told Rubin that he was the networking architect of the company, and that was fine. But we were going to do our own damn [network], and he wasn't going to tell us what to do."

With his sway over networking ebbing, Rubin sought to win a comic victory by penning a series of news flashes that lampooned Cutler's machismo:

Redmond, Wash.—Four programmers died in a freak accident today when David N. Cutler threw his dick on a second-floor conference table. The dick crashed through the floor and into the lab below, killing the programmers and damaging three computers.

Cutler's dick sustained only minor injuries. . . .

Washington, D.C.—A four-foot tsunami, or tidal wave, devastated much of the West Coast today. The Federal Emergency Management Agency called it the worst U.S. disaster ever, estimating damages at $500 billion. . . .

Redmond, Wash.—Rescue workers found the first survivor of the tsunami in the ruins of Microsoft's corporate campus.

David N. Cutler was found clinging to a water fountain. He reported having a pissing match with another Microsoft employee right before the tsunami.

Cutler's only injury appeared to be mild dehydration.

4. BLIND ALLEY

Cutler forced a smile, a paper cup in his hand. Gates struggled with the top of a champagne bottle, his glasses sliding down his nose. Gathered in the hardware lab in late July 1989, the team gawked at Gates, whom most had not seen for months. Then the cork popped and the champagne flowed. Gates saluted the team. People cheered. Cutler lifted a chocolate cake, with the words Power On Portasys (which stood for Portable Systems, the team's formal name) inscribed on the icing. His chin jutted out proudly, a tight smile exposing gritted teeth. More cheers.

Moments before, Gates had grabbed a switch on a makeshift PC powered by Intel's i860 chip. His hair was a mess, and he wore a pale blue dress shirt, open at the neck, and tan pants with a black belt. He had kept this test a secret from IBM and his other PC customers out of concern that they might presume Microsoft was entering the hardware business. Gates never intended to sell this PC, but it was essential to making sure NT was on track. It also might help Microsoft impress potential buyers of NT—*See what NT makes possible!*—and encourage PC makers to adopt hardware designs that were tailored to NT's strengths.

All this seemed far removed from the naked board, crammed with electronics and spread out on a worktable, that Gates stood over. Red, blue, black and gray wires sprouted from the sheet of circuitry like tubes from a recovering hospital patient. A clip-on fan hung on the shelf above it. Gates flicked the switch. The PC surged on.

Cutler was elated. He felt as if he was making history. Microsoft had never built a computer before; Gates had always left the hardware to his customers. But NT was so advanced that machines required to build and test the new operating system didn't even exist. If Microsoft waited for its customers to build even demonstration models, NT would be years late. This was a "big event," Cutler felt, because it came after nine months of virtual anonymity. For the insecure members of the team, one noted, Gates's appearance in the lab "validated our existence."

Of course, many hurdles lay ahead. Even this small step was painful. Just as Cutler suspected, the i860 chip was flawed. This was partly because Intel—worried about cannibalizing its bellwether X86-chip family—seemed to be limiting the i860. In response to prodding from Rob Short, Intel had improved the chip, but not much.

The uncertainty about the chip placed a cloud over NT. The choice of a chip was crucial: The two pieces were as closely related as horse and jockey. No matter how good a jockey, he can't turn a plow horse into a thoroughbred. It was the same with chips and software. Indeed, an operating system depended on a reliable chip. If the chip was a dud, a program could fail with it. NT's portability would someday make a switch to another chip easy and unremarkable. But that would be when NT was well established. Until then, the operating system must be paired with a winner.

Gates hung around after the cutting of the cake, talking with Short and his engineers about the special circuitry in the model and the further work required to turn it into a fully functioning PC. Then Cutler joined in the conversation. The others peeled off, leaving the two alone. Cutler wore tan pants and a black T-shirt with the logo of the sports equipment maker Head emblazoned across his chest. Standing there, his arms akimbo, he looked like an aging health club instructor, his T-shirt so tight against his flesh it seemed painted onto his muscular torso. He spoke firmly to Gates about the work ahead, stabbing his finger in the air, his hand in the shape of a pistol.

The most pressing matter was to run a piece of NT code on the i860. A week later, the team did. The program lacked virtually all its controls, but it managed to display the words "Hello World" on an attached screen. This was the best NT could do, but it made Cutler happy.

The shortcomings of the i860 chip were a growing problem. Just six weeks after the party with Gates, Cutler began searching for a replacement. He preferred a chip from Mips, an Intel rival. The Mips chip seemed superior to the i860, but switching to it would set the team back badly.

Chips weren't the team's only worry. A paucity of code-writing tools slowed progress. "Tools are important because there's nothing you can do on a computer with your hands," one code writer explained. "In the 1960s, you could still open the case and monkey with switches. But today you need tools." And few tools existed for the i860. Since it wasn't reliable enough for ordinary use, programmers had to write code that mimicked, or simulated, the chip. Intel's 386 chip ran the i860 simulator code, but at a snail's pace. It took minutes on the simulator to do things that took seconds on the real chip. Waiting for the simulator devoured time better spent coding. Programmers were impatient. "It was pretty painful," said Wood, one of the guys who didn't like waiting for his machine to catch up with him.

Other tools were poor or useless. The team was especially dependent on debuggers, programs that made it easier to locate and analyze flaws in their code. Generally a code writer only noticed something wrong with his program when it failed; in order to determine *what* was in error, he relied on a debugger, which provided a snapshot of a piece of code. If the debugger contained bugs itself—a common occurrence—its picture would be fuzzy, frustrating programmers even more.

Cutler asked some of his own programmers to create tools, something that was ordinarily handled by Microsoft's tools division. The job of building tools detracted from the main task of making NT, but Cutler felt he had no choice. Tools were a programmer's lifeblood; the quality of his tools was as important as the quality of his specs. Everything about NT was so new—the chips it would support, the code itself—that many of the tools didn't exist. The situation was akin to a novelist discovering at the start of a new book that he must also invent a grammar and punctuation style alongside his work of fiction.

The team also found itself exploring blind alleys—an affliction common to all work that pushes the boundaries of the known. Even the best programmers found that the complexities of their own code, or the interdependencies between their code and the myriad of other pieces that make up a working computer system, mocked them. The i860, for instance, was so flaky that code writers often couldn't tell whether their code or the hardware had caused a crash. Hours were spent poring over a failure only to conclude that their program was correct.

The chip, naturally, wasn't the only culprit. Other hardware might cause code to appear broken. As NT grew in size, the i860 prototype stored the program on a floppy disk the size of a shirt pocket. Someone wrote code to instruct the computer on how to store NT on a floppy. One day NT outgrew the floppy disk; now code was needed to tell the i860 to store NT on a roomier hard disk. Cutler offered to write this code. Everyone thought it would take two or three days. Three days passed; Cutler still hadn't come up with code that would do the trick. A week passed; he still wasn't done.

Cutler, who described himself as "one of these people who just don't make many mistakes," looked as if he had made a foolish one. By now he swore a lot, mostly at himself. Teammates, who had endured countless barbs from Cutler over their alleged inadequacies, showed him no mercy. One constantly ribbed Cutler: "Would you like me to write the code? Or should we ask someone from another group [at Microsoft] to do it for you?"

Cutler was not amused. Insisting that the hard drive was the problem, he bought a new one. It worked; then it didn't. He switched cables. The drive worked; then it didn't. He tried another cable. It still didn't work. Cutler began to think he had bought a bad batch of cables.

Then one day, when it looked as if he'd never figure out his on-again, off-again problem, Cutler told Short: "Something is just wrong here." The words triggered something in him. Short jumped to his feet and flipped through a manual. His face suddenly lost its color. The manual held a disturbing clue. Short had forgotten to install a minor piece of circuitry. Cutler's code had been right all along.

In the midst of all this, Gates anxiously awaited Cutler's first forecast of NT's completion. Two weeks before the first anniversary of Cutler's arrival, Gates met with him and Perazzoli in Microsoft's unadorned boardroom. "For the first time, we promised [specific] deliverables to Bill," Perazzoli said. The schedule was neat and tight; the promises were limited. Perazzoli, who made the presentation in order to free Cutler better to field questions, declared that old OS/2 applications would not run on NT without extensive changes. And DOS applications wouldn't run at all. Neither would existing OS/2 "drivers," or programs that controlled specific peripherals, such as printers (each brand of printer, for instance, usually required its own driver code). This last point really bothered Gates, who felt that preserving the drivers was, as he put it, "mother's milk. You always wanted to do that." He took some convincing, but Gates finally accepted that writing new drivers (or asking the peripheral companies to do so) was better than taking the cumbersome technical steps required to reuse existing drivers.

Given these goals, the team vowed it would ship to manufacturing the final version, or "Golden Master," of NT no later than March 30, 1991. But between then and the deadline eighteen months away, there were a series of goals to reach. These also drew Gates's attention:

Jan. 30, 1990	"Minimal NT up and running"
July 30, 1990	"Code complete"
Oct. 30, 1990	Version for applications writers
March 30, 1991	"Golden Master"

The schedule was aggressive, and keeping it depended on the timely contributions of three groups not directly under Cutler's control.

First, there was the matter of making NT work on Intel's 386 family of chips, which were the PC standard. Gates viewed this task, called a "port," as "a top priority." He had never imagined releasing NT unless it ran on standard PCs. Cutler, however, had no passion for the port. He considered the RISC chip to be the principal home for NT. There was logic to Cutler's bias. He feared that making a version of NT for the standard PCs with a 386 chip would undermine his goal of portability. The standard PC was so popular that his team would be tempted to write nonportable assembly code designed to make NT run faster or perform some special trick that worked only on the 386.

Perazzoli bluntly stated this fear: "To us, the port to the 386 was evil." At the same time, "It was good because there were plenty of 386 PCs out there," and his programmers hungered for the chance to write code on a target machine. While Perazzoli was torn over the port, in practice, he could spare no one for the job. The NT team had doubled since its formation. Several people had joined from Cutler's former Digital lab, but the team still numbered fewer than twenty people.

To launch the port, Gates pried one guy loose from the OS/2 team to start the job, with the promise of two more code writers to follow. The NT schedule hinged on their speedy work.

Networking represented a second dependency. Cutler pushed hard for his own networking group. Until then, he depended on people who worked for Darryl Rubin, whom Cutler had fought to a stalemate. Darryl Havens, who oversaw networking for Cutler, crafted a sensible arrangement with a Rubin associate, which called for the two teams to share work and at least try to agree on goals and techniques. Brian Valentine, Rubin's deputy, credited Havens with making the decisive moves in ending the bitter squabbling between the teams. "Havens is very smart; he's not threatening; he doesn't challenge you," Valentine said. "He doesn't accuse you of stupidity, which immediately puts people on the defensive."

Cutler, however, found little to cheer about in the rapprochement with Rubin's gang. While appreciative of Havens's effort, he saw the truce as merely a pause in the push to gain a networking group of his own.

Graphics, which included the user interface, was the team's third and biggest dependency. Cutler's group had no one working on

graphics, even though this piece of the operating program produced everything visible on the computer screen. "We always, always were going to have graphics," Cutler said. But he knew little
about graphics code. His prior operating systems, despite their
power, provided no graphics. In computerspeak, they supported
"character- " or "text-based" applications only. This suited Cutler
fine; he knew the "secret handshakes" required to control text applications the way many blind people knew braille. But without realizing it, he was living in a bygone time. It was now the age of
visualization, when abstract concepts as well as basic needs and
wants were increasingly expressed in visual terms. From its origins
as a number cruncher, the computer had gone Hollywood; it was
now an image maker of vast power. Thus, graphics in many ways
defined the look and feel of computing.

Cutler was ill at ease with the style of visual computing. Just as he
happily allowed someone else to solve the problem of making NT
compatible with past DOS and OS/2 applications, Cutler presumed
graphics was someone else's problem. And it was.

If Chuck Whitmer wasn't some Hollywood director's celluloid
dream, then he should have been. He was Indiana Jones with a keyboard. A teenage math and chess whiz, Whitmer, born in 1957, was
good enough at physics to gain both a bachelor's and master's degree in four years at the University of Chicago. Then, while studying
for his doctorate at Princeton, he took up gambling, becoming expert at card games. Exploiting his ability to hold six decks in his
head at once, he soon covered his school expenses with blackjack
winnings earned in Atlantic City casinos. To avoid drawing attention
to his skills, he played under various fake names.

Whitmer's work with computers, then limited to assisting him in
his physics studies, took a decided turn toward comprehending
games of chance. With their unlimited capacity for analyzing proba-
bilities, computers were a gambler's dream. He and another
physics student wrote a program that tried to predict instantly the
outcome of a roulette throw. They collected data at casinos, rushing
to their room with fresh roulette results, which they fed to their
program. To refine their model, they drew on data from various

quarters, even filming dealers throwing roulette balls at a gambling school.

None of this detracted from Whitmer's promise as a physicist. He was so smart that during his second year at Princeton the professors graded many of exam questions by comparing other student answers with his.

But programming lured Whitmer away from physics. For someone who could construct and deconstruct puzzles, software held riches beyond the dreams of even the finest physicist. Whitmer teamed with fellow physics graduate student Nathan Myrhvold, who had arrived at Princeton the same year as Whitmer. Joined by Myrhvold's brother, they formed the software company that Microsoft bought for a reported $1.5 million in stock in 1986. The stock would soar in value over the next few years, making Whitmer a millionaire by virtue of that alone. But joining Microsoft proved as big a boon.

Whitmer arrived in Redmond in June 1986, quickly becoming the lead graphics programmer on Presentation Manager, the software personality planned for OS/2. With his grasp of math, Whitmer was attracted by computer graphics, the most math-intensive field in software. One might think that math aptitude would apply across the code-writing world, but this was not so. The logical operations of a computer, while abstract, were abstract in a familiar way. When computers added two numbers together, for instance, they did so in much the same way as people do: One plus one equals two. A computer performed this addition faster than a person, but the route to the answer was the same. This was not so with graphics. When an ordinary person (as opposed to a civil engineer) wanted to draw a circle, he did not apply a special algorithm to his choice of a diameter. He just drew a circle with his hand. Having no hands, computers drew circles—and all the other shapes—by applying mathematical formulas. The better the formulas, the more accurate and versatile the shapes. Not every programmer instinctively grasped that within each physical object, like a core inside an apple, lived a mathematical relationship. This was even true, of course, for the alphabet: The computer treated a letter as a shape, defined by numbers. Whitmer grasped the essence of shapes, and his ability to refine and mold them was uncanny.

Whitmer spent a little more than two years at work on Presentation Manager, helping to finish the program in late 1988. Seeking a fresh start, he began lobbying IBM software executives in December to cosponsor with Microsoft an effort to make a portable version of PM. This would make it possible for PM applications to run on PCs powered by RISC chips and not Intel's X86 family of processors. In April 1989 Whitmer won IBM's support. Microsoft put him in charge of a small group and gave him, in his words, "free rein."

To Whitmer, freedom meant more than refusing to file status reports, attend meetings or answer the phone. Freedom meant more than severing his ties with the annoying OS/2 project, so that he no longer suffered the strains of colloborating with IBM. Freedom meant something more profoundly liberating to Whitmer, who promptly declared himself "dead" and disappeared. His team disappeared with him.

They left behind a curious poster, taped to their office doors. "Sorry, we're dead," the poster announced. When people asked Whitmer's boss for his whereabouts, they heard the official line: "Whitmer is dead."

Of course, he wasn't *really* dead, just out of the loop. He hid unnoticed in another building on Microsoft's campus with several others, forming what management writer Tom Peters has called a "skunk works," or secret project unfettered by the ordinary rhythms of beauracracy. More stylishly, Whitmer called his team the *Undead.*

Before asking the Undead to write a word of code, Whitmer pondered two questions that would have a momentous effect on his graphics program (and, though he could not have realized it then, on the whole course of NT).

The first question was whether the Undead should duplicate or improve on PM's graphics? Whitmer chose the path of improvement for sound mathematical reasons. PM created its panopoly of graphics by manipulating conical shapes and ellipses. The math involved was relatively cumbersome. For his portable program, Whitmer chose as his basic unit the "bezier," a generic curve produced by a mathematical formula.

In choosing the bezier, which served as the basis for a variety of computer-created shapes, Whitmer knew that special hardware existed to accelerate the bezier math, and that Postscript, the most popular approach to forming letters and shapes on the printed page, was derived from bezier curves. Both these facts would give portable PM faster, more flexible graphics.

The second question was which programming language he should code in. By definition portable code was produced by a high-level language; assembly code, by contrast, was tied to a specific processor and hence was not portable. Precedent suggested a language called C, which many programmers knew. While it was portable, however, C was difficult to master and gave a programmer a great deal of latitude, which increased the likelihood of coding errors. A more inspired choice—a gambler's choice—was C++, a newer language that was all the rage among software theorists. By preventing code writers from making mistakes, C++ promised faster results and greater consistency, which would benefit programs that were the work of many people.

Whitmer was attracted by the putative benefits of C++. "It stops you from being stupid," he said. Gates, swept up in the euphoria over C++, encouraged Whitmer to "get out on the frontier" and use it.

Gates promoted C++ to a reluctant Cutler, who complained that important C++ tools were lacking or unreliable and that very few programmers knew the language. Why take the time to learn it, when the C language will do? Cutler asked.

Gates persisted in pushing C++ until Cutler issued a firm and final no.

As Cutler expected, the choice of the C++ language cost the Undead months of code writing, during which they instead learned a language none knew. They started writing code in June 1989, but much of this code later required revising. They were C++ rookies, and for a long time it showed.

In the midst of this, Whitmer, who had kept the entire design of his graphics program in his head, felt compelled to write out his graphics specification. Whitmer didn't look forward to this. He had a furtive side and viewed programming not as a strictly rational act, but as a kind of modern-day alchemy in which a worthless metal was turned into gold seemingly by invoking a magic spell. His followers among the Undead shared this whimsical, magical view of themselves.

As one outsider described the style of the Undead, "They think of themselves as wizards, not scientists. Wizards are dark and mysterious. They act as if success, and the trappings of achievement— money, status, women—are too puny to concern them. These are the guys who sat in the back of the computer science lab and got bad grades, maybe on purpose. They usually aren't broad, but great at one thing. And they don't like to explain themselves."

Whitmer was the king wizard, and if he had to write a spec, he would shroud this activity in mystery. To start with, he wished to write the specs somewhere faraway and with the help of a sidekick. Walt Moore would be perfect, he thought.

Moore was a college dropout, a self-taught programmer from Seattle who'd worked at Microsoft long enough to qualify as a millionaire based on his vested stock options alone. He had curly black hair and wore glasses and a wry expression that left other people off balance. He arrived at Microsoft in 1983, when the great need was for small, tight, clever code. PCs then lacked pep, storage space was thin and internal memory was ridiculously small. On this Lilliputian platform, programs of awesome ingenuity performed tasks that a few years before had been considered the province of far more expensive computers. Moore showed a flair for this kind of coding that could not be discerned from an interview. In person he was shy and indirect; he didn't make a big first impression. Microsoft had initially rejected him for a job, a rebuff so painful to Moore that he hung the rejection notice on his office door for some months after his hiring. He considered the letter to be a badge of honor and did not remove it until Ballmer asked him to take it down.

His speciality was writing the code that made graphics appear on computer displays in the way the program intends the graphics to be seen. In general such code is called a driver; Moore's metier was display drivers. The cleverer the code, the faster the graphics flashed on screen. This was unglamorous but important work. If it was poorly done, customers were unhappy. As Gates constantly reminded people, PC customers really only cared about how quickly their information flashed before them on screen. The display driver was not the sole factor in determining the speed, but it was a big one.

Moore was as much a mystery to himself as to others. At the age of thirty-two, he was a perfectionist, conservative and methodical; his approach to code writing was shaped by his deep knowledge of video games. Moore was a superb player, especially at those games in which an error "killed" a player. "Walt doesn't like dying in video games," a friend said.

His aversion to losing shaped his character, as a person and a programmer. He was single, shy around women, yet he yearned for a great, lasting love. He repeatedly was infatuated with the female receptionists at Microsoft, yet he seemed hopelessly unable to turn an affair of the heart into one of the flesh. Still, he had a dark sense of humor and an appreciation of the absurdities of the powerful and self-important. Moore was a good person to have around when people began to take their goals and purposes too seriously. He reminded everyone of the folly of life.

Moore was pleased to join Whitmer on a spec-writing trip, especially when he learned the destination was Maui. Whitmer told Martin Dunsmuir, his manager, that they wanted ten days in Hawaii and Microsoft need only pay for the plane tickets. He and Moore would cover their own expenses on the island. Dunsmuir agreed, thinking Whitmer was joking.

Whitmer immediately booked two tickets for the earliest flight to Hawaii the next day. He and Moore boarded a 6:45 a.m. flight to San Francisco, where they would change planes en route to Maui. Who should greet them on board but Dunsmuir, who happened to have business that day in California. Startled, Dunsmuir yelled, "You bastards, I didn't think you were serious!"

It was the Undead all over again. Before leaving Whitmer told everyone he and Moore planned to decamp to Tacoma, a dreary city some fifty miles to the south of Redmond. It was a neat ploy, since colleagues mainly conversed via electronic mail, or e-mail. No matter Whitmer's whereabouts, his e-mail address remained "Chuckwh." At Microsoft, e-mail was the most trusted and intimate means of exchanging messages. From any PC, an employee could send a note to one employee or scores of them. They could create the electronic equivalent of a mail drop; Cutler's team, for instance, went by "NTDev"; all messages to this alias could be read by everyone on the team (though not by members of other teams).

E-mail was so ingrained at Microsoft that an employee invariably checked his mail at the start of each day and, if he had a PC at home, before he went to bed. Bill Gates was a tireless e-mail correspondent, who had only a few months before publicly stated that "reading and sending" e-mail was "his highest priority activity each day." Indeed, conversing via e-mail was so habitual that many people were actually referred to in spoken conversations by their e-mail addresses instead of their given names. A person's e-mail name generally consisted of his first name and the first letter in his surname. Gates was "Billg"; Cutler was "Davec"; Perazzoli was "Loup"; Moore was "Waltm."

The e-mail gambit was convincing. Whitmer and Moore responded to inquiries as if they were down the hall. They actually were hunched over laptop computers, either in their rooms at the Maui Westin, or at pool side sipping piña coladas. The only awkward moment arose when Gates unexpectedly summoned Whitmer, via e-mail, to a meeting the next day. After frantically checking the flights out of Maui, Whitmer realized he couldn't make Seattle in time. He lamely begged off.

In the allotted ten days, the two men wrote most of the spec, buying a cheap printer to make sure they had the all-important hard copy in tow when they left the island.

Armed with the spec, the Undead quickened their progress, but the group was still hampered by the birth pains of writing code in C++. At the end of 1989, Whitmer trashed much of the code written in the few months after the Maui trip. With his "ideas and concepts about graphics still evolving," he chalked up the year as an object lesson in the cost of pioneering.

The new year brought a rude awakening. Long-simmering problems came home to roost on January 2, 1990, when Gates let fly a bunch of complaints about the project. Most important, he suspected that the port of NT to the 386 chip was proceeding too slowly.

Even though this wasn't strictly Cutler's responsibility, Gates suggested that the delay reflected Cutler's neglect of the 386 chip. This delay was intolerable because Gates considered the 386 chip to be NT's "ultimate platform."

Gates had also learned of the dispute between Cutler and Rubin, and he brought the two men together that day in a bid at reconciliation. Later the same day, Gates huddled with Cutler, Myrhvold and Ballmer to discuss another dark cloud hanging over the project: Intel's i860. The chip, they agreed, must be replaced with another RISC chip, even though this meant absorbing months of fresh work.

Cutler was caught off guard by the swift onset of crisis. In his zeal to build the kernel—the foundation—of NT, he had lost sight of his project's position within Microsoft and its relationship to the broader forces rippling through the personal computer industry. His blindness was not surprising: Cutler was a stranger to the world of the PC. He was unprepared to appreciate the diversity and number of interdependencies between groups within Microsoft and companies and customers outside it. "None of us knew anything about the PC industry," said Rob Short. "We thought we were the hotshots—and knew what was going on—because we understood the technology. But we didn't see what was happening in the PC business."

Perazzoli, meanwhile, thought the remedy was for Cutler to take responsibility for graphics and networking code, but "Dave didn't want to sign up for all this management stuff." Cutler also didn't find graphics appealing. His Digital operating systems contained just rudimentary graphics and none of the dazzling visual features that owners of PCs had come to love. Cutler's passion was directed toward the foundation of an operating system, not its ornate surface. His enthusiasm for NT's hidden aspects, however, seemed to jeopardize the project. He was the natural leader of NT, but he seemed too reluctant to take responsibility for its disparate pieces. This reticence prompted a few senior Microsofties to "call me on the carpet," Cutler conceded. He brushed aside his critics. No matter what they said, "I knew I was going to deliver. I absolutely knew I'd deliver NT. No question."

Paul Maritz didn't expect a welcoming parade when he came to Cutler's rescue. He didn't get one either.

Though he stood six feet two inches tall, Maritz was an understated person in a company of blowhards. He didn't feel compelled to show off his smarts. But when he spoke extemporaneously, he did so with a crispness and precision that made it seem as if he read from a script. At first blush he seemed overly correct and mannered. But before long he let out a nervous laugh, a cross between catching his breath and chuckling, that suggested the tensions held within him.

Maritz had found a home at Microsoft. Born thirty-four years earlier to an Afrikaner father and a Kenyan-born mother of British parentage, he was raised on a farm in the waning years of what was then the white-settler nation of Rhodesia (now Zimbabwe). He always thought his future lay elsewhere. "My father brought me up to believe that the days of the white man in Africa were over," he recalled. "So from an early age there was no expectation that we'd stay there. We were taught to get an education that would stand us in good stead wherever we went."

In college in Capetown, South Africa, Maritz studied math and economics. For a course on statistics, he wrote a program in Basic. He liked it and entered a programming competition sponsored by the local IBM sales office, submitting a computer version of the game Life. He won. "I found my destiny," he said.

On graduating, Maritz left for London, where he was hired by Burroughs, then a large maker of mainframe computers. After two years, he left to teach at a Scottish university, then moved to the United States to join Intel. He spent five years there in various management posts before moving to Microsoft in 1986. Gates put him in charge of the company's infant Unix and networking businesses. His canvas was large, but he supervised just thirteen people.

In March 1989 Ballmer gave Maritz responsibility for OS/2, though not authority over Cutler's team. In fact, Ballmer wished Maritz to take charge of NT, but Cutler refused to report to Maritz. Since formal duties meant little at Microsoft, Ballmer expected Maritz to oversee Cutler's team and ultimately "make sense" of NT.

For the rest of the year, Maritz, immersed in OS/2, had little time for Cutler. In January 1990, however, he began to look into NT, prompted by Gates's alarm over the lack of coordination between

Cutler's people and other groups at Microsoft. Maritz concluded that NT was an "exercise in technology development," not a product, and a "poorly coordinated exercise" at that. He felt that the situation would improve if Whitmer's graphics group, the networking people under Rubin's command and the NT crew were combined into a single team under Cutler's command. Unless this happened NT would never even become a commercial product.

Cutler, while agreeing that his project was "disjointed," objected to taking on more responsibility. He especially wished to steer clear of graphics. The subject was alien to him, he wasn't "clear [on] how to sort it out," and he was put off by Whitmer's style. Besides, he felt his own team, now consisting of about twenty-five people, was already large. The thought of an even larger team upset him. "I'd rather be in charge of five people than five hundred," he said.

Cutler's bias against big teams was understandable. He was alert to the hazards of spreading himself too thin: The more he took on, the less likely he thought he would be to deliver anything of quality. Still, his allegiance to small teams was a quaint anachronism in an age of complexity. Gates hoped that Cutler would realize that "the whole product was going to look poor" unless someone of his stature filled the leadership breach. Gates felt so strongly about this that he considered ordering Cutler to broaden his duties. He thought Maritz could just "jam [the decision] home" over Cutler's objections.

Maritz, however, preferred not to force things. He viewed Cutler as a powerful but delicate instrument. It was best not to tinker with Cutler. "If you fix the bad things," he said, "you're probably going to screw up the good things." Besides, Cutler showed no willingness to accept such an order from Maritz, who struggled to earn Cutler's civility. As he began meeting regularly with Cutler on NT matters, Maritz often found himself the victim of slights. Once Maritz innocently suggested to Cutler that "We should—" Cutler interrupted: "We! Who's we? You mean you and the mouse in your pocket?"

Maritz brushed off such retorts, even finding humor in Cutler's apparently inexhaustible supply of epithets. He refused to allow Cutler to draw him into a brawl. Instead, he hoped Cutler would "volunteer" for greater responsibility as the shortcomings of the status quo became more apparent.

On February 23, 1990, Maritz offered a challenge that was intended to bring the shortcomings of NT's organization to the surface.
This challenge, which for the first time clearly tied together Cutler
and Whitmer, was to make four Presentation Manager programs
run on NT in time for a demonstration that November at the industry's mammoth annual Computer Dealer Exposition (Comdex). This
was a "huge goal," Maritz believed, because it meant vastly increasing the integration between Cutler's kernel and Whitmer's. In
Maritz's mind his challenge left no room for fudging: "Either you
achieve this milestone or you don't. You can't bullshit."

In part Maritz was trying to teach Cutler the lesson that he had
"no real conception of the huge amount of work that goes into the
operating [program] beyond the kernel." Cutler's team "was a
bunch of guys building a kernel with no delivery vehicle" to the customer. "It's like building a house," he explained. Of course, the foundation must be solid, but there's much more to a house than that.

The Comdex demonstration had another benefit. It would send a
message to rival companies, which claimed that Microsoft wouldn't
release a portable operating program until 1994. Maritz thought NT
might be finished as early as 1992. The demonstration, he said,
"would certainly let people know that NT was *real* and would be
coming in their lifetimes."

Jonathan Manheim was delighted by Maritz's challenge. The leader
of a small group of testers assigned to NT, Manheim was dark and
swarthy, wore a thick mustache, and had a somber disposition that
made his rough-hewn face seem like a mask. But he warmed quickly to others and spoke easily about himself and his emotions in a
way unusual for men who do technical work. Code writers and engineers often maintain the fiction that their own psychology has little bearing on their work. Reason rules. But Manheim, while logical,
was also introspective.

Born in 1950, Manheim was raised in New Jersey, drifted to California in the early 1970s, and began a fitful college career at Berkeley. He took up photography, snapping pictures of street scenes and
selling them to passersby. One day he bought a pair of contact lens-
es and struck up a conversation with the optician, who was about

his age and had also attended Berkeley. The optician and Manheim became friends, and Manheim soon went to work in his eyeglass store. Manheim filled prescriptions and made glasses until the optician asked Manheim to store his business records on a personal computer. Manheim bought his first PC.

Then as now the PC held a curious power over restless, analytical people. To start with, the computer carried a psychological appeal not unlike that of an automobile. Both machines were objects of intense attachment for many of their owners—feelings of attachment that went well beyond the utility of the machines. While illustrating the way in which people can form emotional bonds with tools, the symbolisms of the automobile and the PC differed in an important way. The realm of the automobile extended no further than that of fantasy and enjoyment. The PC, by contrast, was a medium for creation. The utility of a PC arose directly from its software. Writing software required little money and, surprisingly, scant experience. Anyone with enough money to own a PC could fancy himself the next Bill Gates. By the mid-1980s the PC was a machine of dreams and a creator of opportunity. It had sparked a modern-day gold rush. Thousands of people programmed, driven by the desire to satisfy their curiosity, impress their friends and strike it rich.

Manheim was very much a part of this movement. No sooner had he written a program to track sales and inventory for the optical store then he sought to sell this program to others. He imagined selling so many copies that he would no longer have to work in the store but could program full-time. His feverish dreams, however, broke against cold reality. His program sold three copies; but this didn't matter—he was hooked. After work he invariably found himself in front of his PC, typing late into the night, sprucing up the look and feel of his program (the one that wasn't selling). By day he dragged about the optical shop, tired from his nocturnal fiddling. Finally it hit him: He had to learn whether he could cut it as a programmer.

He found a job writing code for a small company with shaky finances. By then he was married, had a child and was looking for something better. His wife's parents lived in Washington State, so he sought a job with the state's biggest software employer, Microsoft. He was rejected. Six months later—having lost his California job when his employer went bust—he moved to Washington without a job. Within weeks of his arrival, he was hired by Microsoft, which was growing so fast it needed scores of new employees at any time.

Manheim started with Microsoft as a contract employee, which meant he was paid for his work but received no benefits. Microsoft often started people as contractors because it was much easier to fire them if they didn't work out. (The benefit of contracting was that the worker received overtime pay, which could mount up rather quickly at Microsoft, where fifty- to sixty-hour weeks were typical and weekend work was unavoidable. Microsoft's salaried workers almost never earned overtime pay; their extra hours were considered as strictly voluntary. Managers believed Microsoft generously compensated employees for the long hours by giving bonuses and stock options.)

Contracting was a good first step for Manheim. Assigned to testing the OS/2 program, he clicked. His maturity and discipline caught the eye of Moshe Dunie, who coordinated the testing of OS/2. In June 1989, Dunie asked Manheim if he'd spend half-time creating a test team for an advanced version of OS/2 called NT. Manheim agreed, on the condition that he could rely on Dunie for help.

At the age of forty Dunie was a graybeard by Microsoft standards. He was unusual in other respects, too. For Dunie, Microsoft was something of a second career—a second life, really. Born in 1949 in the new state of Israel, he grew up in the shadow of the Holocaust. His father, a partner in a small truck company, sprang from a well-off German family of Lithuanian descent. In Germany he had worked as a manager in the family cigarette factory, but he left for Palestine in 1938. There he met Dunie's mother, a Czech who had survived Auschwitz. In Israel she bore Dunie two sons—Moshe and a brother five years his junior. She instilled in them a sense of perfectionism. "When my homework was messy, my mother would rip up the paper, and I'd start again," Dunie recalled. "My mother was very warmhearted about this, though. She did it in a way that didn't hurt."

When he graduated from high school, Dunie, a strong student, was allowed to skip a stint in the army and enroll in Israel's best engineering school. As part of the deal, he agreed to serve his five years in the army following his schooling, but he still had to serve in the reserves each summer. One year, while guarding a kibbutz along the border with Lebanon, he witnessed an Arab attack. No one was killed, but a bomb exploded. The memory stuck with him. Even twenty years later, he had "a nightmare now and again about a terrorist attacking my home or my family."

After college, Dunie was sent by the Israeli Air Force to a secret test range, where he designed airborne weaponry. When his hitch ended, he joined an American aerospace company, managing a team writing the code for the onboard computer of an F-16 fighter jet. In 1981, he joined a Silicon Valley company making energy-management software. Seven years later, he replied to a Microsoft ad and was hired as a manager on the OS/2 team.

Dunie's experience in aerospace and defense made for an unusual résumé by Microsoft's standards. The typical Microsoftie, Bill Gates included, was vaguely rebellious, self-absorbed, prone to flights of fancy and indifferent to rank. In contrast, Dunie respected the chain of command, kept secrets and immersed himself in details. Coming from the field of aviation, where mundane errors could cost lives, he was exact.

For all these reasons, Dunie was drawn to testing, the grubby and anonymous side of programming. He insisted that testing, "though less glorious than making a product," often decided the fate of a program. He was attracted by the field's youth and freedom from dogma. Indeed, testing was wide open. Having grown rapidly, many PC software companies were stretched to the limit simply building their programs. With customers clamoring for new products, testing inevitably had to take a backseat. In addition, though it was eroding, there remained a pejorative attitude toward testing: "Let the customer test the program." That saved the builder money and time, but it frustrated buyers, who came to view the first release of a program as a gamble.

Microsoft's operating programs sold in such great numbers that extensive testing was imperative. Testing stressed various aspects of a program, the aim being to uncover weak links or coding errors. Dunie believed that the tests for OS/2 concentrated too heavily on the underlying pieces of the system and not enough on merely imitating the stresses typically imposed by customers. Dunie wanted to achieve a better balance in testing NT. He also wanted to gain an earlier start. If testers began writing their tests as soon as the pieces of NT were specified, the tests would be ready by the time the code worked.

There was no foolproof method for testing a program, making the tester's lot a humble one. Dunie showed the requisite humility and appreciated the benefits of deference. He displayed none of the raw ego that made code writers in turn brilliant and impossible. Solicitous toward Cutler, he took the attitude: "Cutler's usually right. . . . [and] if something upsets him there's a good reason."

Dunie was small, balding and wore wire-rimmed glasses. A lonely swath of hair stretched across his bald pate, gamely trying to stay put. Greeting strangers with a bashful smile, he seemed naked without a pad or a plan to guide him. He looked like an easy mark, but in crises he turned as hard as steel. His dedication to goals bordered on fanaticism. No matter how tricky or mundane the task, he kept after it, circling and circling, drawing ever closer, until finally he squashed it like an insect.

Cutler at first paid little attention to the testers except to grumble that "not only do we have a test group, it looks like it's going to be a big test group." Cutler had never relied on testers at Digital and considered them superfluous. "Its great to have a test group, but we probably won't need that anyway since the code will be of such [high] quality," he thought. He was glad that Manheim didn't report to him, and he wanted to keep it that way. And when Dunie asked for advice on testing, Cutler said that testing was often superfluous in the early stages of code writing. Testers "tend to find problems that every programmer knows is there," he said.

Cutler actually thought testers were worse than that. Their mere presence, he felt, fostered the dangerous illusion that someone could save a programmer from his sins. Cutler wanted a programmer to test his own code. The rationale for outside testing, of course, was that the code writer had a vested interest in making his code look better than it really was. After slaving over a program, he might not show the honesty required to fully expose errors. Cutler was unconvinced by this argument: "People say you can't test your own stuff. I say baloney."

Cutler's attitude made it harder for the testers, who were resigned to their second-class status, to win acceptance from the team. Wood, as elitist a code writer as any, explained: "A lot of testers feel they don't get respect, and they don't. Its kind of a Catch-22. Some of them don't deserve the respect because they're not that great technically. And those who are good technically are stuck [as testers], which doesn't help them."

This stereotype stemmed partly from a belief that the testers delighted in making programmers look bad. Testers denied that they sought to embarrass anyone, but it was true, as one put it, that "our goal is to kill a program—to cause a catastrophic problem."

If a code writer considered himself a master craftsman, a tester saw himself as a marauder, probing for weak points in code, then cruelly exploiting them. The dominant technique was uncomplicated: Stress a program until it broke. Because NT did many things at once, testing all the possible permutations required repetition. Many "stress" tests would run at the same time. A simple one consisted of opening, closing, reading and changing one file for minutes on end (the file might be a letter or a page from an electronic ledger). NT might fail only when a file closed at the same time as the operating system ordered a document printed.

This was only one side of testing. The other side involved piecing together random clues. Having crashed a program, the task is to discern why it failed. The best testers were masters at deducing the chain of events leading to a failure. They provided code writers with a virtual road map to fix their bug. The worst testers offered little more than a description of the hangup and a half-baked hypothesis of the cause.

Manheim had started testing NT almost exclusively in the fall of 1989, but he was still formally part of the OS/2 team. Other testers straddled both projects too. Maritz settled the problem of divided loyalties by assigning Manheim and six others to test NT full-time in late February 1990. Maritz's challenge to Cutler and Whitmer—to make four applications run on NT by the November trade show—

prompted the switch. This meant that the two programming teams would have to mesh their codes for the first time. This surely would expose technical flaws and mismatches in both pieces. Manheim's group would make it possible to identify these problems more quickly.

The shift scared Manheim because it meant a separation from Dunie, his boss and mentor, who would stick with OS/2. He felt "abandoned."

Work, however, was an antidote for worry. In response to Maritz's directives, old tests were scrapped and new ones written. The new tests aimed at duplicating the basic actions of the targeted applications (The identity of the programs was still a matter of debate, though Maritz leaned toward including the popular spreadsheet and design programs 1-2-3 and Autocad, and at least one Microsoft program, probably the company's word processor). The most valuable tests were disarmingly simple. Presentation Manager allowed users to switch from one on-screen window to another, but only one window could be active at a time. A quick check was to activate a window: If it didn't activate, something was amiss.

Some tests took less than a minute; others groaned on for hours. The results of all tests were logged and analyzed, providing ample fodder for anxiety and edification. In a makeshift buddy system, testers stuck with the same few programmers in the hopes of learning their code faster. Manheim told testers to dig into a flaw, studying it deeply before filing an official "bug report" on the code. Programmers lived to shoot down such reports as a consequence of a tester's feverish imagination, so Manheim encouraged as much deliberation as possible before filing them. "This kind of attention went a long way toward raising the respect [code writers] showed us," one said.

Cutler's growing appreciation for testing was more important, however. Though miserly with praise, Cutler made a gesture one spring day that filled the bedraggled testers with pride. One of his programmers, preparing to make a big change in NT, asked Cutler for his approval.

"So did you have this guy test it first?" Cutler said, pointing at the tester standing nearby. The programmer, who hadn't, quickly surrendered his code for testing. Cutler, who always preferred actions to proclamations, had made his point.

Whitmer's Undead and Cutler's veterans were as different as fire and ice.

The Undead acted like precocious college students who lived in a frat house. They behaved in the tradition of what Whitmer called "the old Microsoft crowd," which reflected the hacker ideal of programming. Hackers were virtuosos who wrote code as much (or more) for the sport of it than to achieve specific aims. They insisted that games often cast light on software's unrecognized powers and at the very least honed their own coding skills. "These games are for testing the mettle of the novice or for playing among master hackers," one observer has written. "They are not pranks to be played on others."

Hackers enjoyed pranks. After six hours of code writing, when the eyesight seemed about to go, an Undead member shot a round of golf—in the hallway. If he had company maybe he played a friendly contest of nerf bow-and-arrows. Another popular pastime was "hoser ball," in which players tried to knock down a phalanx of empty soda cans with a tennis ball filled with pennies and wrapped in electrical tape.

With so many antics, it was hard to tell when the Undead worked. Whitmer insisted on a distinction that Cutler would never grasp: "There are people who like to have fun and others who fuck up." Coding wizards were so good they could afford to cultivate their idiosyncrasies. Whitmer, for instance, preferred to arrive in the late morning or early afternoon and work into the evening. During one stretch, however, he devoted an evening a week to teaching colleagues how to count cards in order to beat the casinos. Whitmer invited those too timid to learn to invest in one of his periodic gambling binges; the minimum throw was five thousand dollars.

Walt Moore, after years of torrid coding, had recently retreated to his office. He sat inside, door closed and blinds lowered. It was as if he'd entered an electronic cocoon. There was a tacit understanding at Microsoft that after someone contributed substantially to the company he deserved to be carried for a time—maybe as long as a year—until he regained his zeal. Moore had shifted into this category. He played video games for hours. He realized he was slipping, but he was not sure why. Maybe he'd done the same thing for too long. Maybe Whitmer had dragged him down. He was such an authority that Moore increasingly deferred to him. He felt stirrings of initiative quenched by this inner debate: "Chuck is just going to reverse me anyway, so why make the decision? It doesn't matter what I think, it's Chuck's product. He makes the decisions, and I'm just a peon here to implement."

Moore also felt that he was the victim of "a deadly spiral." He had spent so many twelve-hour days at Microsoft over the past seven years that his circle of friends had grown smaller and smaller until the isolation became as tight as a noose around a condemned man's neck. It had happened without his noticing it, he felt. "You work a lot and [think], 'Oh, gee, I don't know anybody and the few people I do know are busy. So I'll work some more.' You keep working, you know less people, you do less things. Then pretty soon all you have left is work." Then even work seemed hollow and uncomfortable, becoming a haunted house that maintained a strange hold even as he desperately plotted an escape. Moore was at the point at which he wanted a companion. He'd met his current female infatuation when she cold-called him peddling tickets to the Seattle Ballet. Moore said he'd buy many tickets if she'd attend the ballet with him. She agreed and liked Moore enough to see him again. But she kept the relationship so ambiguous that even Moore couldn't say whether they were dating or just friends.

Another Whitmer coder had the opposite problem: His personal life was too rewarding. Paul Butzi was converting the most visible part of PM from assembly into portable code. Slightly built and of medium height, Butzi was urbane, witty and sarcastic. Even when he fell behind in his work, he still commuted to and from work by bus. He routinely called it a day by 5:30 p.m. And he never worked weekends, devoting them to his wife and two children. Such fidelity to family was astonishing for a Microsoftie. Said Whitmer: "Paul is a family man who happens to work at Microsoft. Other fathers work at Microsoft and happen to have families."

Butzi made no apologies for his domesticity. He'd arrived at Microsoft six years earlier, after a stint at Bell Labs, and now felt he'd proven himself. He could understand why the few colleagues in their twenties with families felt torn between work and family; they were competing with unmarried (and sometimes friendless) coworkers. But he felt that as a veteran he was entitled to a full personal life. He was determined not to end up like one of the Undead who slept at the office so often he seemed to enter his house only to shower. Repeating an old cliché, Butzi said: "Nobody lay on their deathbed wishing they'd spent more time at work."

By contrast, Cutler's team was like a crack unit in the Marines. Members arrived early, usually before 8:00 a.m., and prepared to stick closely to a plan. They liked to have a good time, but only off the premises. Cutler looked down on horsing around on the job. He hated computer games and winced whenever he got wind that one of his people played them in the office. He left his office in the middle of the day for an hour of squash, often skipping lunch. He practically never quit work before 6:30 p.m. Cutler's whole life revolved around NT. Almost all of his friends worked with him on the project. He couldn't understand how Whitmer's crew, with all their laugh and play, could carry their weight. He groused: "They always seemed on vacation."

Cutler wasn't beyond criticism himself. One critic was Naveen Jain, who in the spring of 1990 was asked to monitor how well the two halves of NT—kernel and graphics—meshed. Jain was a "program manager"; his job was to suggest features and changes in NT that might excite or satisfy customers. Program managers at Microsoft helped to define the product even though they didn't write code. Their influence was considerable, sometimes exceeding even that of the chief code writer. But they mainly relied on persuasion; they had no authority to order code writers actually to carry out their ideas. However, when staffers balked, a program manager might hire a contractor to produce the desired code. At best a program manager was a messenger from the marketplace. While the code writers concentrated on finishing *their* product, the program manager studied competing products, gathered intelligence about forthcoming products from rivals and solicited suggestions from potential customers. If a Microsoft product appeared to lack a feature customers raved about, the program manager argued for its inclusion. He often lost these arguments on technical or other grounds, but at a minimum he forced programmers to justify their goals.

Gates valued strong program managers, believing that theirs counted among "the most important jobs" at Microsoft because they "own . . . the vision of the product." Cutler rejected this view. He felt that code writers "owned" their products and bristled at the inexperience of some program managers. He was especially unimpressed with Jain.

Cutler had enough problems without fending off unwanted suggestions from a program manager. The previous October's schedule, which predicted that all code for NT would be written by July 1990, was now hopelessly out of date. The morass of graphics and delays in the delivery of the Mips processor meant that the team would struggle to finish the code that year. To make matters worse, doubts still persisted about the basic design of NT, called client-server. This meant that OS/2's personality stood outside the kernel, which treated it essentially as an application: It was virtually impossible for a flawed application to disrupt the rest of NT. But client-server slowed performance because the personality had to communicate back and forth with the kernel about what the application wanted done. This added a time-consuming procedure to the operations of NT, but Cutler insisted that his team would overcome it. Besides, even if NT ended up running applications slightly slower than normal, it was worth it, he felt. After all, reliability was his preeminent goal. So while "a tradeoff between reliability and speed" was inevitable, he said, there was no reason for panic.

In early May, Cutler began preparing for a May 30 meeting with Gates, his first in five months with Microsoft's chief. Cutler knew that Gates "had never bought into the fact that [client-server] was the best way to build the system." The last thing he wanted was for Gates to revisit the client-server decision in the meeting, because that might force a revision in NT's basic design—something Cutler wished to avoid.

As Cutler feared, the meeting with Gates went badly. Gates attacked the soft underbelly of NT: the graphics piece. Realizing that the choice of C++ meant the graphics code would be very large, he concluded it would require a far larger amount of computer memory than he expected. Gates seized on the slow progress as an excuse to worry aloud about whether Presentation Manager applications ever would run as quickly on NT as they did on OS/2. He was distressed to learn that the port of NT to Intel's 386 chip, which he viewed as the project's highest priority, still wasn't finished. Finally he fretted about the client-server design, which he feared sacrificed too much speed for reliability. Taken together, Gates's concerns underscored Maritz's private view that the NT project was "poorly coordinated" and nothing more than "a technology development exercise."

Rocking anxiously in his chair, Gates thought the NT project was in poor shape. To be sure, graphics "was the riskiest part," and he knew it wasn't Cutler's responsibility but then it probably should have been. Loudly Gates asked the group: "What you're telling me is that NT is going to be too big and too slow?"

Cutler and Perazolli stayed quiet. Maritz said nothing either, knowing that "too big, too slow" was a damning indictment from Gates. Only Jain was prepared to speak. He thought that Gates should know the truth: a chief executive deserved that. There was nothing wrong with giving Gates the bad news now and then promising to reform. NT was "too big, too slow," Jain said. "You're right."

Gates nodded. Then everyone in the room burst into nervous laughter.

Cutler saw little humor in Jain's remark. For a time, he even wished a pox on every program manager who sought to advise him or his team. With his project seemingly on the ropes—indeed, with his career hanging in the balance and the fate of NT the only thing standing between him and the dismissive conclusion that he could not cut it outside Digital's cozy nest—Cutler did not welcome advice or requests from those outside his code-writing family.

"I always push back," Cutler said. "It's like, man, if [these people] were more reasonable about everything, I wouldn't be so fucking uptight all the time. . . . I'm one of these people, I'll buy into anything that's just. I'll work hard day and night. But don't pile anything on me after I've committed to do something that's hard to do."

Little did Cutler realize that his friends at Microsoft had only just begun to make demands.

5. GROWLING BEARS

Cutler, Perazzoli and Rob Short huddled together in one of their periodic "staff" meetings. The brain trust of the project, they often met informally to ponder the future. Cutler liked these small meetings because he could speak his mind without fear of being misunderstood. It was June 8, 1990, and the meeting was prompted by a distant thunder that once seemed unimportant but now upset everything.

The rumbling had begun sixteen days earlier. Before an adoring crowd in Manhattan that included his mother, Bill Gates introduced a new version of Windows. No program had ever so excited PC owners. Throughout the world, millions of people eagerly awaited the arrival of Windows 3.0, the best version yet of a program that for the first time overcame the irritating limitations of DOS, including the awful memory barrier that hampered so many applications. Moreover, Windows made it possible to control a PC by pointing at pictures called icons, or pulling down menus on screen and making choices. Equally important, Windows 3.0 superseded the DOS command system.

Gates had promoted Windows for seven years with scant success; now the wild reception for this improved version altered the software universe beyond recognition. Suddenly the successor to the DOS standard was Windows. Windows' ascendance paralleled Gates's own rise, prompting *The Wall Street Journal* to describe him in May "as the single most influential figure in the computer industry."

Cutler wondered whether it was now his turn to pay homage to Windows. He despised changing gears and had long resisted entreaties from Gates to find a way to run Windows on NT. But OS/2 wasn't selling, despite IBM's support. As Perazzoli said, the question of the moment was: "Should our product be called Windows NT?"

Cutler shuddered. That wasn't his decision. Ballmer and Maritz controlled the outside of NT—the way it looked to the customer— while he controlled the inside. Still, Perazzoli had a point. Why buck a trend? Maybe NT *should* ride the Windows wave. Cutler told Perazzoli: "We ought to start looking at Windows manuals."

Paul Maritz was thinking along the same lines. Responsible for Microsoft's side of OS/2 and for NT, he found it increasingly difficult to balance OS/2 and Windows and to keep IBM, Microsoft's biggest customer, happy while pursuing Microsoft's destiny. OS/2 and Windows were two incompatible ways of controlling a PC. By promoting both, Microsoft confused customers and applications writers. The company also wasted money and talent. Microsoft had about 150 code writers working on future versions of OS/2 at an annual cost of roughly fifty million dollars.

It was an uphill battle trying to convince Gates and Ballmer that the time had come to part ways with IBM on the development of software. Formerly, the sale of Microsoft's operating programs was based "on a very simple premise," Maritz said. "You get the business with IBM and everything else will take care of itself." Now he felt that it was time to shatter this simple equation.

Throughout the spring and into the summer of 1990, Maritz told Gates and Ballmer, "We have to choose the Windows horse or the OS/2 horse." The choice threatened NT, which was critical to Microsoft's future. NT would never get finished unless "we got really serious" about it, but Microsoft "didn't have the resources behind NT to even make it into a product," Maritz insisted, because of all the time and money spent on OS/2.

Maritz told Gates and Ballmer that, under the circumstances, he was sure to fail as Microsoft's OS/2 chief. "Unless our strategy changed, I felt I was wasting my life. Why would one want to endure the tension, the stress and the pain if you're on a strategy that has no clear chance of winning?"

There was one good reason: IBM might view Microsoft's withdrawal from OS/2 as a declaration of war and retaliate. If IBM dumped Microsoft as a supplier of basic software, scores of companies that made functionally identical copies (or "clones") of IBM's PCs might also dump Microsoft. Because of this risk Maritz's plea to dump OS/2 fell on deaf ears at first. Ballmer couldn't really conceive of Microsoft succeeding without IBM's full backing. He took for granted conflict between the two allies. IBM and Microsoft were like two bears screwing in the woods: "The distressing sounds you hear are only the bears changing position."

By late July, Gates had revised his view. Windows was his top priority now. He'd long resisted this conclusion, but now he considered it "the most obvious thing in the world. It wasn't something I decided. Windows was happening. It was futile" to deny it.

With OS/2 relegated to the bench, Gates was excited. Microsoft's popularity was now so great that he bet that PC makers would never turn against the combination of DOS and Windows simply to support IBM. Besides, Gates was tired of IBM's incessant whining about restraining Windows. "You can [improve] Windows later," IBM executives kept telling him. "Just give us a couple of years to get dignity for OS/2." Gates now believed OS/2 was mortally wounded, a victim of Microsoft's prowess and IBM's sclerotic culture.

So Gates sided with Maritz. NT would assume the Windows "personality," by assuming those of its attributes that were visible to the customer. NT also would be redesigned to run applications written specifically for Windows. But Gates added a wrinkle to his position. Given the depth of IBM's attachment to OS/2, Gates reasoned, abandoning the program altogether would only trigger a nasty split with IBM. Why not maintain a pretense of cooperation by convincing IBM of the merits of an operating system that hosted both Windows and OS/2? NT could be designed to do this, Gates reasoned.

If IBM accepted this, Microsoft could continue to describe Cutler's program as "NT OS/2." Even though it contradicted his rhetoric about the need for a single software standard, Gates was prepared to tell IBM: "There's no reason to think two [program personalities] can't be of equal importance" to customers.

This was a bold stroke. By denying reality, Gates's tactic would freeze IBM long enough for Microsoft to install Windows as the standard for computing. Gates would peddle this apparent compromise to IBM and rival software makers, while Maritz and Cutler's team pursued the real objective internally.

Maritz was overjoyed. Finally NT would become part of the winning Windows family, spanning everything from small notebook computers to big machines running NT. He prepared to pull the plug on OS/2 and shift many of its 150 programmers to Cutler's team, where they would give NT a Windows makeover. To allow Gates and Ballmer publicly to maintain the fiction that OS/2 was alive and well and had a place in Microsoft's future, Maritz resigned himself to supporting a few programmers who would finish a greatly scaled-down version of an OS/2 personality for NT. But those familiar with Maritz's plans knew better; they began calling Cutler's program by its true name: Windows NT.

On August 1, 1990, Maritz asked Cutler and Perazzoli, "How do we move to a Windows plan?" The wedding date wasn't set, he cautioned, but it might not be long before NT and Windows were married in a discreet, private ceremony. Shaking his head, Perazzoli thought, "This is a bombshell."

Three weeks later, on August 20, Gates, Ballmer, Maritz, Cutler and Microsoft's other operating-system leaders gathered at the Schumway Mansion, near Microsoft's campus, to discuss the merger of Windows and NT. As one participant put it, "Out of the ashes of OS/2, NT is reborn."

The swing in favor of Windows wrecked the team's schedule. It rendered moot the challenge issued by Maritz in February 1990 to make four OS/2 programs run on NT in time for fall Comdex. The switch to Windows meant the team would have nothing to display at the mammoth trade show. This wasn't surprising, since some code writers, especially Whitmer's Undead, now had to trash months of work. The shift to Windows also raised tough technical questions about NT's ability to support old Windows and DOS programs—questions that Cutler had long hoped to avoid. When news of the marriage between Windows and NT spread, some members of his team, one said, "were screaming with agony inside."

Others were relieved. Darryl Havens, an original member of Cutler's crew, "didn't like OS/2 anyway" because it lacked reliability and wasn't much of an improvement over DOS. "It was better to have something else," he thought, "regardless of what it was."

Perazzoli agreed. For months he'd wondered whether NT should adopt the Windows personality. Hoping this would happen, he had avoided resolving some technical matters with the OS/2 team on the assumption that "it would be an incredible waste of time."

Technical preferences aside, the success of Windows was a windfall for Cutler and colleagues. Most had received sizable stock option grants on joining Microsoft, partly to compensate for their reduced wages. At other companies such stock grants might return 10 to 25 percent profit to a grateful employee over five to ten years. A doubling of value would be a bonanza. But lately Microsoft's stock had soared—with no limit in sight. Demand for Windows transformed Microsoft from the leader of the software pack into a giant looming over the rest of the industry. The company's net profits were especially impressive; an astonishing 25 percent of sales flowed to the bottom line. Options granted to Cutler two years earlier, while substantial at the time, were now breathtaking. And the stock price seemed a cinch to double over the next few years, given the company's bullish outlook.

Even at the current stock price, Cutler's options now were worth at least several million dollars. Havens and Perazzoli, meanwhile, were assured of clearing high six figures. Even the team's rookie programmer, hired fresh from Princeton the summer before, would reap a few hundred thousand dollars within three years. This kind of money could buy a lot of loyalty and hard work. It also made for independent-minded programmers.

Cutler had mixed reactions to the shift from OS/2 to Windows. On the one hand, the move "made a lot of sense," he said. "OS/2 went away. We didn't have to deal with IBM. It was pretty obvious this was a good thing to do." Still, the rapid changes in strategy were reminiscent of his days at Digital, where too many of his projects were altered as a prelude to cancellation. He worried that NT might have a similar fate.

Ballmer reassured him. The bright side was that finally—*finally*—NT had a large target market. Some portion of Windows owners would adopt NT. This put Cutler in a much better position to define the next generation of PC software, placing him at the apex of technical power in the computer industry. Besides, NT would still meet the goals closest to Cutler's heart: portability, reliability and the ability to provide an alternative to Unix, the splintered high-end operating program.

This last goal was crucial to Cutler. "Unix is like Cutler's lifelong foe," said one team member who'd worked with Cutler for nearly two decades. "It's like his Moriarty [Sherlock Holmes's nemesis]. He thinks Unix is a junk operating program designed by a committee of Ph.D.s. There's never been one mind behind the whole thing, and it shows. So he's always been out to get Unix. But this is the first time he's had the chance."

Ballmer also reminded Cutler the shift meant he was free of IBM. Cutler asked about Ballmer's promise that NT would still sport an OS/2 personality. Not to worry, Ballmer assured him, someone else could take care of that. Indeed, OS/2 was now so unimportant to Microsoft that Ballmer had assigned a tiny team in Israel to create an OS/2 variant of NT. The Microsofties hated OS/2 so much they couldn't even bear to have someone working on it in the same continent. What's more, Cutler didn't even have to check on the Israelis; someone else would do that.

Cutler soon learned that the Israelis were probably the only part of the NT team that lay outside his domain. Maritz wanted Cutler to oversee every aspect of programming, including networking, graphics and compatibility. He also asked Cutler to run the test organization. The man who never wanted an empire was getting one. Maritz felt it was the only way to curb Cutler's penchant for "pissing at all the other guys sideways. I knew it was the only way it would work. Otherwise it would've been an impossible task to mediate" the disputes between Cutler and the heads of other groups. Even after Cutler's team made a fragile peace with Darryl Rubin's networking group, Maritz still noticed that there "was a two-inch pipe with piss going back and forth between the two teams." Maritz, who after the debacle of OS/2 very much needed a success in NT, couldn't abide any further infighting. He told Cutler, "You can't complain about these portable graphics guys [the Undead] and these other guys [in networking and test] not doing their job. Because they're all going to work for you."

Cutler refused. He still wished to write as much NT code as he could. "I lead by example. I don't ask anyone to do what I won't do." He couldn't write and review code as well as manage a group of two hundred people. "I can't think or imagine having more than one hundred guys work for me," he told Maritz.

To satisfy Cutler, Maritz "reluctantly" withdrew testing from Cutler's domain and began talking with him about the two people—one for graphics and one for networking—who would join Perazzoli as Cutler's lieutenants. Needed, Maritz thought, were managers who could stand up to Cutler's "steel," yet show "velvet to people underneath them."

Even as Cutler wrestled with his newly expanded team, technical matters demanded immediate attention. Given the shift in Microsoft strategy, the most pressing one was how to make writing Windows applications for NT seem familiar. Writers of applications programs had spent much time learning the hundreds of "secret handshakes," known as APIs ("application programming interfaces"), that enabled an application to obtain a service from Windows. Theoretically Cutler's team could create brand-new APIs for NT, but there was every reason why the NT APIs should resemble the Windows APIs. Applications writers would still have to write new versions of their programs if they wished them to swallow data in gulps of thirty-two bits—one of NT's big advantages over DOS-based Windows. But working with similar sets of APIs would make it easier to do these conversions. And making life easier for applications writers would increase the likelihood that they would write programs for NT.

On the matter of APIs, Cutler relied on the most eclectic code writer on his original team, Mark Lucovsky. "I don't care what [the code] looks like, just make it work," he told Lucovsky.

Cutler's guidance was in line with Microsoft's tradition of giving its programmers free rein. "We mostly hire people who have to be constrained, not motivated," said a veteran.

Lucovsky fit this mold. After graduating from California Polytechnic in San Luis Obispo, he had burned through a few jobs and landed at Digital West in 1987. He so impressed Cutler and Perazzoli that, when they joined Microsoft, they thought it essential he come with them. Lucovsky was twenty-nine years old, married and the father of two children. He was smart but immature. A jack-of-all-trades who awed colleagues with his intimate knowledge of NT's vast terrain, Lucovsky nevertheless angered teammates with his skepticism and self-serving judgments. He was relentlessly critical of others, constantly probing for weaknesses. "Until you prove otherwise, you're wrong and he's right," said one critic.

Quick with a wisecrack, Lucovsky often wore a sly grin on his cherubic face that seemed to say, "I know something you don't." He once brashly greeted the arrival of Helen Custer, a female technical writer whose job was to write a volume on the innards of NT, by suggesting that she document his code for him. (Many programmers so intensely dislike writing plain-English descriptions of their code that documentation has been termed "the castor oil of programming—managers think it is good for programmers, and programmers hate it!") Custer, who held an undergraduate degree in computer science, was offended. "I'm not going to be your lackey!" she told him.

He laughed dismissively.

Many people felt that Lucovsky was a jerk. He was hard to manage but showed the pep and initiative that every team needs. Even more valuable, Lucovsky sought to understand how the many pieces of NT interacted as a system. Large programs, like any large structures, are built in pieces, which then are stitched together. Most builders learn their own piece and perhaps a little of the surrounding ones, but not much more. Lucovsky had a rare ability to learn the intricate details of his own pieces and at the same time clearly see how *all* the pieces fit together.

He knew his own mind, too. An instinctive troubleshooter, he pursued solutions across organizational boundaries. He never asked permission. He had an air of superiority and sparked feelings of envy and irritation by insisting on having the newest and best PCs. After Perazzoli, his boss, pulled strings to obtain a snazzy big monitor for him, Lucovsky boasted about his new equipment to colleagues still toiling on older models. And if that didn't ruffle enough feathers, he stirred up hostility by openly criticizing others when he saw a botched job. Once Custer asked him for feedback on a draft of a chapter about the kernel, and Lucovsky returned the draft with "NO!" written in block letters across the cover. Custer was devastated. Lucovsky found her writing so poor, she felt, he couldn't even muster the concern to tell her why.

After nearly two years of what he considered "tinkering around, getting a style," Lucovsky felt that with the switch to Windows the NT team finally had "a clear focus." He also felt the team had no time to lose; unless it defined the APIs, someone else would. It might be another group within Microsoft. Lucovsky's biggest fear was that IBM would convince Ballmer, its staunchest ally within Microsoft and Cutler's boss, to allow it to define the APIs. This would be a disaster. IBM would try to make the APIs look like those required for OS/2. And IBM also might give short shrift to those APIs that had no correlate in DOS-based Windows; these APIs enabled applications writers to take advantage of NT's distinct powers.

Lucovsky, in a race against an imagined rival, felt the team should propose its own APIs as soon as possible. He enlisted Steve Wood in the effort. He and Wood had worked together before; Lucovsky even had a habit of polishing the code submitted by Wood, which often ranged across so many aspects of NT that Wood lost track of the intricacies himself. Lucovsky was more fastidious than Wood, but otherwise they had much in common: tremendous concentration, the ability to produce a lot of code fast, a distaste for excessive documentation and self-confidence bordering on megalomania. Within two weeks, they wrote an eighty-page paper describing proposed NT versions of hundreds of Windows APIs. Many of these were straightforward conversions; others required some ingenuity. The effect, in most cases, was to hide from the applications writer the underlying differences between Windows on DOS and Windows on NT.

An example of this involved the way a writer from another software company creating a Windows application requested internal memory. He was used to asking for either local or global memory, depending on the size of memory needed. If he wanted thirty-two bytes of local memory, he wrote:

X = local alloc (LMEM_zeroinit,32)

NT, however, had a uniform memory type; it made no distinction between local or global memory. But to make the applications writer feel comfortable, Wood and Lucovsky chose to retain the older Windows API style.

Soon others joined in writing APIs for their parts of NT. A large number were written by a group, led by veteran code writer Scott Ludwig, which had been charged with making Windows programs run on OS/2. Now Ludwig's target was NT. The software concepts were the same, and though new code was required he and his colleagues could draw on knowledge gained from their prior effort. Whitmer, whose Undead were now officially part of Cutler's team, supplied many graphics APIs. Even Ballmer got into the act, reading the proposed APIs, circling those that weren't identical with the old ones, and sending dispatches to Cutler asking for explanations of the discrepancies. A program manager coordinated the API effort and canvassed applications writers for their advice. He even organized a gathering of applications writers at the Microsoft campus December 17, 1990, at which they reviewed the more than one thousand APIs created by then.

Not everyone was happy with the team's outpouring of APIs. IBM's code writers, still laboring under the illusion that NT would host OS/2, pestered Ballmer about seeing the APIs. On January 17, 1991, IBM's people finally got a peek. Sensing trouble, Cutler skipped the meeting. Perazzoli went in his place, opening the meeting with his usual warmth. He then invited Lucovsky to describe the APIs. After hearing about ten of them, one IBM engineer realized they bore a strong resemblance to Windows APIs. "Couldn't you have carried over even one OS/2 API?" he asked.

Lucovsky, happy to rub salt in IBM's wound, answered honestly. "No," he said. "Our goal is to make it easy to go from Windows to NT."

Shouting erupted as the IBMers got the message that Microsoft was abandoning OS/2. One IBMer jumped to his feet, then pounded his fist on the table. Lucovsky, who had fifteen more slides to cover, kept on talking. But for all the impact his words had, he could have been silent. The IBMers felt conned. This whole notion of NT hosting both Windows and OS/2 was a charade. Gates, Ballmer and the rest of them would say anything to keep IBM as an ally, but their actions were clear. Now the IBMers squirmed in their seats, eager for the meeting to end so they could report this shocking news to their bosses in Armonk. Watching the meeting unravel, Perazzoli felt the IBM-Microsoft—the era's most important industry alliance—died that very day.

The shift to Windows, while freeing Microsoft from its profitable but restrictive alliance with IBM, had a nightmarish side. NT was now expected to run existing DOS and Windows programs *unchanged*. This would be a boon to customers, who would not have to throw anything away, but it meant that innovators had to lug the past on their backs as they forged ahead.

In principle, compatibility was straightforward. For years, designers had accommodated old programs, written for an obsolete operating system, by *emulating* the old environment within a new context. Cutler himself, in designing Digital's VMS operating program, had taken steps to ensure that certain older programs would remain useful. This practice was well established. It worked best, however, with small numbers of applications that had a great deal in common. DOS and Windows programs were shockingly diverse. Even if the team somehow found a single structure to put behind them, success would only lead to another programming hurdle. Once DOS and Windows applications ran on NT, customers might expect them to run as fast as normal; otherwise, they could continue to run the applications on the old operating system. So getting applications to run under NT was only half the battle; the other half was getting them to run as fast or faster than they did before.

In the early months of the project, when Gates and Cutler spoke often, the two would discuss at length the question of compatibility. Gates would muse aloud about the possibility of running on NT programs of virtually every pedigree: Unix, OS/2, Windows, DOS. "Can we mix and match?" Gates would ask. Cutler was leery of this. He would review Gates's wish list and plead: "You mean you want all these things?" Though Gates always said yes, Cutler managed to avoid ever explicitly promising anything other than OS/2 applications on NT.

Now Cutler's wiggle room was gone, and so were his personnel constraints. Until August his team had still been too small to tackle much more than the guts of NT. Now Cutler had more than a hundred programmers at his disposal, mostly refugees from OS/2. Included among these was a soft-spoken Englishman who played classical piano and flute. Matthew Felton considered music to be his "big passion," but he had programming in his blood. His father, George Felton, was among England's leading code writers in the 1950s. His work was so influential that colleagues named an early operating program "the George" (after George visited his son at Microsoft, a teammate cracked that perhaps they should rename NT "the Dave"). And Felton's mother had been an early programmer too, leaving the field in 1953 to raise her four sons.

Felton joined Microsoft in 1987, after a stint with a British computer maker. On the OS/2 project he led the team charged with making DOS programs run on OS/2. After three years, he was considered an expert at coping with the oddities of DOS. He achieved his mastery through an elaborate sleight of hand. Code was inserted into OS/2, its sole purpose to present a DOS program with a piece of the operating system behaving just as DOS would. Felton was quite happy to do the same for NT. The code would be different, because NT's design bore little resemblance to OS/2's, but he was confident: "I've done it before; I can do it again," he said.

Then one day Perazzoli sent someone to Felton's office with a message: Could he and his team please handle the work needed to get Windows applications on NT too? Excited by the prospect, Felton took a big gulp and accepted.

Felton didn't expect much help from Perazzoli and Cutler; these were the same guys who a year earlier had recoiled at the idea of making DOS and Windows applications run on NT. Just so they knew what to expect, Felton gave them a tutorial on the problem, which boiled down to finding a generic way to fool DOS and Windows applications. Think of an application as a husband who calls his wife to tell her when he'll arrive home at the end of the day. Think of NT as a master impersonator who must imitate a certain wife, depending on which husband calls. This wouldn't be so hard if each husband just conveyed the time of his arrival. The husband might say *anything*, but NT must still answer in a manner that convinces the husband that it is his wife on the line. Felton hoped that a model, planted inside NT, could serve as this impersonator, accommodating all DOS and Windows applications. Only time would tell if Felton was right. As Cutler listened, he grew more anxious. Felton "could almost see his stomach churning."

Just as the personality of NT changed, so too did the character and organization of the team building it. By their sheer numbers alone, newcomers put their stamp on Cutler's tribe. Instead of one "base" group of about twenty-five people, NT now consisted of three coding groups of about thirty-five people each. A fourth group, consisting of about thirty testers, checked the progress of NT. Perazzoli still headed the base group, which was now about twice its earlier size. Leif Pederson, an OS/2 refugee, was in charge of the graphics group, which itself consisted of three fairly autonomous units, including Whitmer's Undead. A third group was headed by David Thompson, who brought with him a gang of refugees from Microsoft's networking team. The testers were led by Moshe Dunie. Then there was Rob Short's small hardware group, still building prototype PCs.

The team's sudden expansion altered the relations between Cutler and the rank and file. He was no longer viewed as a familiar patriarch whose mercurial personality was accepted. Most of the new people were afraid of Cutler and his temper tantrums. They spoke with him only at their own risk. That they came from OS/2 and networking, objects of Cutler's scorn in the past, heightened the newcomers' need to prove their worth.

To be sure, some newcomers won instant acceptance. Felton, for instance, brought an entire group with him; he simply transferred loyalty from one flag to another. Other new managers also had a leg up in the race to gain credibility. Skillful managers who wrote code were the rule at Microsoft. Gates had a notion that only solid code writers should manage and all managers of code writers should keep writing code. This was a wonderful antidote for the illness that afflicted most software companies, in which managers were prisoners of their programmers. Schedules were missed, products failed, budgets were busted—all because the people on the top never could figure out what their modern-day wizards had done. Indeed, some initially successful software companies suffered spectacular collapses because of management's ignorance of code. At Microsoft programmers *were* the managers.

In her six years at Microsoft, Lee Smith had proved herself as a code writer on various projects. In her mid-thirties, she was technically astute, highly disciplined and took pride in helping others. After high school she had performed as a dancer; now she was fanatical about fitness: She rowed with a crew team four or five times a week and lifted weights. It showed. From March to October she wore only a tank top, shorts and running shoes around the office.

When asked to manage an NT group, Smith at first declined. She felt "burned out" and worried about proving herself again. Cutler's ex-Digital gang was intimidating; they acted superior to the Microsofties. "Would I be able to work myself up to the feverish pitch needed to impress these guys?" she asked herself.

Still, the role was appealing. She would supervise a small group, maybe four or five people, who would write the driver code that controlled pointing devices called mice, keyboards and storage disks. Not ready to leave Microsoft, and in search of a project, Smith joined the team. She felt an immediate rush of adrenaline. "NT was the place to be," she said. "It was the place where the really gung-ho people were."

Nobody made a big deal of it, but with her arrival Smith became the highest-ranking woman on the team and the only female manager.

Women were a rarity on NT. Until the switch to Windows, Therese Stowell had been the lone woman code writer on the project. Hardly a nerd, she was blond, blue-eyed and had style. (Most men on the project considered it a fashion statement merely to don clean clothes. T-shirts and jeans were the norm, with Cutler—dressing like a high school gym teacher—setting the tone. Surrounded by this frumpy bunch, Stowell looked like a young starlet.)

She discovered her flair for programming at Brown University, where she was among the best computer students in her class. She knew she wanted to write code for a living when, as a senior, she grew so engrossed in a class assignment that she programmed for two days straight, quitting only when "I saw little orange bugs crawling across the screen." (The bugs were a hallucination.)

Microsoft hired Stowell out of college. After two years on OS/2 she switched to NT in September 1989. Havens recruited her to assist Steve Wood, who was then working on giving NT an OS/2 personality. Wood, whom she considered a legend, stuck up for her with the skeptical Digital guys. Sentimentality wasn't in Wood's act, but there it was. He felt protective toward Stowell as a fellow Microsoftie among the Digital crew. That Wood never questioned her ability or knowledge buoyed Stowell, who felt that among this collection of ten-year veterans she was "absolutely the lowest person on the [NT] totem pole."

Wood put Stowell to work on the piece of NT that would make it possible to write text—and text only—in a window on screen. This feature was called the console. Many programmers used it all day long. Console text looked like the output from a teletype. All text was the same size and font. Stowell's code would also create the movable segments on the screen—these were the windows with a lowercase *w* that inspired the name Windows—that contained the console text.

Stowell very quickly cut a striking figure within NT. Perazzoli arranged for her to have the office next to his, and she decorated it in a retro-hippie style that astonished Perazzoli, who was old enough to have been a real hippie. She burned incense and hung colored lights from the ceiling and love beads in her doorway. She started her day slowly, reading her e-mail while sipping a Tab. The first can invariably led to others, since she found it hard to write code without "chain-drinking Tabs," as she put it.

After a year, Stowell still thought Cutler did not respect her abilities; for whatever reasons she didn't seem to measure up to his

standards. Stowell held her ground, even when Cutler himself criticized her code. It was hard: Shouting wasn't part of her style, but
she kept her balance, and the few other women programmers who
joined the team later admired her for it. "She makes computer science seem cool," one said. "You think you have to be ugly and bor-
ing to go into computers, but you don't. Therese is lovely and hip."

Indeed, Stowell realized the whole image of code writing as a
masculine pursuit was a distortion. The leading edge of programming had not always been a world without women. At the dawn of
digital computing after World War II, when programming was still
viewed as an unglamorous activity bordering on clerical work, male
hardware engineers enlisted women to write code. By the early
1950s women had made a substantial contribution to the field. The
pioneer in making it easier to program was a woman, Grace Hopper. But Hopper was sui generis; she was a role model who in a few
short years became an anachronism. By the 1960s, programming
was a hot field: Jobs were plentiful; salaries were high; men took
over the field. By 1965, the year of Stowell's birth, there was scant
room for women in software.

When several other women, including Smith, joined the project as
part of the OS/2 migration in September 1990, Stowell saw her
chance: Organize!

She imagined an electronic forum. The company's e-mail system supported dozens of so-called bulletin boards, on which a
group of people could exchange ideas. Why not a bulletin board for
women programmers—not only the ones in NT but elsewhere in
the company?

She would call it Hoppers, after Grace Hopper, her heroine.

Other women warmed to the notion. Ellen Aycock, one of Microsoft's first female programmers, was among the newcomers to NT.
She quickly found Cutler and certain of his cohorts to be among
"the most difficult people I'd ever worked with." Their style, she discovered, was "total confrontation. The person who shouts and curs-
es the most is right. It was the way of NT. And everybody from OS/2
was a bozo. That was the word thrown around."

Aycock agreed with Stowell that while women programmers were not overtly held back, the "harsh and unproductive" milieu meant "women weren't valued as much," maybe because they refused to act with machismo.

Stowell also turned to Smith for aid. Certainly she would help; it was time for Microsoft's women programmers to get to know one another better. Smith had tried to bring women together years ago, but found them too wary even to meet for a pot-luck dinner—as if a mere meeting were a show of disloyalty. Of course it wasn't: Only a blind and deaf person could deny that "women expended a lot of extra energy just educating the men around them." Smith even felt that men judged her not for herself but for all women. She felt that future women code writers might be judged in the light of her performance—as in, "We had a woman once and look what happened." It was partly for this reason that Smith rarely relaxed on the job.

On October 12, 1990, on a Friday afternoon, Stowell called to order the first meeting of Hoppers. About twenty women attended. Beyond launching a bulletin board, the women weren't sure what to do. Stowell figured something would come to them sooner or later.

The Hoppers bulletin board caught on quickly with the women on the team. Stowell was pleased, feeling less isolated and more aware of the issues facing women.

And there *were* issues. "It is infinitely harder for women to prove their worth on this project," said Steve Wood, Stowell's supervisor. Wood allowed that the bias against women wasn't "deliberate" or even "conscious" but it took longer for a woman to convince male peers of her technical talent. And when she did, it only took one "screw-up," Wood said, for the old skepticism about her ability to resurface.

Stowell conceded that perceptions of bias were elusive. Things were going well for her. She drew wide praise for an improvement to the console, her major piece of NT. At first, the only way to insert characters into console text was to overstrike existing characters. "This was," as Perazzoli put it, "a royal pain in the ass." Stowell worked hard to make it possible to insert blocks of characters into the console text. Her coworkers considered this a cause for joy.

When she was finished, Stowell received perhaps fifty congratulatory notices.

Yet Stowell knew that she was an anomaly. Relatively few women pursued careers in programming. Although numbers were rising modestly, she felt Microsoft might attract more women if the atmosphere at this and other software companies were more welcoming. She wasn't asking for special treatment, but was it necessary that the workplace become an unending stream of "male-to-male combat?"

It was hard, of course, for Stowell and the other women to say what would improve things, to spell out what they were *for*. But they knew what they were against.

Bit-map nudes.

"Bit-map" referred to a technique of displaying vivid images on a computer screen. Nudes were, of course, naked women.

No one had ever done a scientific poll, but quite a few men among the NT team enjoyed viewing nude images on their screen. A program controlled the appearance of the nudes, which tended to appear when the PC was otherwise idle. Too often, Stowell and other women found themselves visiting a male colleague to talk about code, only to find another woman's breasts pictured on the screen in front of them.

"It was something we could point to and say, 'This is wrong,' " said Jane Howell, NT's only female hardware engineer and a Hoppers founder.

The nudes became a rallying point for the Hoppers women. To lay the basis for a united front, Stowell went to Lee Smith, the senior woman on the team, for a favor. Smith kept an enormous poster of a scantily clad female body builder on her office wall. Would Smith mind taking that down? Stowell asked. It wouldn't look right if the women complained about the nudes displayed by men and then someone brought up Smith's poster. Smith agreed; she immediately took the poster down.

The nude-loving men on the team conceded less readily. They argued that the nudes were displayed only in their own offices. Microsoft had a tradition of "anything goes" within an employee's personal space. Musical instruments, stereo systems, elaborate fish tanks, potted trees were all allowed. And the walls had never been slapped with any limitations.

This was different, the women insisted. Wood agreed, dismissing male rationalizations as "total bullshit."

When persuasion failed, Stowell, Howell and the others petitioned Maritz for redress. Maritz, who oversaw the entire project, was sympathetic to the women's position but reluctant to ban the nudes outright. Swayed by the argument that a person's office was a sanctuary, he dispatched the following proclamation: "The issue is the display of bit-map images of nude figures, which are offensive to many in our community. Please exercise common sense in this regard."

While the women considered it a victory simply that Maritz addressed the matter, they found his statement weak. From then on, when they discovered offensive bit-maps, they complained directly to the company's personnel department, which reprimanded the offenders. Before long, nudes were banned.

As NT grew more complicated, so did the management of the project. Cutler and his chief aides—Perazzoli, Thompson and Pederson—faced difficult and diverse choices. They often felt flooded by possibilities, leaving Perazzoli thinking that the project ran "right on the edge of chaos." More control wasn't the answer, however. "It seems like a little dose of management is needed," he said. "Yet you can never give a little management. You always give too much. Its a very precarious position, *under*managing. Yet you have to be there to succeed."

Cutler himself certainly didn't *over*manage. Usually he tried to stay out of the way. Cutler believed that talent won out and was best displayed in small teams consisting of a few people. While it looked as if his programming groups had grown to an elephantine size, they were actually collections of small teams. Perazzoli, for instance, oversaw about a half dozen technical managers, or "leads," who in turn looked after four or five people each. Sometimes, when the problems were discrete enough, a lead split his group in two, spawning two leads who reported to him. At the same time, each of the programming groups had one or two senior code writers, called architects, who designed large, important pieces of code. The idea was that the fewer minds applied to a piece, the greater the consistency in the design. The architect's spec then served as a blueprint for one or more programmers to implement. There was room for flexibility too. Architects sometimes fixed bugs; implementers occasionally designed programs.

Reporting, however, was loose—a crazy quilt, not a hierarchy—and to make matters more confusing, it was a fluid crazy quilt at that. Formal reporting lines were often ignored. Programmers weren't expected to seek approval from their leads whenever they made a decision. Many ignored their leads altogether. The leads, meanwhile, had their own coding to do, so they sometimes lost track of their code writers. In the end, people sought help from whoever could give it to them—within or without their immediate group. While this style reflected Microsoft's freewheeling organization, it also flowed from Cutler's leadership. "I'm not a process person," he said, referring to his distaste for following elaborate organizational procedures. "People have to understand that process is to help get the job done, not an end in itself."

Chuck Whitmer had too much to do. He was the manager of the graphics group, in charge of eleven people. He was the group's architect. He coded a lot. And people from other groups often sought his advice on how to get existing applications to run on NT.

Realizing he needed help, Whitmer turned to Microsoft's tallest employee, Kent Diamond. Standing six feet six inches tall, the skinny twenty-eight-year-old Diamond got things done without sacrificing his easygoing manner. A native of Mountain View, California, he earned a double major in computer science and economics at Berkeley. He joined Microsoft in 1985 as a programmer, then was dispatched to the OS/2 project to keep one of its pieces on schedule. The job meant, as he put it, "running interference with IBM." In the spring of 1988, he was sent to Tokyo to rescue the troubled Japanese release of OS/2. His mission done, he returned to the United States.

Diamond was pleased to accept Whitmer's offer. After OS/2, it was a relief to work on an operating program IBM had no hand in. He felt people at IBM worshiped hierarchies. Each employee worried about his little piece of turf and nothing else. Diamond still recalled with amazement the time an IBM programmer, hacking away at OS/2, watched the program crash to a halt. The guy studied his screen for a minute, then said, "Wow, what a nasty problem. Glad that isn't in my code." He restarted his PC and went back to work, never even reporting the bug.

At Microsoft that would never happen. People stepped into the breach. No one said you had to, but it felt good when you did. Graphics was just such a breach, Diamond felt. He quickly diagnosed the group's problem:

> Total confusion. I had eleven people working for me who had almost no clue what they should be working on. The troubles were deeper than just the change to Windows. Chuck had not been able to devote enough time to management. He neglected to assign work to programmers. Most were given small tasks that would take a few days. As their tasks were completed, they returned to Chuck for fresh guidance. Overloaded, Chuck couldn't get them started on something else quickly. Lots of time was wasted. In addition, many tasks were ill defined. Chuck knew what he wanted but didn't have the time to explain it carefully. Again, more wasted time.

The group was behind, missing deadlines. "It was not good," Diamond said. But it wasn't that hard to fix either. Over a month he hammered out clear assignments and schedules with the code writers. This helped but was no panacea. Diamond knew the group remained in a difficult spot: "There was a ton of work to do—and not much time to do all this work. The schedules were very tight. Shipping this product was not going to be easy."

And that was if the group delivered just the features Whitmer had promised. As managers defined NT more precisely, the wish list grew—for graphics and everything else. To protect the group, Diamond reacted warily to pleas for more, agreeing to a new feature only if he could drop an old one. "We can do it, but it will cost you something else" was his refrain.

Diamond quickly gained a reputation for excessive caution. Behind his back, people called him "an old lady." Cutler had mixed feelings about Diamond. He looked down on indecisiveness but liked people who tried to stem the rising tide of features. Diamond's trouble was that he couldn't tell when he faced a real emergency.

One crisis had erupted involving the graphics part of the client-server code. Time and again, Cutler had hoped to dispel doubts about client-server. In his design, the kernel code treated the entire graphical portion of the operating system, including the Windows personality, as an application. It was a classic design choice. Client-server ensured reliability but degraded performance. It was probably Cutler's most momentous decision.

Gates, however, was never at peace with it. In November 1990, he raised fresh questions about how this design affected the speed of popular graphics-intensive programs such as AutoCad and Corel Draw. It was late to revisit this old dispute, but he worried that these programs might run too poorly on NT, drawing complaints from fans.

Cutler wanted to quell this new revolt against client-server quickly. He hoped a demonstration of NT's probable speed would quiet critics. To perform the demonstration he needed some code from the graphics group. Diamond and Whitmer, who learned of Cutler's concern through their boss, Pederson, didn't realize that Cutler wanted the code immediately. They assumed they had months to prove it was possible to speed up these type of applications, which was exactly what they planned to do by the next March.

That wasn't good enough for Cutler. One day he cornered Whitmer and Diamond and exploded over client-server. Didn't they realize that the success of the project depended on improving it?

Whitmer was dumbfounded. "Wow, Dave!" he said. "Leif [Pederson] told us you were concerned, but we did not realize you were *that* concerned."

The next day Diamond put three people on the task.

With graphics under fire and the group's work load mounting, Diamond searched for ways to bring his code writers closer together. They already had a warm-weather barbecue every Friday, when they gathered at one of the fields on campus to play softball or croquet. But Diamond sought a forum where they could exchange technical insights in a relaxed way.

His solution was to turn an odd-shaped piece of the hallway into a lounge. Joggers used the space to weigh in, and the scale stayed put. Diamond added a couch and an espresso maker. He also installed a white board in the hope that his folks would rough out solutions with the handy marker.

The graphics team—ten men and a woman—grew attached to the lounge. Sometimes people played, but often they discussed their work. Diamond's office opened onto the lounge. He heard the conversations. He knew.

No other group had a lounge, however. This was perhaps because the quirky layout of Diamond's offices was not duplicated anywhere else in Building Two. But more likely there were no other lounges because Cutler opposed them. It didn't take Diamond long to realize the "enormous downside to the lounge. The political costs were very high." Cutler would pass the lounge, note the presence of a few programmers and equate them with goof-offs. Diamond privately fumed that Cutler only thought the worst of his people. The group might have gotten off to a slow start, but they were on track now. Diamond blamed Cutler's stubborn animus toward Whitmer and company on what he called the Gerald Ford syndrome. "Early in his presidency, Ford fell coming down the stairs of *Air Force One*," Diamond explained. "A few days later he slipped while walking across the lawn. Suddenly he was the klutzy president. There was no going back. Even though he was one of the best athletes ever to occupy the White House, to this day he cannot shake the reputation." The lesson was plain. Cutler's mind worked the same way, Diamond felt. "A reputation had been established. Once you are on his bad side, there is no recovery."

Cutler could dismiss a person too handily and hold fast to a negative image of someone. "It takes quite a while for somebody to actually drop to the bottom of my esteem, but when they get there, digging out of that is unbelievably hard," he allowed. "It takes a long time for that to happen, so most people never get there. But the ones that do just stay there."

His harsh judgments of graphics seemed hypocritical to Diamond's allies. Besides being an avid skier, Cutler played squash at noon, some weeks every workday. So Whitmer wondered where Cutler got off questioning the fun had by the graphics group. Why did Cutler cast aspersions on their good times when no one begrudged him his recreations?

Cutler saw the worst in graphics. "He worried about that group all the time," an intimate said. "He saw them as loose cannons." While overly harsh, Cutler's paranoia was fueled by some disquieting signs. Despite Diamond's enthusiasm, Walt Moore was sinking deeper into the malaise that afflicted him. Moore was one of the veterans on the team. He was expected to produce a load of display-driver code. The other parts of NT could be great, but without Moore's code a customer would see nothing on his PC screen. Though an expert at display-drivers, Moore was barely getting any work done. He'd long wanted to train someone to replace him, so he could switch to something else, but it never happened. He could recall code he'd written ten years ago, but nothing fresh came to mind.

Friends tried to cheer him up. "Everybody was rooting for Walt," said one teammate. "Everybody tried to encourage him to get the job done and feel a part of the team. You can't help but like Walt."

The collegial support failed to lift Moore's spirits. Shuttered in his office, he spent hours mastering a computer simulation of the ancient Chinese game of strategy called Pai Gow. Whitmer, who liked to wager at Pai Gow, had introduced Moore to it. A dealer presents four dominoes to a player, who has three choices on how best to arrange them. To novices, the game seemed entirely random, the outcome utterly dependent on the hand dealt. Or was it? On one of his gambling trips Whitmer had leafed through a book entitled *Pai Gow With Tears* and run across this observation: "It is understood that to employ an optimal strategy a player would need a concealable computer." Whitmer took this claim as a challenge; he sought to prove that he could play Pai Gow as well as a computer but without the machine by his side. His goal was to memorize the best strategy to apply to each of the 3,620 distinct hands of Pai Gow. The easiest way to study the possible hands was by practicing against the computer simulation. Moore, who instantly saw the allure of outwitting the Pai Gow dealer, had written this training program in about eighty hours. The program embodied Whitmer's views on the best approach to each hand. Play the hand "wrong" and the program displayed what Whitmer considered the "optimum," or best, way of playing it.

Moore practiced Pai Gow on his office computer each day. Mastering a game was a hacker thing to do (and Moore was nothing if not a hacker). Whitmer challenged Moore to play 500 hands without error, which he considered an indication of competency.

That was tough. So far, Moore couldn't top 400. Five hundred hands without an error seemed far off. Still, it felt good to have a goal.

By early January 1991, the project's new structure and strategy were in place and many technical issues had been put to rest.

Client-server was a done deal. Cutler's people had demonstrated to Ballmer in a head-to-head comparison that Diamond had dubbed the "Pepsi Challenge" that Windows applications ran just the smallest percentage points slower on NT than they did on DOS. This was a "taste" test, of course; it would be many months before NT's ability to emulate Windows was sufficiently advanced actually to run Windows applications fast. But the debate over client-server was over—and mercifully, Cutler felt.

The approach to compatibility was set. The group under Felton would write the code for the NT version tailored to the Intel X86 chip family, which at present was the principal target. An outside company called Insignia Solutions would write the code enabling the Mips version of NT to run Windows and DOS applications. The choice to reach outside the Microsoft group, while ultimately made by Maritz, was considered "the best bet" by Cutler. Insignia had proven expertise in making DOS and Windows programs run on computers using non-Intel chips. Cutler saw no reason to duplicate code Insignia could produce more quickly. After all, "we had no expertise in this," he said.

Perhaps the only unfortunate result of choosing Insignia was that even after months of discussions a formal contract between the two companies still required polishing. At best Insignia would begin "work in earnest" in February.

The schedule represented another bright spot. At least there was one. Before, Cutler and Perazzoli had a sense of when the project might end. But this was always a loose, seat-of-the-pants estimate. In January 1991, Cutler and his lieutenants committed to a series of milestones and an ultimate ship date. The most important applications writers working for other companies would receive their first sneak preview, or "beta" version, of NT in August 1991. By October 31, 1991, NT's code would be complete. This Halloween deadline for "code complete," as the team termed it, meant no new features and just choice revisions after this date. Testing and bug fixing would push the actual release date—when NT shipped to customers—into the second quarter of 1992.

While the schedule looked solid, any combination of perfectly understandable delays could derail it. There were still many unknowns. Estimating the length of a job was notoriously difficult—and NT's features were not set. The uncertainty over a proposed file system was typical of the many choices facing the team. The file system is a central part of any operating system because, as its name implies, it organizes the way data is stored and retrieved. The choice of a file system colors the experience of both program writers and customers. As a result, a new file system meant a major adaptation for these two communities. The team had yet to decide whether to create a new file system for NT or merely carry forward older ones formed for DOS and OS/2.

There were dozens of other decisions still to be made too. Until they were made, the team's schedule was a glorified security blanket. It was easy to punch holes in the schedule, and someone was about to do just that.

Robert Muglia was the latest program manager assigned to NT. The previous ones had been defeated by Cutler's will when they tried to influence NT's design. On other Microsoft teams program managers defined many of a product's features. Not on NT, at least not yet. The team's first program manager, Naveen Jain, was young, inexperienced and swiftly routed by Cutler. Then another program manager arrived, a meticulous native of Argentina with an MBA from Stanford. Cutler ignored and then routed him too.

Then came Muglia. Excitable and relentless, he had a pleasant disposition and good manners. He was born in Connecticut, educated at the University of Michigan and worked seven years for a maker of telephone equipment before joining Microsoft in 1987. Muglia quickly acquired a reputation for persistence, wide-ranging knowledge and authoritative opinions. "He knows what to fight for and what not to fight for," one colleague said. "And he has a great nose for detecting problems, jumping in and understanding every last detail."

Maritz, who was growing impatient with the inability of program managers to make a dent in Cutler's organization, personally selected Muglia for the job and expected him to stick. Persuasive and well spoken, Muglia was determined to win a role on the team. With a comeback for every apparent rebuff, Muglia insisted that a computer program, while certainly inspired and created by code writers, must reflect the currents of the market and the desires of customers. No great program was created by slavishly following the market or crudely regurgitating the requests of shoppers. But creators lived in a cocoon. The very demands of their craft made it hard to step outside the bounds of their imaginations.

Muglia was bent on bringing the outside world to the men and women making NT, leavening the code writer's intelligence with the wisdom of the bazaar. He regarded Cutler's abilities highly but knew he would inevitably clash with him. He expected the first battle to come over NT's schedule and the program's features. NT would take a lot longer to finish and needed many more features to appeal to the ordinary customer, he felt.

Yet influencing engineers was difficult in the best of situations. They often dug in their heels, refusing to modify pet ideas. There was a kind of macho about this embrace of engineering "purity." Muglia found Cutler to be "the biggest, hardest-assed development manager in the whole world." The only advantage Muglia had over the preceding program managers was that he reported directly to Maritz. But that would help only so much: Muglia was about to enter a world where Cutler was a force of nature. He ruled the way the wind ruled, or the sun or the rain. Muglia would survive by his wits, if at all.

"I still hadn't figured out how to deal with Dave going in," Muglia later said. "But it was apparent that caution was advised. Step lightly, and at least have your facts straight."

With the project more than two years old and NT assuming what appeared to be its final shape, Gates now cast his gaze elsewhere. He hardly ever spoke with Cutler anymore; they almost never exchanged e-mail either. This was partly Gates's way of paying Cutler a compliment. Most Microsoft projects lacked leaders of Cutler's caliber; Gates was breathing down those guys' necks. He felt he couldn't offer Cutler much help. "My ability to add value to a project that Cutler's running is a lot less than some other Microsoft projects," he said.

There existed a gulf between Gates and Cutler, which neither wished to measure. Theirs was an ambiguous relationship, but it worked best that way. They were allies but not friends, partners but not collaborators. Cutler toiled within the confines of Gates's domain but had carved out a separate realm for himself. His allegiance to Gates was rarely tested and never questioned. This arrangement bore fruit but little warmth. Gates sometimes acted as if he thought Cutler was a know-it-all who dismissed Gates's advice and achievements too readily. He eschewed casual conversations with Cutler because he felt "always a little leery about saying the wrong thing" to him. Cutler, meanwhile, saw Gates as someone who could tell him "what he was signed up to do." While he wanted Gates's approval, Cutler didn't look to him for advice and succor.

Even during the periodic reviews of NT's progress, there was little chance for Cutler and Gates to speak privately. Maritz, Perazzoli and others attended these meetings, which had the air of a performance. "They were never spontaneous," Perazzoli said. "There were tons of slides, and we always had a demo. We always showed Bill something so he'd know there was progress and that we were spending his money wisely."

Rather than express their frustrations to Gates, Cutler and Perazzoli preferred instead to complain to Maritz or Ballmer. "That's how we wanted it to be," Perazzoli said. "Bill's too powerful. You don't want to expose yourself. If he doesn't like what you're doing, he'll tell you no. Then there's no recourse."

6. DOG FOOD

Should we or shouldn't we?

The question of whether or not to create a new file system for NT gnawed at Gary Kimura. It was a momentous decision. A file system organizes the contents of a hard disk or a floppy disk into files and folders. Constantly relied on, a file system is a crucial piece of the operating program, defining the customer's experience with a PC almost as much as the interface.

The choice facing Kimura was stark. On the one hand, the team could stick with the existing DOS and OS/2 file systems. The advantage lay in their familiarity. Customers and programmers already used them. There would be, as the marketeers at Microsoft said, a smooth transition. On the other hand, neither file system met the level of reliability sought by Cutler, who wanted NT to be able automatically to reconstruct files and data disrupted by the failure of a PC. Such an innovation risked upsetting NT's schedule. Given all the work to be done, there was barely enough time to complete a new file system for the first release of NT.

Kimura, the technical lead for file systems, had weighed the pros and cons for many months. An incisive thinker, he was quiet, sometimes aloof, but spirited when challenged. Slender, sinewy and of medium height, he had a swimmer's body. His hair was black, his eyes and mouth small. Born in 1956, Kimura was raised in Seattle.

His parents—American-born children of Japanese immigrants—had met in a government internment camp during World War II. After the war, his father ran a landscaping business. Kimura attended the University of Washington, obtaining a doctorate in computer science in 1984. He first considered a job at a Digital lab in Palo Alto, but a researcher there urged him to visit Cutler's lab in Seattle. He did, and Cutler hired him.

One of the original members of the NT team, he arrived at Microsoft a week after Cutler, on November 7, 1988, with the initial wave of converts from the Digital lab. He found the first months at Microsoft rough. The unfamiliar people and surroundings depressed him. His mood enlivened when he started reviewing the file system for OS/2 before Christmas. He found it had too many points of failure. Limitations on the size and number of files also were strikes against the OS/2 system. At Cutler's behest, Kimura wrote a memo summarizing his criticisms with all the academic precision he could muster. The memo sparked controversy, ending up in the hands of Gordon Letwin, the author of OS/2's file system. Kimura was delighted to have caused a scuffle. "When we started pissing off other groups—that's when I started feeling comfortable," he said.

For the next year, Kimura scrambled to adapt both the crude DOS file system and the leaky OS/2 file system to NT. This was needed to ensure that NT could read data created by DOS and OS/2 programs. The twin tasks were essentially translations into the portable language of NT. Kimura was unenthused. "It was straightforward work, a lot of it," he said. "There wasn't anything exciting about it," he said.

By the summer of 1990, Kimura was far enough along to turn his attention to a new file system. But he needed help. As it was, Kimura was improving the two other file systems as well as refining a program that initially launched, or "booted," NT when a PC was switched on.

Seeking to bolster Kimura's team, Cutler invited Tom Miller, who had worked with Cutler for nearly fifteen years at Digital, to join the project. Miller, a forty-year-old specialist in file systems, was also among those who had followed Cutler out of Digital. He had joined Microsoft's networking group but kept tabs on Cutler's team. The idea of working with Kimura on NT appealed to Miller. He thought this might be his last chance to create an operating system from scratch. Writing such software was "a dying art," he thought. "No one will do a system like [NT] again, ever." Just a handful of companies had the resources and market clout to embark on a new operating system, and even they often chose to refine an existing system rather than build a completely new one. A new technique in programming, which relied heavily on recycling code, augured ill for those who wished to write operating systems from scratch. Young people weren't as attracted to operating systems as they once had been. The field of software had become so diverse that university professors now stressed the importance of mastering tools, techniques and applications; the operating system was widely viewed as a given. For all these reasons, it was hard for Miller "to imagine anyone, any time soon, building another modern operating system from the ground up." Believing NT could be "the last of a breed," he thought Cutler's team might be remembered "as the best operating system team ever assembled!" Miller longed to partake in NT's creation.

While grateful for Miller's enthusiasm, Cutler dismissed the suggestion that his team was on a historic mission or that NT was the last of anything. To be sure, NT's ambitions were uncommonly large, but the operating system hardly marked the end of an era. He rather believed that NT was part of a wave of future operating systems that would host multiple personalities. He also knew enough about the frontier of computing to realize that software not even on the drawing board yet would someday overshadow NT. Most important, he was aware that a basic shift in the way people handled information was under way and that this shift would be likely to spawn even more intricate operating systems. At best, NT would serve as a foundation for these systems, which would probably not become standard until early in the next century.

These new software systems were inevitable because advances in computing and communications promised to allow the ordinary person to gain the same mastery over motion pictures, still images and audio recordings that he now possessed over the printed word. Indeed, the shift seemed likely to create a new kind of literacy: multimedia. The roots of this new skill lay in the fact that sound and images were expressible in digital form, as strings of ones and zeros. The audio compact disc was the most popular example of digital media, but increasingly motion pictures and photographs would be stored digitally too.

The great advantage of digital media is that it can be stored, retrieved and massaged by a computer—at lightning speed and with unerring accuracy. Software provides the means of control, making it possible for a person to browse, identify and even modify motion pictures, still images and audio recordings as easily as he can write, copy or edit text on a computer today. Not all of this information will be under one person's local control. Wishing to look at a film or hear a recording only occasionally, he will receive a given selection over an electronic network. Computer programs will act as guides, or agents, for consumers plugged into these networks, which also go by the name "information highways."

Creating these electronic servants loomed as a monumental software problem: NT was to be a first step toward this goal. In the decades ahead, new software services, aimed at managing and massaging multimedia data, might rest on the edifice of NT. So Cutler hoped that NT would have a long life. The Unix operating system, against which he often measured NT, was nearly twenty years old and still evolving in useful ways. "Perhaps NT will be lucky enough to last as long," he mused. "Only time will tell."

When he invited Miller to join NT, Cutler promised him the chance to create a new file system. For Miller, who was an expert in techniques of restoring files and processing requests in high volumes, this was another major draw. His arrival cheered Kimura. Stout, slow moving and unpretentious, Miller looked like a weatherbeaten sailor. His face was pocked like the side of an old boat, his hair was sun-bleached sandy blond and he wore an odd collection of loose-fitting shirts and pants better suited to the beach than the office.

After lengthy discussions with Kimura and others, Miller was ready to write a specification for his new file system. Dubbed NTFS, the proposed file system ran into opposition even before Miller could precisely describe its features. Cutler, of course, needed no more convincing, but others opposed a new file system. Still furious about

Kimura's criticisms, the OS/2 leaders opposed it. They argued that their file system was as good as anything Cutler's gang could do, and if it wasn't they'd make it better. Marketeers, meanwhile, worried that a third file system would confuse customers. Microsoft had to support the two existing ones, so a third would burden program writers with the need to provide for another format.

With so much controversy over the file system, Cutler needed Maritz's approval to move on. Though skeptical, Maritz was reluctant to reject something Cutler wanted so badly. And the technical arguments in favor of NTFS were strong. The ability to restore "lost" files would be a major benefit to customers. Maritz also was swayed by the complaint that OS/2 couldn't support very big collections of files, those larger than four gigabytes. If it was to be the backbone of a company's entire information network, NT might need to manage even larger files. Maritz decided that Miller could write a spec for NTFS, but he reserved the right to kill the file system before the actual coding of it began.

Miller gathered some pens and pads, two weeks' worth of provisions and prepared for a lengthy trip on his twenty-eight-foot sailboat. Miller felt that spec writing benefited from solitude, and the ocean offered plenty of it. But he had worked on enough specs "to know that if you do something entirely in isolation you won't get the best crack at it. You need someone to at least bounce ideas off of." Kimura, the obvious trip mate, couldn't come. He had a date with the other file systems. Rather than sail alone, Miller arranged with Perazzoli, who officially took care of the file team, to fly in a programmer Miller knew well. He lived in Switzerland.

In August, Miller and his sidekick set sail for two weeks. The routine was easy: Work in the morning, talking and scratching out notes on a pad, then sail somewhere, then talk and scratch out more notes, then anchor by evening and relax. "You can't do this stuff too intensely," Miller said.

On the water, Miller pondered dozens of technical questions relating to the file system, but he thought most deeply about recovering and restoring files in the event the computer lost power or totally failed. This was the feature that would make or break NT's file system. Certain versions of Unix, the high-end operating program that Cutler sought to outdo with NT, were able to restore files following these situations. But when a PC lost data from a file, it usually lost it for good. This was because unless the PC was specifically instructed to store new entries in the permanent storage of a hard disk, it would save time by keeping many minutes' worth of entries in speedier, temporary DRAM memory. In event of a failure, this memory was always wiped clean.

Miller's answer was to create a duplicate record of all entries. The first record was the ordinary record, which resided first in temporary memory and then in permanent storage. The duplicate entry would live in a special log, which would be sent separately to the hard disk. This log would not contain entries made at the precise moment of the failure, but everything until a few seconds before the disaster. Miller called this state the "last known good." Once the computer came on again, the files in this state would appear.

While conceptually breathtaking, "last known good" posed a disquieting practical problem: It robbed the PC of some of its performance because of the need to post duplicate entries. Entries usually were duplicated by two computers running in tandem. Bank teller machines, stock exchanges and other organizations that could not survive an instant without their current computer records relied on this hardware solution to maintain a backup. Miller sought to accomplish something similar through software and in a single computer. This was tricky, but Miller thought he possessed the beginnings of a solution. He envisioned a special log as the safeguard against the loss of data. He also saw a way to reduce the time it took to put an entry into permanent storage, which meant that the special log might not slow down the computer much, or at all.

Bobbing on the Puget Sound waves, the scheme sounded great to Miller, but he wondered how his intricate notion would play on dry land.

At the end of his sail, Miller had the raw stuff for his spec. He then spent a week at home typing his notes and polishing the language. He finished with a fifty-page description of the guts of a new file system, which met both his and Cutler's aims. But back at Microsoft, he ran into a wall. Despite Cutler's support, Miller found that he, Kimura and two colleagues were swamped making the DOS and OS/2 file systems run faster and better on NT. Work on the new file system had to wait.

By February 1991, the demands on the DOS and OS/2 file systems were overwhelming. Cutler, armed with a schedule, was urging the team to "eat its own dog food." Part macho stunt and part common sense, the "dog food diet" was the cornerstone of Cutler's philosophy. "We're going to run on the program we build," he insisted. Eating dog food meant there would be no escape from facing the flaws and imperfections of NT. Even while immersed in his own piece of NT, a code writer would confront all of its weaknesses. By controlling the operations of a code writer's computer, NT would define the quality of his life. If at first NT tasted no better than dog food, all the better. Code writers would feel an urgent need to raise the dietary level by quickly fixing the errant code and writing more durable code in the first place.

Since the project's inception two and a half years before, programmers had written their code with the help of the OS/2 operating system. Now they would do so on a computer controlled by NT. With complicated programs, the sooner the pieces were assembled, the sooner certain kinds of bugs emerged. Among makers of complex software eating their own dog food was not unusual. Only by eating dog food could creators find bugs that stemmed strictly from the interplay of the pieces of system software.

With the shift still two months away, the tension was already rising. Cutler wanted NT in as good a shape as possible because once programmers lived on a strictly NT diet they would immediately suffer the shortcomings of NT's immaturity. The two existing file systems had to improve so that everyday work could occur more smoothly.

Kimura had other worries when it came to deciding whether his group should build a new file system from scratch. An unexpected rival to the new file system had surfaced. It was a new Microsoft project, code named Cairo, whose chief was James Allchin, a highly regarded code designer with a reputation just a notch below Cutler's. Allchin didn't want Kimura and Miller creating a new file system.

Allchin, whose shock of white hair spawned his nickname, Great White Hope, had joined Microsoft a few months before, lured away from a rival. He saw the Cairo project as the successor to NT and the means of realizing Gates's goal of "information at your fingertips." This slogan neatly encapsulated the future of computing, according to Gates. He imagined people leaving behind a world in which they retrieved information by mastering applications. While applications were powerful, they made people chop information into separate boxes. For example, a letter to client Bob Jones could be found by opening the word-processing file that held letters. A record of money owed by Jones was in a spreadsheet. Jones's phone number and address might be in a third application, an electronic Rolodex. Wouldn't it be easier, Gates wondered, for a person to find all this disparate information with a single request rather than by opening three separate applications?

No one really knew the answer. As a rallying cry, "Information at Your Fingertips!" smacked more of salesmanship than engineering, coming at a time when Microsoft's programs were about as easy to use as an unassembled children's toy. Cutler, battling to keep NT on track, cast a skeptical glance at Cairo, which he viewed as pie-in-the-sky. Allchin recognized that he walked "the edge between research and engineering"; he had to avoid "the pitfall of 'grandiose' projects that never get done or that are so fat and slow they can't be used." Nonetheless, he wasn't bashful about extolling Cairo's virtues.

High on Allchin's priorities was a new file system to manage the hidden wizardry that would stitch together disparate pieces of information to satisfy a single request. Miller and Kimura thought they could extend their file system in order to do the job, but Allchin disagreed. In February 1991, he pressed Maritz to kill NT's proposed file system because he thought it would undermine support among program writers for a Cairo file system. But, in a show of admiration, he asked that Miller and Kimura be transferred to his Cairo team. Cutler saw the attempted raid as a compliment but opposed the departure of his file-system mavens. Maritz worried about supporting too many file systems but refused either to kill NT's proposed file system or give Allchin Cutler's people. Miller and Kimura knew nothing of the tussle for their services.

The menace of dog food and Cairo left Kimura uneasy. He worried about uncertainties, working them over in his mind. Like a record skipping, he kept asking himself: "Should we or shouldn't we?"

The crowd of 250 people, gathered on March 12, 1991, was larger than usual for a lunchtime "tech talk" on the Microsoft campus. But there was a reason for the large audience. The secrecy surrounding NT was about to be lifted, at least for these Microsoft colleagues.

Lou Perazzoli leaned over a microphone jutting from the podium. With Cutler speech shy as usual, it fell to Perazzoli to describe the goals of NT and the team's progress. "If we all could be like Lou, we'd be in great shape," one colleague said. Though he seemed enthusiastic, confident and optimistic, Perazzoli worried that NT was taking longer to build than expected. When he'd left Digital for Microsoft to join Cutler, he joked that he wanted to complete a product before his hair turned gray. As he hunched over the podium in the harsh light of the auditorium, his thinning mane looked silvery. Clearing his throat and speaking in a sing-song voice, he began a detailed review of the program's features. Then he gave a sketchy report on the work finished so far. Finally he made a curious confession: "NT is sort of a chameleon operating system. First we were doing OS/2. Then Windows started selling millions of copies" and NT changed its skin. Perazzoli was proud of how quickly the team had made this about-face, saying the adjustment took only three months.

After his talk, Perazzoli fielded questions. His fellow Microsofties wasted no time in putting him on the spot: "When will NT ship?" they asked. "I was told not to talk about schedules," he answered, smiling. The next challenge, he said, was to switch the whole team to computers controlled by the latest version of their very own NT, itself a work-in-progress. "Once we do that," said Perazzoli, referring to the practice of eating dog food, "we can get an idea of how good the performance is, what needs to be improved and what the bug rate is." The first "eight guinea pigs" would switch on March 26.

The next several months would say much about whether NT would be finished during the first half of 1992. The team could promise a "code freeze" by Halloween or Christmas, but "the real trick" to avoiding massive delays was "to test [NT] all along," Perazzoli said. "We want to be running on it. We want to subject ourselves to our bugs. [If we do], we figure we'll get them fixed quicker."

The conversion to dog food unfolded in three stages: first NT without graphics, then with graphics and finally networking.

In the first stage, code writers switched from OS/2 to a version of NT that lacked both graphics and the Windows personality. Perazzoli's "guinea pigs" included himself, Mark Lucovsky and six other code writers who were collectively known as the "Pioneers." Besides their daily work, the Pioneers logged every abnormality found in NT. There were plenty. Perazzoli noted fourteen serious shortcomings on his first day. The most common was the unexplained failures of NT. These crashes, besides exhausting patience, destroyed data.

Since NT was so unpredictable (and wasn't yet able to send and receive e-mail), each Pioneer did housekeeping chores on an OS/2 computer in his office. "You quickly learned what you could and couldn't do on NT," said Lucovsky. When something went wrong, Lucovsky wasn't bashful about pursuing the suspected culprit. "I'd grab whoever seemed responsible and pull them in." If the victim resisted, Lucovsky said, "I need you now."

As more programmers ate dog food, they were astonished by NT's crudeness. "I was totally flabbergasted by the difficulty of getting things done with NT," said one. "It seemed like every time you typed a command [NT] didn't work, and you had to go off and find out why." This meant questioning teammates, thus sharply raising the number of daily interruptions and making it hard to write any new code. The writers of NT's central pieces often found themselves hectored about a mysterious bug, regardless of their responsibility for it. Almost no one liked the interruptions, but Cutler considered them unavoidable. Practical concerns made him an incrementalist at heart. Even code based on the best specs and designs usually only improved a little at a time. This was tedious work, often avoided. So Cutler favored bothering code writers, whom he suspected always wanted to write new code and forget about yesterday's mistakes.

The drive for dog food turned the Build Lab into the project's nerve center. Located on the first floor of the building which housed the team, the Build Lab was where each new test version of NT was electronically sewn together. Each "build" contained the latest additions and changes to NT. A new one usually came out each week. The construction of a build was only partly automated; each required the helping hands of at least one technician. Officially part of the test group, the technician or builder blended the latest submissions from code writers with the existing pieces of NT that were held in a "source file," which was essentially the master copy of NT.

Each build was a snapshot of NT at a given moment in time. On completion, the build was given a number and distributed to both testers and programmers. They quickly decided whether the latest build was an improvement over the last one. Especially strong builds were fondly recalled; sometimes, code writers stuck with those builds until a decidedly better one came along. Cutler didn't approve of this practice. He wanted people to work on each new build. As a matter of principle, he liked his builds served fast. The sooner a build arrived, the sooner testers could bang on it and code writers could refine their creation. Because the only way to really evaluate code was to run it.

In the earliest days of the project, the code for NT was so small that programmers made their own builds. A few zealots still did. But since August of 1989, code writers could rely on an official build made by Kyle Shannon. Youthful and exuberant, Shannon was ready for anything. He stood five feet eight inches tall, weighed about 160 pounds and kept his brown hair cropped short, exposing a silver hoop earring that hung from his left lobe. His hazel-green eyes sparkled with mischief, belying his zeal for hard work. Shannon epitomized the spirit of the Build Lab and, in many ways, of all travelers to the electronic frontier. An autodidact, he learned fast, convinced his destiny lay in software.

Shannon was born in Seattle in 1964, the son of a mail carrier and a restaurant worker. At the age of twelve, he took a fancy to computers, saving all his paper-route money and buying a Radio Shack PC. After high school, he worked for a series of restaurants, then enrolled in a two-year college, gaining a degree in business programming. He went to work taking care of an accounting firm's computers, then in May of 1988 took "a major pay cut" to join Microsoft, the rising corporate star in the Seattle area.

Microsoft asked Shannon to feed floppy disks into duplicating machines. This activity was as close as the company came to manufacturing. The disks, which eventually landed in the hands of customers, contained copies of Microsoft programs. The job paid $5.25 an hour. Shannon accepted, knowing he was starting with Microsoft as the high-tech equivalent of a janitor. But he badly wanted a job at Microsoft; he wanted a future.

Duplicating disks, Shannon worked four ten-hour days and a mandatory eight hours of overtime on Fridays. He kept tabs on many machines at once. After nine months, he won a transfer into the belly of Microsoft, joining the OS/2 build team. In August 1989 he began building NT once a week. The task was fuzzy. On the appointed day of his first build, Shannon arrived at the offices of the NT team. Microsoft was known for its meager training. "Sink or swim" was the rule for rookies. But Shannon's initiation stretched this maxim to the point of absurdity.

Steve Wood was the first person Shannon met, which was fortuitous since Wood whipped out a three-page description on building NT. Sitting before a computer, Shannon carefully took the first step. It didn't work. The second step didn't work either. Nor did the third.

Shannon told Wood that his instructions had failed. Wood looked unconcerned. He dismissed the build instructions as "old news. Just try this," he snapped, then blurted out some computerese. Shannon tried Wood's commands. No build.

Next he found Lucovsky, who playfully asked why he even wanted to build NT. "There are twenty testers who want to write test apps for NT, and they need a build to do that," Shannon said.

"To hell with the testers," Lucovsky answered.

By now Shannon was confused. He was off to a bad start.

He then found Perazzoli, who happily offered assistance. What a relief, he thought. Unfortunately Perazzoli didn't seem to know how to work a personal computer. DOS seemed as foreign to him as Greek. Shannon's hopes of building NT were dashed. Out of pity, he showed Perazzoli one of the simplest DOS operations—how to copy a file. It was like breathing life into a clay figure. Perazzoli suddenly ripped through a combination of commands that resulted in a completed build of NT. Then he explained to Shannon what he had done. Perazzoli's directions made sense. Shannon left thinking that Perazzoli "must be like Einstein. He can't answer a phone but can code like crazy."

Shannon's experience illustrated the peculiar ways of the NT team. Everything was in flux. Cutler liked his people to wear many hats, and they did. Decisions came from all over. Coders and testers were demanding. Quick on his feet, Shannon learned to ride the waves. He did the first eighty builds on his own. "I was strictly a service," he said. "I serviced everybody in NT."

Much of the job was routine. At first, Shannon built a new version of NT every Wednesday, starting at about 7:30 in the morning. By then he had all the submissions, or "check-ins," that were needed to bring the build up to date. Cutler considered the quality of a check-in to be the truest measure of a code writer. Nothing made him angrier than when a programmer failed to test his code before submitting it to the build lab. He expected a programmer to do more than simply convert the code into the lower-level language understood by the computer (a conversion done automatically by a compiler). "Even code that compiles can crash the system," Cutler said. "So they can't just write the code, see that it compiles and check it in. They have to test it." It maddened Cutler that even now many programmers, out of laziness or stupidity or both, "failed to understand the importance of absolutely high-quality check-ins."

If a code writer wanted to avoid scrutiny, he or she could check in electronically, preventing anyone from reviewing a piece of code for accuracy or style. It was up to the code writer to hew to the proper standard. When building, Shannon determined only that a check-in met the minimum standard. If the code compiled, then Shannon meshed it into the new build.

This was the first hurdle. When completed, the build had to be distributed, or "propagated," across the team. Once in use, the build might die unexpectedly due to faulty code. When the person whose code "broke" the build was identified, there was hell to pay. "If you break the build," Cutler often said, "your ass is grass, and I'm the lawn mower." The authors of bad check-ins came to dread the sight of Cutler.

Shannon, of course, took care not to botch the build himself. The process was highly automated—computers did most of the grunt work—but Shannon certainly could hit the wrong keys or muff the proper sequence. He started the process of creating a new build of NT by typing: \\KYLESH. CD\MSBUG. Then he typed: Run "Building.cmd kylesh ntdb ntos. After the build was finished, he typed: CD\NT\RELEASE\BIN\I386.

Shannon initially leaned on Lucovsky for guidance, but after a year he knew his routines well enough to train several former OS/2 builders who had joined him in handling the expanding task of building NT. In March 1991, Shannon's life took a new turn. Dog food came to the build lab. The goal was to build NT on computers controlled by NT. Shannon faced this prospect with trepidation. He remembered months when he couldn't keep NT running long enough to finish a build. "It was kind of a hairy nightmare," he said. "We used to call it living on the bleeding edge."

Now NT was still bleeding, but it was also building. Shannon and his fellow builders started eating dog food, too.

Cutler believed that the makers of an operating system should trade additional features for time. Better to release the first version sooner with less. His was a less-now, more-later ethic.

Robert Muglia, the program manager, took a different view. Wishing to open the project to the vitalizing influences of the market, he reviewed the plans for every aspect of NT. In many ways, he found the product thin. The team's work, while impressive, was only "great raw material" for a saleable product. Important features were not planned, or planned features missed the point. Officially Muglia's prime weapon in the battle to "expand the scope of NT" was a "product one requirements document" that briefly described NT's features. This document was akin to a contract between engineering and management. Muglia inherited one from the previous program manager, but he quickly went about revamping it, penciling in scores of additional features. Most changes were small and intended to make NT more useful.

Cutler's bile rose every time he heard a call for a new feature. "It drives him nuts," said one intimate, "because it interferes with his ability to deliver on his commitment. With his experience he knows that you put more stuff in and the schedule just goes out, even if you pretend it doesn't." As much as Cutler fought against the rising tide, it became harder to reject new features. Feature mania fed on itself. And it wasn't just the marketeers either. The programmers kept getting bright ideas about this or that. "As time passes, invention thrives," Cutler often said.

To the novice, unbridled invention seemed a boon. But Cutler well knew that each additional piece of NT greatly increased the interactions between pieces of the operating system, giving rise to many more unexpected bugs. "If they [program managers] had to go through this grueling experience of trying to ship this thing," Cutler said, "I think they'd have a little different outlook on how much work we can do, how much we can take on. As it stands they have this endless list of shit. The list is always twice as long as what we can do."

In meetings Cutler listened cynically as the program managers prattled on:

Their favorite line is to walk in and say, "We aren't going to sell a copy. Nope, if we don't add this feature, the whole product is fucked. Absolutely fucked." And there you sit, having spent years of your life, night and day, working on this thing, and this guy tells you he can't sell the product because it doesn't have this feature.

So you're forced into this position of saying, "Well, I'll just have to work harder, I'll put in more time, because we have to have this feature, or nobody will be able to sell NT." Well, after a while you learn that as soon as you get one feature done, hey there's another one. And I just hate that. I *hate* that!

Muglia, who had no desire to become an object of hatred, quickly learned that it was suicide to attack Cutler directly. "I never want Dave to say no to something," Muglia said. "Because once Dave says no it is very hard to undo his decision."

Better to take his case to rank-and-file code writers and their managers; they were less likely to recoil in horror at a request to make NT more appealing. Or if that didn't work, Muglia could hire an outside code writer. Once Muglia had a rough piece of code in hand, resistance to his ideas often melted.

Muglia urged his junior program managers to act boldly. When one whined that a programmer ignored him, making it impossible to write a certain spec, Muglia responded: "You're acting like a victim. Just do it." The advice was correct. After circulating a proposed spec, the program manager suddenly gained the code writer's attention.

With Muglia unafraid to push his suggestions to the limit (or abandon his poor ones quickly) he achieved what he termed "a tenuous balance" between program managers and the code writers. The evolution of the new file system well illustrated Muglia's effect on the project.

One issue that bedeviled the file system was the way files were named. Hastily created a decade ago and limited by primitive PC electronics, DOS did many frustrating things. Naming files was one of them. DOS restricted file names to a maximum of eleven characters, which had to appear like this:

xxmiller.tom

Because of this, people couldn't give memorable names to their DOS files. It was preferable to call a file about a jazz trumpeter *Miles* or perhaps *MilesDavis* but DOS wouldn't allow that. A file name must have no more than eight characters, then a period, then three characters. The nearest a DOS name could come to Miles Davis was *MilesDav.isx*. That wasn't exactly easy to remember.

With more powerful PCs and more planning, it was easy to create a program that allowed so-called long file names. OS/2 created files such as *TomMiller* or *Holiday.On.Ice* or any combination of 255 characters. But when someone using a DOS application, with its short names, tried to find a file bearing a long OS/2 name either in his own PC or from another PC, reached via a network, it wasn't possible. The OS/2 files, if they had long names, were not visible through DOS (or Windows, for that matter, which then relied on the same file-naming technique). As a result, few OS/2 customers bothered to switch to long names. The short, inconvenient DOS names persisted.

The plans called for NT to embody this unsatisfactory status quo. Muglia objected—for good reason. Gates wanted a change and regularly "beat me up on this subject," Muglia said. "It was one of those issues he would bring up at every opportunity, and even when there wasn't a good opportunity, he'd still bring it up. In no uncertain terms, he would tell me how stupid we all were for not providing some sort of mapping" between short DOS names and the longer NT names.

Yet Muglia realized that any solution would "open up an enormous can of worms. The mapping needed to happen automatically, yet be clear to the user and not cause any compatibility problems."

It took two weeks—"the longest weeks I can remember," Muglia said—to sort out an approach. Miller and Kimura batted around ideas with Lucovsky, the project's top troubleshooter, and with other Microsofties. They finally agreed that each new NT file would automatically receive two names. The first would be chosen by the user. If a long name was selected, NT automatically created a second name that conformed to the limitations of DOS but resembled the long name.

Miller and Kimura were left to work out the unanswered questions. The two most vexing were: What if someone didn't like the pre-assigned short name and wanted to change it? Or what if the name was identical, through a sheer fluke, with the name of an existing file? These were real riddles, but Muglia asked them not to modify their file-system schedule even though they were tackling this added feature. Revising the deadline might anger Cutler, whom Muglia had kept out of the discussions. Miller and Kimura swallowed hard. The solution to the puzzle posed by DOS names was in view, but making it work would take time. Fortunately the problem was an interesting one. They agreed to solve it and stick with their current schedule.

The expanding scope of the file system mirrored the challenges facing NT as a whole. In terms of an earlier analogy, the operating system had outgrown the downstairs staff of a home. It was now more accurate to view NT as the service staff of a large hotel.

Instead of one family seeking aid, hundreds of guests wanted attention. This required an enormous staff. Instead of a cook preparing food for a single dining room, teams of chefs were cooking for a few restaurants full of diners. Instead of a housekeeper, there was an army of housekeepers. Whereas the house made do with locks on doors and windows, the hotel took elaborate security measures and stationed guards in the lobby.

Since Hotel NT was under construction, the services it would offer guests were only being tested. So there was much discussion among the people managing the project about which frills (and how many) to provide in addition to the traditional basics. Of course, the beds would be made in the morning, but should they be turned down at night? Should there be a phone in the bathroom as well as one near the bed?

Then there were debates over ways to improve on the usual service, which would perhaps give the hotel an edge over rivals when it opened. It might take guests five minutes to check out; with better ways of processing payment the time could be cut in half. The locks on doors were strong, but guests might feel safer with a customizable security system in each room.

There were really no right answers regarding the fine points of Hotel NT. There were only compromises.

Should we or shouldn't we? By late March, it was clear that the schedule for the new file system was unrealistic. The spec was to be finished by April 30, 1991. The code was to be "functionally" complete by July 15 and ready for final testing a month later. When he blessed the schedule, Kimura said, "We need to get this done fast." Now he saw that the strain of caring for the older file systems was taking away from work on the new one.

Kimura wanted out. He wanted to drop the new file system from the plan for NT. Perazzoli, his boss, concurred. He sympathized with Kimura in the situation he was facing and was about to advise several other groups to scale back their ambitions for NT. He still had a faint hope the team could reach "code complete" by Halloween. But if they didn't scale back now, the team could treat that deadline as a charade. This was no one's fault. Scheduling was never easy; the bigger the project, the larger the degree of error. "With software, you know what you have to do," he said, "but it's always a big surprise how long it will take."

Miller opposed abandoning the file system. He was solely responsible for recoverability, its outstanding attribute, which he thought of as "my big thing." After having worked so hard on the old file systems, he felt he would regret not pushing ahead with the new one. Kimura was unconvinced. They argued. The two men rarely argued about large matters, usually keeping their disagreements to small points. The divisions between them were often lost on outsiders. Miller, for instance, preferred leaving only one blank space after making the notation // (which marked the start of a coding comment). Kimura liked leaving two. They argued endlessly about this point, with Kimura always concluding: "Two spaces is how *you* do it."

Kimura won the argument about the file system too. On April 1, he drafted a memo advising that the feature be dropped. "It is a matter of priorities," he wrote. "All of us would like to see NTFS available by the first release. . . . [But] NTFS will still get done" for a later release. On a printout of the memo, Miller scribbled: "We have begun and will continue to work on NTFS."

At Perazzoli's behest, Kimura held the memo for a few days until Cutler returned from a holiday. (To the annoyance of some teammates, he took his holidays. To be sure, he kept long hours on the job, but he played as hard as he worked. He tried midnight skiing, when he couldn't get away any earlier, and then what is called heliskiing. A copter dropped him and his party on a mountainside and retrieved them later. The skiing was excellent, and there were no crowds.) When Cutler was on vacation, work ground on. But the file system was such a big feature that Perazzoli wanted Cutler's approval before dropping it.

Cutler refused to give it. On returning, he promptly reversed Perazzoli's decision. He wanted a new file system for NT. He had lobbied too hard for it to give up now. Like it or not, Kimura and Miller were back in business.

Stage two of dog food—graphics—swept over the team at the same time. By late May scores of programmers were writing code with the help of PCs controlled by a version of NT that lacked Windows graphics. Eschewing graphics simplified matters. Naturally, NT without graphics was smaller, ran faster and had fewer bugs. Cutler, who had never worked with graphical software in his years at Digital, took well to this version. But in Muglia's eyes this "lite" edition of NT was a poor substitute for dog food. He thought that Cutler "didn't give a shit about DOS or Windows compatibility or about the graphical user interface [GUI]. Everyone was nervous that Dave wouldn't run the GUI." As the weeks went by and the team stuck to its text-only diet, Muglia fretted that Cutler would never add graphics to the dog food.

Muglia's anxieties were understandable. Cutler wasn't keen on adopting the Windows version for his own use; he had never routinely done his work with applications that were controlled by graphical commands. He wondered whether "I'd want to switch or not." But if he didn't switch to the Windows version of NT, a raft of important code writers might not switch either.

Then one day Cutler switched. No fanfare, he just did it. Muglia was relieved; a confrontation had been avoided.

The third and final dog food stage involved networking. In this phase the computers that stored the team's files and served as the hub of its network would switch to NT, abandoning OS/2's Lan Man networking program. The shift was inevitable. The team wanted NT to control both the individual desktop PC and a new breed of PC known as a server. A server enabled a network of PCs to share files and applications; this made it easier for groups of people to work on the same documents and share information as well as printers, disk drives and other devices.

Demand for servers was rising; these super-PCs were rapidly displacing far more expensive mini- and mainframe computers. The server was critical to the future of both NT and Microsoft. With NT, Microsoft hoped to shove aside networking rival Novell. Gates expected NT to win a wide following first on servers and only later on individual PCs. Just that month he had circulated a memo in which he predicted that NT would not dominate the desktop until at least 1995.

The first step was to convert the team's servers to NT. This posed certain difficulties. When NT crashed on an individual's desk, that was bad but it only hurt one person. When it crashed on the network, everyone's work was hampered. The sharing of files and information and hardware came to a halt. Moreover, it became impossible to receive the latest build of NT.

The impending switch put the networking group and its chief, David Thompson, on the spot. The group was an amalgam of old Microsofties, ex-Digital men and young guys a year or two out of school. Thompson had worked for Digital for five years, for a time even sharing the same building as Cutler, passing him in the halls but never meeting him formally. Thompson joined Microsoft in April 1990, in time to feel the chill between Cutler and Darryl Rubin, who had tried but failed to prevent Cutler's team from dictating Microsoft's networking future.

Thompson had begun as a manager in Rubin's camp, but with the revamping of networking in September 1990 he joined Cutler with some code writers in tow. It was a nice fit. Thompson, who saw work in black-and-white terms, liked that "the first thing Dave does is make it clear to you that it's important to meet expectations." Thompson wasn't skittish when Cutler poked fun at him. Though his heart "would beat a little faster" when Cutler really lit into him, Thompson didn't retreat readily. He had a quick wit, and he was willing to trade barbs with Cutler.

At first, Thompson's goals were modest. NT would exchange files and services with Microsoft's current networking programs. But as Muglia and the program managers fed back opinions from customers, Thompson raised the goals. In time, networking became "a moving target" for his team. By the spring of 1991, he'd promised that his piece of NT would make it possible to exchange files and services with computers controlled by the Unix operating program.

The fresh ambitions for networking made it harder to finish a test version for the team's own use. Cracking the whip, Thompson imposed a July 31 deadline for a dog food edition. It looked like a stretch. To lend drama to the push, Thompson made a bet with one of Rubin's sidekicks. The wager "kept us a little looser. It did help motivate us," said one teammate. If his group missed the deadline, Thompson promised to don a woman's bathing suit and swim across an artificial pond on Microsoft's campus. The pond was known as Lake Bill.

David Treadwell was a good soldier. If he could help it, he would keep his leader from diving into Lake Bill.

Treadwell was soft-spoken, athletic and 23 years old. While an undergraduate at Princeton University, he had been so highly sought after that Gates himself telephoned to urge him to join Microsoft. Treadwell arrived in July 1989, becoming the lone rookie in Cutler's team of veterans. To a man, they were at least ten years his senior and hardly eager to teach him the ropes. His boss, Perazzoli, made it "real clear to me he didn't want a lot of interruptions. He wanted me to figure things out on my own." It was sink or swim, and he swam. One teammate told him encouragingly: "Nobody minds if you ask a question, just as long as you've researched it enough and clearly put in the effort to find the answer on your own."

Treadwell took the advice to heart. He was a quick study, rarely relying on others for aid. Asked to work on NT's networking piece, he was swept up in the team's rivalry with Rubin's networking team. Before long he was pounding his chest like a Cutler vet. Why shouldn't they write networking code from scratch instead of adapting Rubin's stuff? "We think we can do it better," he said. "Fewer bugs. Faster."

He charged ahead, in his first twelve months writing an astonishing fifteen thousand lines of code. By some measures that was several times the output of the average programmer. On the one-year anniversary of his arrival, he was given one of just two coveted rookie-of-the-year awards personally bestowed by Gates. With his reputation rising, he did something that had apparently never occurred to anyone on the boast-happy NT team: He downplayed his accomplishments.

By the middle of 1991, after two years on NT, Treadwell had mastered programming under fire. But just when he thought he'd steeled himself against every attack, he faced a new enemy. With Thompson's deadline looming, his network code was on the blink when used in combination with a certain Compaq PC. Instead of sending a correct page of text across the network from the PC, the text contained this string of characters near the start of every page: 3ffffff fffff7.

The pattern disrupted otherwise normal data; it was the only corrupted data on the page; and it occurred at random intervals, anywhere from three minutes to twenty hours. Data corruption, as the team called it, was a deadly sin, worse in some ways than a crash. At least when a program crashed, destroying data, the loss was circumscribed. With this kind of bug, there was no telling the extent of the damage.

Treadwell first identified the bug on May 26, a Sunday, and it soon sucked in other people. After three weeks of fiddling, with no solution, Treadwell, Gary Kimura and a colleague named Mike Glass dedicated the third weekend in June to getting a line on this bug. Four other people, including Perazzoli and Havens, pitched in too.

During the weekend Treadwell grew convinced that the code was fine. So did Glass, an expert on the interplay between PC hardware and software. Born in Iowa thirty-three years earlier, Glass had attended six colleges in nine years and had begun programming a decade ago for four dollars an hour. Before joining Microsoft in November 1990, Glass had worked as a programmer for the PC maker Compaq, the second largest buyer of Microsoft's programs. On the NT team, he wrote code that enabled the operating system to "drive" different pieces of input-output hardware: disk drives, keyboards, network controllers and the like. Tall and thin, Glass had chiseled features and a dreamy look in his eyes that suggested to some a sudden departure from an ashram. Once attracted to a problem, he never let go. "He wants to get a solution now!" a friend said.

After studying Treadwell's code, Glass was puzzled as to why it behaved differently on different PCs. To him, that pointed to a hardware flaw. Cutler asked Rob Short, the team's hardware guru, to investigate. Short subjected various PCs running the code to a battery of tests. Convinced that software was the culprit, he bet Glass a dinner that he was right.

Glass and Treadwell, while defending their viewpoint, agonized over the situation. "Data corruption," Glass said, "is the worst thing that can happen to you in computing." Treadwell, an avid volleyball player, couldn't visit the court while the bug lurked out there. He had bad dreams too, seeing himself and Glass searching endlessly for a solution. In his dream they never found the bug.

"Reality mirrored my dream," Treadwell said. "I'd come in late at night, trying to find the bug, and I never would. What made it even worse was that we were running hard to finish [the first dog food version], and this bug totally prevented it."

In his precarious state, Treadwell seemed offended when Short needled him and Glass, talking about the bug every time he saw them working on something else. "I tormented them," Short confessed. He offered no apologies. His attitude was: "We're going to fix this because it isn't going away otherwise."

In his lab, Short tried to narrow down the problem, making a list of everything they knew that happened before the failure occurred. Glass, meanwhile, huddled with Compaq's engineers after Cutler guessed that the company's networking hardware was at fault. A few more weeks passed. Then, in mid-July, Glass stumbled on what looked like a breakthrough. An engineer at Adaptec, which made devices used in Compaq and other brand-name PCs that controlled the input and output of data, casually sent Glass a month-old errata sheet. It described a bug that fitted the pattern vexing the team.

This was it! Suddenly Glass was furious. Over the past six weeks of chasing this bug, he'd spoken several times with this Adaptec engineer. Once he'd even described the bug in detail, only to have the engineer tell him he'd never heard of it. He was appalled.

While relieved that he'd come to the end of the mystery, Treadwell felt angry too: "I spent so much time on this. It was a whole month for me. One month is a lot of time for one bug."

At least Glass won the bet with Short, who paid for an expensive dinner for Glass and his wife.

Thompson wasn't as lucky. Because of the mysterious bug and other delays, his networking team missed the deadline for completing its dog food version. But instead of swimming the pond, Thompson won a reprieve. It cost, though. If his team missed the August 31 deadline, then he'd swim Lake Bill along with Treadwell and four other network coders.

The group made it easily, finishing the first networking version of NT in mid-August. There was no time to celebrate, however. Fellow programmers soon reported many bugs. This had the salutary effect of speeding improvements, but it made life miserable for the network coders. To quell the yelps from victims of the frequent network crashes, Thompson outfitted his guys with beepers so that they could field emergency calls after hours. Treadwell and the others felt put upon by the vagaries of their code. Thompson wasn't exactly applying balm to his people's wounds: "Don't tell me you don't handle a technician's job," he told them. "If it's broken, fix it."

It wasn't as if they had a choice, either. The more vigorous code writers were distressed to lose their PCs for even a minute. They complained instantly about the latest outrage wrought by the network. "When will it be available?" was their plea.

How quickly these team members forgot the difficulties brought on by the switch to dog food! Since March 1991 the team had been buffeted by two waves of change: first switching to NT without graphics and then to NT with graphics. Both shifts had interfered with the progress of code writing by exposing weaknesses in existing code, forcing people to spend hours and sometimes days making revisions. This bedeviled Kimura and Miller in their bid to create a new file system. Now that the team's network depended on dog food, Thompson's coders couldn't go anywhere without a helpful teammate telling them: "You probably know this already—the server's crashed."

7. SHIP MODE

"No, we have to do better than this!"

And with that, on August 12, 1991, Paul Maritz shattered the tidy world of two technical leaders and a half dozen code writers.

Maritz was disappointed. By this point, NT's value to customers should have been clear. According to the schedule, the program was supposed to be essentially finished within three months; yet at best NT's code was 80 percent complete. Though not officially Cutler's boss, Maritz actually oversaw the project. Although it was unusual for him to meddle with the guts of NT, he was dismayed by its weak security features. Now he jeopardized the schedule by asking the team to consider scrapping its work on security and starting over.

Security was something customers fretted about too. Because computers make it so easy to view, copy and transfer information, adequate protection against tampering was vital. This was perhaps less so for individuals or small groups, but large organizations needed at least a modicum of protection. The enemy wasn't just outsiders seeking entry into a computer network for the purposes of theft or vandalism; so-called viruses also menaced unprotected networks. But most customers had a more common concern: The main priority was retaining a measure of privacy and control within the organization. Certain people must view sensitive financial information, for example, while others must not. A manager may wish

143

an employee to view certain records for only a few months; afterward the normal restrictions apply. A new employee must gain quick access to certain records and an available printer or sit needlessly idle.

Mainframe and minicomputers, which were designed to support large networks, generally accounted for security by giving wide-ranging authority to a network administrator. When a new employee joined a company, the administrator issued him or her a password and a list of "permissions," or electronic areas he or she could visit. The password, which was typed into a computer when a person "logged on," set the boundaries for a person's electronic travel.

At the outset of the NT project, Cutler treated security as an afterthought, another item on a long list of features. Gary Kimura initially handled it, but he also ran file systems, which kept him too busy to pay attention to security. About a year into the project, in January 1990, Cutler asked Jim Kelly, an old pal, to take charge. Kelly wore glasses, a short brown beard and, though in his mid-thirties, had a freckle-faced, boyish quality that belied his stubbornness. After handling security for Cutler at his Digital lab, he had arrived at Microsoft with the original crowd but only just now joined the NT team. Moody and taciturn, Kelly was devoted to Cutler and fiercely loyal to the Digital clique. He was rigid, combative and dictatorial—a Cutler clone though without the original's élan.

Kelly immediately found himself in a hole. "Security was a Johnny-come-lately to NT," he realized. Given the late start, he thought it best to roughly duplicate the security offered by Microsoft's Lan Man networking program. This meant that the burden of security would fall on a network administrator, leaving the person at the PC with precious few options. If a person required access to many different groups within an organization, they would have to rely on numerous passwords. This was a hassle. Even worse, when someone left an organization, the administrator had to cancel each password. Not only did that take time, but it wasn't always easy to track the number of passwords a person held.

Reaching even this level of security, however, proved difficult. In early 1991, Kelly lost two code writers to the new Cairo project. Then in April, Cutler and Lou Perazzoli, concerned about missing the Halloween "code complete" deadline, asked Kelly to slice away security features in order to finish his code more quickly. At the same time, Kelly felt that Robert Muglia, the chief program manager, was "bugging me because I'm not doing enough with security. Well, naturally, I'm resistant when my own bosses are asking for less."

Muglia, however, thought that security should be greatly expanded; he would not let the issue die. He argued that customers would love more security options and fewer passwords. His dream was to offer a single log-on: one way for the same person to enter different groups, even those separated by security walls. Muglia was vague on the engineering details, but he was supported by the managers of Microsoft's internal computer network, who said they would not use NT unless its security was improved.

Muglia's concern prompted Maritz to review the situation. He gathered the principals together: Muglia and his aide Keith Logan; Kelly and his boss, Perazzoli; a programmer named Cliff Van Dyke; and Jim Horne, who led the group that handled the security piece that was visible to the user. Probing the team, Maritz asked, "What happens if I want to give someone access to a spreadsheet on my machine?" The answer was that the network administrator had to arrange it.

Maritz was unhappy. He wanted something quicker, easier: "You mean if I want Bill Gates and only Bill Gates to see this spreadsheet, I can't do it myself?"

No, he couldn't.

Maritz sent them back to the drawing board: *We have to do better than this!*

Kelly took the decision hard. He felt pushed into taking the risk of revamping security for a dubious reward. Not to mention that just trying to satisfy Maritz would wreck the time schedule—that was guaranteed.

He wasn't the only person who felt bad. Maritz's order sent Jim Horne into spasms of anxiety. A native of Quebec, Horne was among a number of Canadians working for Microsoft. Cutler's team had a half dozen at least, the result of the company's taste for graduates of the University of Waterloo, Canada's top-rated computer science department, which annually supplied Microsoft with more new hires than any other North American university. A physics student who taught himself programming, Horne was more self-consciously artistic than anyone else on the NT team. He worked as a radio reporter after college and once wrote a science-fiction novel over a weekend. He played percussion in an orchestra and hoped to conduct one day. Oddly, he fell in love with the maligned OS/2 after attending a conference and pursued a job at Microsoft as a programmer. He was hired in the summer of 1988, then joined NT two years later with a flood of newcomers who swelled the team's ranks of code writers to about one hundred.

His first time on a large team, Horne watched closely as Cutler forged an effective community from diverse members, marveling at his keen sense of direction. Yet even Cutler found it hard to manage the collective creation of software. With tongue in cheek, he declared that the ideal software team consisted of one person. Horne could see his point: "There's a big jump between a program one person can keep in their head and a program created by four or five or seven people," he thought. "And then the jump to one hundred programmers is almost incomprehensible." Cutler's role was akin to that of the director of a motion picture, Horne observed. "He's relying on the talents of all these people he's gathered. There's all sorts of creative differences over direction, and eventually the director says we'll do it this way or that way." Cutler's challenge, he felt, was "to get all these talented people to believe in a schedule and a message."

Indeed, Cutler displayed all the hallmarks of a great Hollywood director. He imposed his tastes and vision on a cast of stars and a crew of talented technicians. He sustained the integrity of his vision by refusing to pander to the marketplace while skillfully gaining the financial resources required for his immense undertaking. Like an Orson Welles, he relied on his skills as an actor and technician as well as a director, making his involvement in his creation more intimate and immediate.

The cinematic image stuck with Horne: "When I see a movie now and watch the credits roll by at the end, I think, 'Yeah, it's like they're building NT.'" Horne's own role was designing and building the user interface, the way programs looked and felt to someone using them. He saw poetry in the presentation of a program. Like many code writers attracted to interfaces, Horne viewed code writing as a mysterious activity; the rationality instrumental in writing code was merely a patina over a strange and wonderful force: "You wave these magic spells over this little box [the computer], and if you get the correct incantation it does tricks for you," he said. "It gives you a feeling of power."

Yet Horne worried about the sense of omnipotence that programming spawned. It was too easy for managers to insist that everything was possible in code. In particular, he feared that Maritz's aspirations for NT's security would result in a software "nightmare."

Horne, Kelly and Van Dyke met often and traded dozens of e-mails over the next six weeks. They discussed alternative models that would satisfy both Kelly's insistence on rigorous protection and Muglia's desire for a single password and freedom from a network administrator. The group never found common ground. "A number of proposals floated, but nothing really fit the bill," Muglia said.

Eager to settle the security question, which threatened to upset the schedule for the entire project, Maritz reconvened the key players on October 4, 1991. Arriving twenty minutes late for the meeting, he proceeded to assail them for failing to reach an agreement on their own. "You've taken too long to come up with an answer," he said impatiently. "We've run out of time. You'll have to do what Lan Man does."

Kelly was relieved. He'd held out and won. Muglia froze; mimicking Microsoft's existing Lan Man networking software meant that NT would not meet any of Maritz's special requests. This decision would play into the hands of Microsoft's archrival Novell, whose Netware software would surely satisfy Maritz's litmus test sometime in the future. Unwilling to walk away empty handed, Muglia suddenly challenged Maritz, his boss and mentor.

"Paul, you're just wrong. It won't work," he said. "You can't sell NT like this." He pleaded for a few more weeks, arguing that a butchered schedule was better than a poor product. "We're onto some solutions," he said. "There are answers."

Maritz relented. He gave them more time.

Cliff Van Dyke welcomed the reprieve. He was still growing accustomed to PCs. Before joining Microsoft a year earlier, he'd worked thirteen years on bigger computers for Harris, a defense contractor. Now he was part of a wave of engineering veterans who had beat a path to Microsoft, the most successful software company in the world.

Van Dyke was studious, low-key and disciplined. He wore wire-rim glasses, and even with a full beard his wife thought he resembled Radar O'Reilly, the skittish factotum on the TV series *M*A*S*H*. Because he was older than most of his teammates, his experience and temperament allowed him the luxury of treating his code writing like a faucet. He turned it on and off at will. His work hours were on the low end of normal for Microsoft: 8:30 a.m. to 6:30 at night, and no weekends. "But those ten hours at work each day, I'm really at it," he said. "I'm a full-bore kind of guy." His routine struck some as mechanical, but was actually ritualistic; his even keel sustained his creativity. While many hotshot coders boasted of working round the clock, snatching pieces of sleep now and again, Van Dyke saw his talent as a renewable and finite resource. A person can bear only so much code in a day. Paradoxically, "When I push harder on hours, it takes me longer to find the right answer," he said. Time with his family—a wife and children—sustained him too. By steadily progressing on a problem and believing less was sometimes more when it came to productivity, he avoided pitting family against work. "Microsoft will consume as much of my time as I let it," he said. To defend yourself, "you just walk out. You go home at the end of the day."

In the unfolding security drama, Van Dyke saw himself as "a small player." Within a week of the Maritz reprieve, he became a big player, thanks to his decision to take a fresh look at a concept he had applied to an unrelated problem. The concept was called "pass-through authentication." In one swoop, it realized Muglia's wish to make one password do the work of many.

"Pass-through" depended on a related idea called "trusted domains." A domain is a group whose members share the same security status. If two domains have a trusted relationship, every member of one domain "passes through" to the other. The network administrator forged links between domains, making a password good for one domain good in the other. One domain potentially could form trusted ties with all the others. But once established, the domain automatically accepted the password from every member of a "trusted" domain.

There was still Maritz's question of how to make a spreadsheet on his PC available to one person—say, Gates and only Gates. This required individuals, as well as the network administrator, to grant permission to view files, use printers and the like. A model, which the group called "flexible administration," seemed to allow for both central control and individual differences. But it did so in unwieldy fashion: Performance was abysmal and "security holes" abounded. Keith Logan, standing in for Muglia, wasn't surprised. Though elegant in theory, "flex admin" proved the old adage, "The Devil is in the details."

As the details became apparent, the model grew more complicated. Instead of treating all domains alike, the model called for two types: local and global. Then Kelly and Van Dyke wondered if they needed a third domain type to accommodate those cases that didn't quite fit either of the categories. But this made Horne's user interface, which he was already constructing, too confusing for customers. Kelly and Van Dyke instead wrote special code to handle the cases covered by the third type and stuck with local and global domains.

By late October, Horne was riding an emotional roller coaster. "We lived in fear, as we wrote more and more code, that we might someday discover a fatal flaw in the fundamental design," he said. There was added pressure because the entire schedule for NT had been set back several months mainly to provide for these revamped security features.

To protect himself, Horne concocted fall-back positions. Logan, a fellow Canadian, was impressed by Horne's thoroughness, even though he felt it was a hollow exercise. "Horne kept thinking about what would happen if we fail," Logan said. "In my mind the only real contingency plan was start over."

Horne drew inward. At home, he refused to talk about his job, frustrating his wife, Karen, who was curious. "If I started talking about it, I'd begin thinking about failure scenarios and get anxious," he said. "I didn't want that." Yet Karen felt cut off from her husband.

A Ph.D. meteorologist, she had given up a professorship in Canada to follow Horne to Microsoft. While the company arranged a work permit for Horne, Karen lacked one, making it impossible for her legally to hold a job in the U.S. A specialist in the arcana of cloud and ice formation, Karen occasionally took freelance jobs abroad, consulting for far-flung electricity suppliers worried about the affect of ice on power lines.

Karen refused to accept Horne's silent suffering. She laid down a rule: He was to tell her "the most important thing that happened at work" each day. Realizing the drift in his marriage, Horne grabbed this lifeline. His daily nugget from the front cheered Karen.

It did little for Horne's own mood, however. He brooded over weighty matters; with the cloud hanging over security, he grew somber and silent at times. Then he bought a black Miata convertible, the Special Edition model with tan leather seats. Horne usually took little notice of cars, driving an aging but sturdy Mazda 626. The Miata, by contrast, was an impractical two-seater that screamed "Joy ride." At $24,000 the car also was an extravagance. Yet because of the rising value of Microsoft's stock, so many Microsofties owned Miatas that some called it the "corporate car." While Horne's choice of wheels was "not exactly unique," he immediately felt the palliative effects of owning a Miata and found "the stress of the security hassle easing."

The first few weeks after buying the Miata, Horne acted like a teenager who had just discovered driving. After work, he took Karen for an evening spin. She enjoyed the attention, although the Miata sometimes made her uneasy. Whenever Horne put the top down, she squawked. Sitting so exposed in this expensive plaything, she felt painfully conspicuous. She told her husband: "I'm just not a top-down kind of girl."

In September 1991, the revamping of security went largely unnoticed as the team pushed to complete a working version of NT in time to demonstrate in October at the mammoth Comdex computer show in Las Vegas. This would be the first public showing of NT. It was critical because it was aimed at those people Microsoft hoped would write the first applications for their new operating system.

Without programs especially tailored to NT, customers might never appreciate NT's powers.

The Comdex deadline, which was hard and fast, drove Cutler to new heights of intensity. Yelling, pounding on walls and cursing became commonplace. The only outrage he didn't commit, Cutler later joked, was to throw his desk out of a window. Why all the histrionics? "I just wasn't used to working in a place where things got so screwed up so often," he said.

At the same time, Cutler scrapped the October 1991 date for finishing the final code for NT. His new finish line was April 1992. If the code was in good shape by then, he thought it would still be possible to begin selling the finished edition of NT by the end of 1992. But this would take some doing. He was appalled by the slovenly condition of the code written by many on his team. Too few of them shared his zeal for getting the code right the first time. This galled him. At times like this Cutler would visit Perazzoli in his office, close the door and bemoan his situation. "We have a bunch of fucking jerks working for us," he said many times. "How are we ever going to get NT done?"

On September 27, 1991, twenty-five days before Comdex, Cutler sent a long and spirited memo to the team's code writers. He sketched out a plan that called for building four versions over the next two weeks, any one of which might end up as the build released to the public.

"Our schedule is very tight," Cutler wrote:

> There is very little margin for error. A single careless [mistake] that causes us to do a rebuild, or otherwise lose a build day, can easily blow 25% of our chances to meet our schedule. Please take a minute to think about how this relates to the changes to the system you are currently making. Also understand that each build we have done over the past several weeks has had some sort of killer bug or build breakage. These things take time to fix. Countless wasted hours are spent nursing broken builds or finding bugs.
>
> Our track record for producing robust and reliable builds on time and without a lot of babysitting is not good.

"What I am asking for here is not rocket science, but you would be surprised how often this is not done," he went on. Then he gave various examples of proper procedure, emphasizing the benefit of expecting the worst: "If you add new functionality [to NT] . . . be prepared for it to fail. And please make sure you can [undo] the change if we run into a problem with it in the builds. This is extremely important! We are under a code freeze. If new stuff is checked in, and [the build] breaks as a result, it is usually a frantic exercise to try to figure out how to work around the problem."

"Frantic" was right. The Build Lab at times seemed about to collapse in disorder. Kyle Shannon and the few other builders were outmatched by the scores of people who flung code at them. At Cutler's behest, Mark Lucovsky, the team's most versatile programmer, filled the gap. He tracked check-ins on a white board in his office and managed the now twice-weekly builds. Before each build he compiled a list of proposed changes, then spoke with each code writer about the rationale for the change and its affect on the stability of NT. Lucovsky's opinion carried weight; he probably understood the mosaic of NT better than anyone else, including Cutler. And he didn't tiptoe around fellow code writers but battered their egos with criticism. "If Lucovsky didn't write it, everything is a piece of shit," said one colleague.

Lucovsky played mother hen as the builders stitched together new versions of NT from their computers. The process could take hours, and the builders tried to reject any new code writers' submissions that arrived after they began their build. But some code writers ignored these rejections; they screamed and whined when they couldn't add something to the build at the last minute.

To keep code writers at bay, Lucovsky bullied, bluffed and blocked people. "A lot of guys wanted to sort of throw stuff in," a builder said, "but Lucovsky was very good at stopping them." At times, he simply locked the code writers out. The door to the Build Lab was controlled by a computerized lock, installed to protect the many computers inside. Almost everyone knew the combination, so Lucovsky removed the battery from the lock when he wished no interruptions. Tardy code writers, punching at the keypad, found themselves locked out. The less mature ones banged on the door, but Lucovsky often let them suffer.

Lucovsky rubbed a lot of people the wrong way. He once insulted Moshe Dunie, the test chief, so badly that he was compelled to apologize in writing. Lucovsky obeyed but went on to tell Dunie that his apology was forced. Even his own wife, Cindy, balked when learning of his actions. "I've heard how he is at work, and I wouldn't want to be around that," she said. "If he treated me that way, or the kids, we wouldn't be married."

To his credit, Lucovsky disliked people who pulled rank. He felt the builders deserved respect and that code writers unfairly abused them. To lift morale, he issued each builder a construction hard hat, which Cindy had dressed up to display the letters NT on the front and the name of the builder on the back. Lucovsky insisted the builders wear these hats, as a matter of pride, in the weeks leading up to the public debut of NT.

Shannon's boss, Mitchell Duncan, was glad to see spirits rise in the Build Lab. Born on Chicago's South Side, Duncan was the youngest of six children, the son of a public school teacher. A good athlete and strong student, he graduated from the city's highly rated Lindbloom Technical High School. An African-American, he attended Howard University, one of the country's leading black colleges, where he studied electrical engineering. Paying his way through school, he held a series of jobs with corporations, his last with Microsoft, where he worked in the OS/2 Build Lab in the summer of 1988. A year later, he returned full-time, joining a week before Shannon arrived. The two men, born one day apart, became best pals, their friendship flourishing even after Duncan's promotion to Build Lab chief.

With the abandonment of OS/2, Duncan switched to NT. Accustomed to the formal and deliberate builds conducted jointly with IBM, Duncan was unprepared for the breakneck, freewheeling style of NT. From the start, he felt that his own boss, the hard-boiled Dunie, had "basically tossed me to the lions."

Sink or swim! Duncan swam, fitfully at times. Besides running the Build Lab, he kept track of the equipment needed for the growing test team and monitored some tests. This aggravated him, but not nearly as much as the blasé attitude of the code writers. They drove him crazy, acting like spoiled children, taking pleasure in irritating others and falling to pieces when they didn't get their way. Duncan barely kept himself from thrashing a few of the worst offenders.

In the run-up to the release of NT at Comdex, Duncan felt the strain. There was no easy antidote for Build Lab trauma. It wasn't just the pressure leading up to the twice-weekly build, but the greeting afforded each new one. "Every time I put out a build," he said, "I knew I'd get crapped on."

In mid-September, a month before Comdex, the team released a trial build to a few dozen outside programmers. The push left Duncan teetering. He took everything so seriously, trying to please the various contending factions that collided in the Build Lab. He said yes to too many requests, and it wore him out. The morning meetings, led by Cutler and attended by anywhere from a dozen to two dozen middle managers on the project, also bruised him. He often drew sharp looks when he explained a delay in the latest build. But lately, with Cutler occasionally spelling Lucovsky in the Build Lab, Duncan felt his "excuses" were viewed more sympathetically. A taste of the lab gave Cutler an appreciation for the disorder menacing the build process, which Duncan alone could hardly solve.

To relax, Duncan formed a flag-football team with Shannon, enrolling in a league for Microsofties. Duncan played quarterback and called the plays. Shannon played defensive end and blocked for Duncan on offense. Even after the team won its first few games, Duncan still felt low. He asked for a transfer out of the Build Lab.

Dunie, ever the trooper, hid his shock. Leave the team? Now? That was impossible. He praised Duncan's work and firmly told him that no shift was possible until NT cleared more hurdles. Duncan stayed put, unhappily.

Of the four build candidates for the Comdex release, the team would likely choose the one that performed best on the daily "stress" tests. The results of these tests came to be seen as an essential indicator of the program's health, as it grew in size and power.

Stress tests consisted of a shifting mix of programs especially written to expose NT's flaws. The tests usually ran all night long, on more than one hundred personal computers. Each morning, a few stress "doctors" gathered the performance statistics created by the tests themselves. They compiled an overall average, which was akin to the team's daily temperature. High marks usually made for a cheerful 9:00 a.m. meeting, when the team's leadership discussed current issues. Low marks might sour Cutler's mood and trigger a hectic search to discover why the newest build stank.

The mix of stress tests changed over time. On any given night, "stress" consisted of a collection of five tests running simultaneously. Each was a program written by a member of the team. One basic test was called Tilt. It called for an unchanging series of five actions:

1. Create a file.
2. Open the file.
3. Write the letters A thru Z in the file.
4. Check file for accuracy.
5. Close the file.

These operations were commonly performed by every PC. The failure to complete any of them usually crashed a machine, signaling a coding error of some severity. Tilt ran all night. Once a specified number of files had been created, all the files were deleted and the whole process was repeated. In concert with other tests, Tilt could run for days.

S. Somasegar, the author of Tilt, was one of the project's original testers and now the lead stress tester. Earnest and thorough, Somasegar puzzled over ways to crash a program, but he reserved his hardest thinking for the question, Where should I look for weaknesses? When preparing tests in advance of the Comdex release, he tried to assume the mentality of applications writers who would receive NT: "What sorts of things will a software developer do with an early release? He wants to make progress on app. He knows a great deal about writing code and will be curious about the deep insides of NT. What are the things he won't be able to work around? Whatever those things are, they have to be right."

Unlike some testers, who felt the sting of their second-class status, Somasegar genuinely preferred writing code for tests rather than for the program itself. "The advantage is I get to play with different parts of NT. To see it whole." Most code writers immersed themselves in small pieces of NT, never understanding the interplay between the parts. They were narrow specialists, whereas testing spawned a surprising number of generalists. "When you're testing," Somasegar said, "you often find things that are outside of your area. But you still have to follow them up. You end up learning about the guts of [NT]."

Born in Madras, India, twenty-six years earlier, Somasegar was a Tamil. He never spelled out the initial S in his name, in keeping with the Tamil practice of identifying oneself by only one full name. After studying engineering in a university in India, he wrote his first program in 1983 with the aid of punch cards. He attended graduate school in the United States, first at Louisiana State University and then at the State University of New York in Buffalo. In January 1989 he joined Microsoft, working first on OS/2 and then on NT.

Work made Somasegar happy. He looked "fondly" on all of his tests. He could not say why, but his mood soared whenever he exposed a flaw in NT. He felt rewarded by his hard work. While espousing the very American belief in the virtue of toil, he held on to his Tamil culture, returning to India in order to interview prospective wives offered by a marriage broker. A confident, attractive woman named Sandhya accepted his proposal after a few telephone conversations and a single meeting. She was the daughter of a retired government official, shared Somasegar's caste (Brahmin), held a college degree and had a brother living in Detroit. They were married in June 1990. After a fifteen-day honeymoon in southern India, they flew to the United States, where Somasegar soon shifted to NT and began working long hours. At times, Sandhya joined him in the office in the evening, reading a book or napping on a couch.

Besides designing stress tests, Somasegar spent much time tallying test results and investigating flaws exposed by those tests. He usually arrived at work before 7:00 a.m. in order to identify problems early in the day so the code writers could address them quickly. To a code writer, there was a grim-reaper quality to Somasegar's appearance at an office door. But his habitual calm helped. A strict vegetarian (on religious grounds), he seemed genuinely pacifistic. While he endowed with great seriousness the enterprise of exposing and fixing coding errors, he evinced no self-righteousness. If anything, he approached programmers, who understandably were sometimes defensive when confronted about a flaw in their code, with a great deal of respect. "When you approach them right, you don't have a problem," he said. The secret: "Be prepared. Do your homework before you talk about a particular problem."

Even then "there was always a lot of tension between programmers and testers at Microsoft," said one tester. "The programmers were very condescending. Their attitude was: 'You guys can't code, so you test. Because you're not as studly as us.'"

When a tester was correct about a problem, a code writer listened—sooner or later. But separating right from wrong was hard. It wasn't always clear who was responsible for a bug, or even if there *was* a bug. It was harder to argue about the results of stress tests. Statistics had weight, a force of their own. Still, it wasn't until September 1 that Cutler, at Dunie's behest, first asked his code writers to run stress tests automatically on their PCs at night. From then on, everyone launched a wave of stress tests on their PCs when they left their offices at night. Only those who were constructing a private build of NT or simply working through the night were exempt from the stress requirement.

Stress uncovered an increasing number of bugs, showing once more that testers were Cutler's conscience. While no match for Cutler, Dunie had the power to withhold a release of NT, forcing Cutler to keep his programmers at work until quality reached the desired level. In October 1991 even the best builds were so flawed and limited in performance that Cutler and Dunie both yearned for better results. Choosing a build to release at Comdex would unfortunately be a matter of accepting the lesser evil.

When Cutler and Dunie finally picked a build for the Comdex release, they declared a temporary ban on further changes in the program on Sunday, October 6. This froze the build, making certain "what is really in and what is out" of it, as Cutler noted.

Within less than twenty-four hours, however, three alterations were made to the build by code writers who had the technical means to modify the program. Cutler exploded. "I guess everyone didn't get that [earlier] message," he wrote. While acknowledging that the changes in the build actually fixed irksome bugs, he flatly declared: "We cannot continue this uncontrolled mode of operation." He then detailed the seven-step review process for any further fixes to the build. If after clearing this review, a fix still corrupted the build, "all hell will break loose," Cutler warned.

"I will admit that these rules are cumbersome," he conceded, but insisted that without them "we will never" make the Comdex deadline.

Later the same day, Cutler issued to the team a "'must be fixed' bug list," which contained those bugs that "should get all the effort" of code writers. He classified the most prominent of these bugs as "showstoppers." As the term (which had been used before at Microsoft) indicates, a showstopper bug was serious enough to "stop the show" performed by the operating system and thus was grounds for holding back the release of a build because it might trigger an embarrassing or unacceptable failure in NT.

It took another ten days to clear all the showstopper bugs. By then there was little time to spare. Comdex would open just four days later, on October 21. The team still needed hundreds of copies of the chosen build, which Microsoft couldn't produce on its own. NT was so large now that it made sense—in terms of both packaging and cost—to store the program on one optical disk. These were the same thin and shiny compact discs that contained recorded music. When formatted differently, these disks held 425 times as much data as a floppy. NT would easily fit on one optical disk. Maritz, who would attend Comdex, imagined happy programmers holding the test version of NT in one hand.

Relying on an optical disk had its risks, though. For one thing, Microsoft needed so many that it arranged for Sony, the largest supplier of compact discs in North America, to handle the job from its disc-duplicating plant in Indiana. Muglia fretted over the possibility of a screwup. The actual process of duplication had been tested and shown not to mar NT itself, but Muglia worried that Sony might mislay the master copy of NT or ship the wrong discs. He dispatched one of his program managers to the company's plant in Terre Haute, Indiana.

David Weld, whom Muglia selected for the task, had carried out sensitive missions before. In 1988, he helped manage the winning political campaign of his uncle, the governor of Massachusetts. Almost alone on the team, Weld was urbane and worldly in the manner of an up-and-coming member of the Eastern Establishment. He attended Dartmouth, where he studied Russian in preparation—his mother thought—for a job with the CIA. Instead, he took a job with Arthur Andersen, the multinational consulting firm, and then returned to school for an M.B.A. He had joined Microsoft six months before in order to bring organization to the code writers making DOS and Windows programs run on NT.

Weld flew to Indianapolis on Thursday night, arriving early the next morning. He kept himself alert by holding a disaster scenario in mind: "Maybe Sony gives me back Madonna on a disk. It's not impossible." He rented a car, stopped at a McDonald's for breakfast and coffee, then drove through cornfields and past a prison. He found the Sony plant by 10:00 a.m. Handing over the program, Weld then took a tour of the plant. Sure enough, he saw boxes of audio disks piled everywhere, maybe even ones by Madonna.

Sony held up its end; the disks were fine. Weld flew to Las Vegas, carrying seventy pounds of disks onto the plane. He checked the rest as luggage. All of it arrived.

Microsoft's decision to show an unfinished NT at Comdex elated Perazzoli. Ever since he'd joined Microsoft three years earlier, he'd worried that at any time the winds could shift and the company could cancel his project. His experience at Digital had left him gun shy. Now that Maritz had publicly shown off NT and made promises about its availability and features, Perazzoli reasoned that Microsoft would never cancel NT. The company had staked out too much territory too publicly to retreat now.

"We're in," he thought. "We'll make it. Just a question of when."

This newfound confidence meant much to Perazzoli; he and the other Digital alumni still regretted spending so much time on unrealized efforts. Cancelled projects were a notable part of a programmer's career. One team member, who had formerly worked at AT&T's Bell Labs, recalled only writing specifications for prototype products during his entire time with the company. Invariably, after finishing the specs, the project was cancelled. Coming away empty handed so often made him feel sad.

After Comdex 1991, it looked as if Perazzoli's instincts had been correct. Raising the curtain on NT was a watershed. Microsoft had grown so powerful in the computer industry that simply the expression of its intention to release NT prompted a wave of interest. Within weeks of Comdex, industry observers were gushing about NT's earth-shattering future. The influential *PC* magazine called NT "the operating system to end all operating systems" and predicted that it was "nothing less than the modern reinvention of the operating system."

As for Microsoft's claim that NT would host DOS and Windows applications, *PC* magazine declared: Forget it. "Every major operating system vendor, upon unveiling a new OS, has announced backwards compatibility. None has ever delivered what they promised, and I see no reason for this time to be different. So I think we can safely dismiss the hyperbole: backwards compatibility is the first thing to go in the hectic final phases of development."

To Perazzoli, who read almost everything written about NT in the thick computer journals, these were fighting words. Others may have reneged on backwards compatibility, but Microsoft would not.

Cutler, too, saw promising signs in the Comdex release. "This is a significant accomplishment that has required many hours of frustration, looking over dead system carcasses and the occasional raising of a voice here and there!" he told the team. "But the important thing is that you made all this happen, and I hope you feel as good as I do about our progress over the last year."

"If you look back on what has been accomplished over the last couple of weeks, it is truly astounding," he went on. "The number of bugs that were fixed with scant few regressions [errors introduced by fixes for bugs] was remarkable. I hope we can continue this level of system integrity. . . . Thank you for the dedicated work."

In his rah-rah message Cutler avoided mentioning his one great disappointment. The Comdex release of NT only worked on Intel's X86 chip, the central processing unit of the standard PC. The team's goal was to create a version of NT that also controlled PCs powered by a RISC family of processors from Mips, an Intel rival. By having two flavors of NT, the team would establish the operating system's portability. It would prove that NT, properly customized, could run on other chips. Though the code was slightly different between the Intel and Mips versions—about 5 percent of the code was tailored to each chip—they were to be functionally identical. This meant that a customer using the same application on either an Intel or a Mips PC would see the same thing. Moreover, NT could be easily adapted to new chips as they emerged. This was a boon to customers because it assured that their current software would run on future gee-whiz chips.

Since the start of the project, Cutler had emphasized the importance of creating two versions of NT in tandem. This kept code writers "honest" by forcing them to write their code in portable languages, rather than lapsing into chip-specific assembly code.

Proudly dubbing himself Mr. Mips, Cutler was more enthusiastic about the version of NT designed for the Mips chip. This was partly because Cutler was a pioneer. No code writer had ever put PC software onto the fast, new-fangled RISC chip. The other reason was tactical. Cutler feared that the Mips version would receive short shrift unless someone of his stature defended it. It was all too easy to tailor NT to Intel's X86 chips, giving the program greater performance but at the cost of portability.

This was the path advocated by Muglia, who was convinced that Intel chips would power virtually every PC for years to come. "Screw Mips," he said. The team should "focus on the Intel version and let Mips drag behind."

To Cutler, Muglia's position was stupid. If the team let the Mips version of NT lag behind, within months there would be no Mips version. Without a constant effort to keep the two versions in line, they would drift hopelessly apart. Day to day Cutler's top priority was to keep the two versions on an equal footing. As one code writer put it, "That guarantees your portability and verifies your design."

Even with Cutler's vigilance, it was hard to maintain the Mips version. Code writers were well aware that nonportable assembly code was faster, so they sometimes slipped such code into the Intel version. "Every time we code something in assembly language, Cutler wants us to work hard to port it to Mips, or justify why we can't," said Chuck Whitmer, the graphics programmer. "So he was our conscience on portability."

Another drag on the Mips version was the chip itself. When Mips sold Microsoft on the chip, "it was a spec, it wasn't a real anything." The design changed constantly, making it hard for Cutler's team to adapt code for it. Even when it was delivered in sample quantities in April 1991—about five months later than Cutler expected—the chip had "more bugs than desired, but there was a lot of pressure to get it out," a Mips engineer said.

While Mips fixed most of the bugs, Cutler and Rob Short's team spent the summer of 1991 making the chip work with NT. This amounted to building the first Mips PCs. The hump was the daily grind of identifying the flaws in the chip (those places where its performance deviated from the specs, which was the target pursued by NT's programmers). Immersion into the Byzantine realm of chip electronics diverted Cutler's attention from perhaps more pressing matters. But without such an effort, the Mips version of NT—and the entire portability effort—might have been abandoned as too troublesome.

Cutler was willing to do anything to help improve the Mips version and his commitment to the portability of NT, including holding the hands of those teammates who were writing code on the Mips version or testing it. "If you have problems, come and see me and I'll try to help out," he told them on September 1. One team member, who usually carped about Cutler's rudeness, said he had "never before worked with a leader of a large project who took such a hands-on approach."

The struggle to unify the two versions of NT was just one of Cutler's worries. To his endless frustration, people were still adding features to NT or the features themselves were still ill defined.

A few features were added almost by accident. Steve Ballmer, the public spokesman for NT, added one without realizing it during one of his frequent speeches to customers and industry insiders. Ballmer's practice of praising the unfinished program was standard procedure in the software industry, in which rivals promised so much, so soon, that one wag coined the term "vaporware" to describe such touted but incomplete programs as NT.

Ballmer's feature was "fault tolerance," a technique that protects against the loss of data from the failure of a computer or its storage devices. This was accomplished by essentially storing every piece of data on two different devices. In the fall of 1991, when everyone on the team thought NT was at least six to nine months from completion, Ballmer promised that NT would offer fault tolerance. This was news to the team, which was still debating whether to include it in NT. With Ballmer's enthusiasm as the nudge, two programmers agreed to forge ahead on fault tolerance. The late start, however, meant that the design for fault tolerance was not set until almost Christmas Eve 1991. It was impossible to actually finish coding the fault tolerance feature in time to ship NT by mid-1992.

Even long-planned features were behind schedule. For example, NT's file system was in such rough shape that testing of it had still not begun by the end of 1991. The work of Tom Miller, Gary Kimura and Brian Andrew, the third code writer on the job, remained hampered by the need to care for the older file systems. This was time consuming. "When something goes wrong with the file system, its easy to blame the file system, even though the source of the error may lie elsewhere and often does," a code writer explained. "So they can't just shut the door and work on NTFS." Besides, creating NTFS was a bigger job than expected. Having wrestled with the decision of whether to include a new file system with NT, Maritz now worried that it burdened the project. Miller and Kimura, he suspected, had "way underestimated the complexity of what they were trying to do. These guys were naive."

Compatibility, or running DOS and Windows applications on NT, lagged too. Like the file system, compatibility was withheld from the October 1991 release to applications writers. Led by Matt Felton, the compatibility team had proved its basic concept. On May 8, 1991, the group saw its first DOS program run on NT. It was a simple computer game called Reversi. Six weeks later, the first Windows application ran on NT; it was Word, Microsoft's word processor. These demonstrations, however, fell far short of the standard for compatibility demanded by customers or even the team's testers. When he heard "rumors" of a Windows program running on NT, Jeff Brown, the chief tester for Windows compatibility, raced to Felton's office. He'd been waiting for weeks to begin testing Windows applications on NT. When he saw Word running on NT in Felton's office, Brown leaped with excitement. "Now we're ready to start," he said. His judgment was premature. Under the strain of testing, Word and a few other Windows programs collapsed. "We'd just play with them and they'd fall over," Brown said.

The problem was that these programs often shared little beyond a skeletal structure. This made it difficult for Felton's team to create a general model that accommodated hundreds of diverse DOS and Windows applications. Still struggling with the model in late 1991, the team had a long way to go. "We weren't doing so well," said Weld, the program manager aiding Felton. "We had a few apps running, but I couldn't install a popular Windows app on NT and expect it to run."

The other disquieting sideshow was the graphics group. Kent Diamond had brought better management, but the group's code wasn't measuring up to Cutler's expectations. The practice of writing code in C++ continually upset Cutler because it created so much confusion and inefficiency. Yet it was deemed too late for graphics to switch to the more tractable C language. Cutler, simmering, "never let [the group's reliance on C++] go unpunished for long," Diamond noted. "He always had to get a jab in."

A second dispute arose from Whitmer's year-old decision to build a new model for NT graphics rather than just adopt the old Windows model. "My original hope," he said, "was that we could have a [graphics] engine that was pure, not corrupted by the old sins of Windows." Whitmer resisted a withering attack from those who insisted that programs on NT should look identical to those on Windows. Whitmer countered that, when it came to graphics, the differences would be so "minute [that] no one will notice."

Many felt Whitmer was wrong. Customers would see the differences. Still guarding his "pure" position, he gave NT two modes of graphics. The first, which kicked in whenever NT hosted an old

Windows or DOS program, created identical graphics. The second mode made superior graphics but took over only when NT ran new Windows applications. Whitmer's decision seemed like a retreat, but he could tell himself: "I've still got my beautiful graphics code."

This controversy privately distressed Muglia. It had slowed progress on graphics compatibility, complicating the schedule. And it had stolen energy from the graphics group. Muglia now worried that Whitmer and Moore, the group's leaders, might not be able to push graphics over the hump because they had worked such long hours on past projects.

The group's random merriment still drew objections, too. During the drive for Comdex, a spirited game of hoser ball broke out, led by Walt Moore and Donald Sidoroff, another veteran programmer. Sidoroff was a sight. Big and hulking, he drove a motorcycle to work, dressed like a Hell's Angel and visited prostitutes while on Nevada gambling trips. He often gave Moore advice about wooing women, once telling him, "Women like men who take charge."

Moore shot back: "And you like women who take charge *cards.*"

Despite his bluster, Sidoroff was ashamed of his social ineptitude and privately struggled with the daily pressure of writing code. "People break under stress in different ways" and turning to prostitutes "was the way I broke," he said. Wrestling with his inner demons, he found in programming "the only good part of my life." But colleagues rarely saw evidence of his joy; he made them uneasy. Women teammates felt he leered at them, while men were intimidated by him.

Sidoroff felt misunderstood. "A geek all my life," he was almost thirty and had gone on his first date only a year before. Though he soon stopped visiting prostitutes, his bad-boy image stuck, fueled by his great size and furious temper. Once he frightened a coworker who had parked a sports car too close to his motorcycle. Sidoroff left a note on the car, demanding the coworker meet him to explain this act of rudeness and promise never to do it again.

So it was no surprise that Sidoroff played hoser ball with less grace than a prima ballerina. As he and Moore alternately rolled the tennis ball filled with pennies, slamming it into rows of spent Coke cans, the game grew loud. Diamond, viewing the scene, wondered whether to crack down or cut them slack. Moore and Sidoroff had just finished a successful two-day hunt for a pernicious bug; they were celebrating. Diamond's impulse "to tell them to tone it down was tempered by the work they had done." He let the game go on.

Diamond's bosses rebuked him after learning of the episode. He then called a graphics meeting and reluctantly banned hoser ball forever from the hallway. But he feared it was too late to undo the damage. "The reputation of the lazy [graphics] workers had been reinforced."

Graphics did have a few straight arrows, young code writers who joined Microsoft direct from school and showed the requisite zeal. But Muglia and Cutler worried about these impressionable souls. Would they lose their work ethic by aping the eccentric elders in the group?

It was an open question, but the novices hardly matched their seniors. Consider Patrick Haluptzok, who joined graphics in January 1990, during the flowering of the Undead. Married and a father of two at the mere age of twenty, Haluptzok hardly matched the profile of the Microsoft youth. After all, veterans such as Moore and Whitmer were bachelors, and code writers five years Haluptzok's senior still had trouble landing a date no less managing a marriage. Rather than a nerd, Haluptzok looked like the all-American boy. Tall, clean-cut and studious, he showed a rebellious streak that seemed unbecoming of someone with a crewcut. While respectful of authority, he challenged elders on his own terms. Only his transparent ambition struck a wrong note with those around him.

Raised in a small town outside Minneapolis, Haluptzok was the son of a prosperous junkyard operator. He married his high school sweetheart, a tall blue-eyed blond named Chenoa. A year older than her husband, she had dropped out of college to join Haluptzok at MIT, where he took a degree in mathematics and she gave birth to two girls.

Though he programmed little in college, Haluptzok attracted Microsoft's attention with a perfect grade-point average. The company offered him a job "not because I knew how to program, which I didn't, but because they believed in hiring smart people who'd then learn how to program." He took the job because it promised wealth and excitement. His starting salary at Microsoft was $34,000, 20 percent less than the highest offer from among six other suitors. But none of the other companies offered stock options with the potential to make him rich.

For his first two months, Haluptzok sat alone in his office, learning to program in C language. Whitmer gave him a book and expected him to teach himself: *Sink or swim*. In college he'd studied programming theory, assuming he'd learn actual coding techniques on the job. Now he worried he might not learn them quickly enough. He often wondered when Whitmer would walk into his office and fire him. Even when he mastered the rudiments of programming, his inexperience plainly showed. Handed a problem, he needed help in forming a coding plan.

Haluptzok picked up more quickly on the spectacular wealth of some coworkers. "They've achieved what I want—lots of money," he said. Indeed, people ten years older than he had reaped millions from their tenure at Microsoft; the company's skyrocketing stock price promised to inflate their holdings further. To Haluptzok it seemed "like they won the lottery." Hundreds of code writers at the company had either cleared at least a million in cash or would soon. Some drove sixty-thousand-dollar sports cars and lived (sometimes alone) in majestic, waterfront homes. Haluptzok wanted the same for himself and his family.

Of course, this opulent future hinged on his code-writing skills. After handling odd jobs for nearly a year, he tackled the part of NT that manages colors on screen and matches them accurately. This palette code created colors by scurrying between the application, which specified a color, and the computer's display screen, which revealed it. Writing the eight thousand lines of palette code in a few weeks, he was determined to win the distinction of bringing color pictures to NT for the first time.

He reached this milestone in March 1991. To ensure his credit, he designed a demonstration that displayed his picture on a computer screen. He left the demo running for weeks. Paul Butzi and a graphics mate decided to alter Haluptzok's code so that his clean-shaven face sprouted a mustache. But anticipating some sort of prank, Haluptzok had made that impossible.

Seeking praise, Haluptzok showed his code to Cutler, whom he no longer feared. Haluptzok had a Mips PC in his office; Cutler flocked to those programmers who actually wrote code on Mips because this helped ensure NT's portability. Another reason for their bond: Haluptzok carried out small, code-writing tasks for Cutler, sometimes dropping his own work "to finish what was on Cutler's hotplate." Sometimes he felt overwhelmed trying to keep pace with both his own job and Cutler's extras. He once asked Cutler which he should cut back on. Do both, Cutler answered.

Haluptzok also gave Cutler reports on work-in-progress by his graphics mates. This made it easier for Cutler to press the group to finish certain tasks, since he was still largely in the dark about the goings-on within graphics, and Whitmer especially resisted sharing inside dope. Haluptzok spoke freely, seeing Cutler as part friend, part father. "He talks to you with the authority of your dad," Haluptzok said. "You want to follow him."

When his spying for Cutler came to light, Haluptzok endured accusations of brown-nosing. He shrugged them off. Sure, he curried favor. "I always try to be Cutler's buddy, to talk with him, find out what he wants done." Why not? Haluptzok felt he could learn much from Cutler, and he was grateful when this "industry icon" listened to him. "With his power level, Dave could totally shit on you," Haluptzok said. "But he doesn't. He's a real guy. He makes me feel important. I go to talk with him on important decisions on NT and he gives me full attention. He talks with you like you're someone worth reckoning with."

To make a name for himself on NT, Haluptzok pulled out all the stops. His routine hours were 8:00 a.m. to 6:00 p.m., Monday through Friday, with an hour break for lunch. Then he drove a few minutes in his yellow 1985 Volkswagen Golf to his $810-a-month, three-bedroom apartment. After two hours with his kids, he returned to the office about 8:00 p.m. and usually worked three more hours.

His work load increased when the team entered "ship mode." This was the period, usually four to six weeks in length, prior to an important release. The push for Comdex marked the onset of "ship mode." Immediately after the team finished the Comdex release, the race was on to create a unified Mips-Intel test edition by December 1991. This meant that "Patrick practically lives at Microsoft," his boss noted. "He's Mr. Motivated."

Chenoa Haluptzok was not Mrs. Motivated. She puzzled over the case of her disappearing husband. She wished him great success and admired his confidence and abilities. But she viewed his work skeptically, puzzled as to why people made such a fuss over a computer program. When Haluptzok excitedly talked about his work in bed late at night, Chenoa invariably fell asleep. Tough and with a touch of wickedness, she grew so angry her first summer in Redmond that she talked of organizing a Microsoft Widows Club and imagined that a picture of a black widow spider would make a suitable logo.

She wanted her husband to accept that ordinary life rolled on regardless of the ups and downs of NT. She didn't mince words when one day she gave him a list of "things pissing me off":

1. I should not have to pick up dirty clothing off the floor. When you take your clothes off, put them in the laundry.
2. You do not need to dirty four different plates to make one salad.
3. Bring dirty dishes to the sink when you are done eating. Even your three- and four-year-old daughters do better than you.
4. Recycle the newspaper when you're done reading it. Don't leave it lying on the living room floor.
5. When you put the kids to bed, put their p.j.'s on.
6. If you see the garbage is full, empty it.
7. If you're hungry, get up and eat. Don't ask me what there is.

Then something happened to brighten Chenoa's mood. Haluptzok sold the first batch of Microsoft stock he received, netting seventy thousand dollars in cash after taxes. Most of the money went for the down payment on an eighteen-hundred-square-foot home, just a few minutes' walk from his office. When they moved at the end of October 1991, Chenoa was overjoyed. She felt that the sacrifices of the past two years had been worth it and that she "finally had something other than her kids to sink my mind and energies into." As she peered out her kitchen window at her two daughters playing in the backyard, she thought, "Microsoft is a wonderful company. Sure, it's tough. But look what we get."

Chenoa's contentment was short-lived. After Haluptzok had a bad month in ship mode, her anger flared again. Instead of presenting her husband with a list this time, she tried disciplining him with a child-rearing technique called "the Box." She put a large box in her garage, and whenever Haluptzok left books or clothes or stuff lying around, she put them in the box. It usually took a week before Haluptzok noticed something was missing. Then he spent an hour or so cleaning out the box.

The box didn't solve the problem of Haluptzok's prolonged absences, however. Pressing toward the December release, he worked upwards of seventy-five hours a week. Some days Chenoa would only see him for fifteen minutes in the morning. Often alone with her two daughters, she longed for the familiarity of Minnesota, where she'd have the loving help of her own parents, two sets of grandparents, two aunts and sundry other relatives (nearly two hundred in all). In Redmond, she had no one. At times she broke into tears, pained by the realization that her husband poured more energy into his job and his relationships at work than into her and their children. One day in early November, she harangued Haluptzok: "I'm the one you live with! I give you the emotional support you need. I followed you to MIT when you attended school. I'm the person you'll grow old with. So why am I always the one on the back burner?"

Haluptzok tried to quiet Chenoa by reminding her that the project was nearly over. The new code-complete deadline was April 1992. "Just a few months more, and things will ease off," he said.

Chenoa flashed a chilly grin. She didn't believe him. For almost a year, her husband had spoken of the project winding down, of a time when he would work less. But each time her hopes rose—each time she imagined herself with a full-time husband and a real family life—"there was always some excuse, some reason why the deadline slipped. Something always drew him back to work."

She couldn't stand it any longer. The last straw came when Haluptzok told her he was going skiing with Cutler for four days—

without his wife and kids. Chenoa fumed. If he was leaving, so was she. For Thanksgiving, she flew to Minneapolis with her two daughters. She was pregnant and planned to stay with her parents for the holidays, returning in the new year.

Haluptzok said he would join his family for Christmas.

Cutler ended 1991 on a rising note. Despite the rush to unify the Mips and Intel versions of NT, he had gone skiing with teammates in mid-December. He went every year at this time to Whistler Mountain in British Columbia. He said he felt guilty about leaving, but it didn't show. When he returned he helped to put the polish on the second release to applications writers, which would run on both Intel and Mips PCs. Finishing the release was hard. The team seemed close to meeting its standard in order to gain a respite over the Christmas holidays, but day after day, as Christmas approached, something stood in the way of NT's release.

"There was a lot of tension in the air," said Perazzoli. "Every day we thought we're ready to ship [NT] only to find another showstopper." The delays were torturous. "This was a painful period," said Perazzoli. "There was no progress." One major obstacle: the team was testing NT more intensely than ever, which exposed errors in the tests themselves. Whenever a flaw was found in a test, it called into question the quality of fixes and of NT itself. Perazzoli wondered whether the team had unwittingly wandered into one of those horrific infinite loops that sometimes brought a permanent halt to progress on a software program. The history of code writing was littered with examples of programs that never were finished because, perversely, each attempt at fixing a flaw spawned other problems. In the worst case, the only way out of this situation lay in scrapping the program and starting over. This seemed a remote possibility for NT, but it was a haunting one nevertheless. "We realized if we didn't pick up the pace we might never finish," Perazzoli said.

Then, a few days before Christmas, Cutler convened a meeting with the team's leaders and told a story about how molten steel can be pushed through a little hole to produce a finished piece of metal. The technical term for this process was "extrusion," and it was what Cutler wanted the team to do now: "Extrude" an acceptable version of NT within twenty-four hours. "The only reason we won't release it is if [NT] won't set up," he said. "Otherwise it's go."

Cutler's brute-force approach helped the team over the hump. The unified Mips-Intel version of NT was released two days before Christmas. The milestone had taken months longer to reach than expected, but Cutler was proud of his team.

"Achieving this milestone has required much longer than we anticipated and has required continuous attention to fixing bugs," he wrote. "It simply would not have been possible without the extra effort everyone put in. This is a significant accomplishment that we all are very proud of. By hosting our own development and running our own file servers on NT we have gained a level of quality not found in many other systems this early in their development life. Thank you for your effort."

Cutler was being polite. The strain of leading such a large team, whose members had such varying levels of experience and expertise, weighed on him. Though he claimed to thrive on stress, it maddened him that his troops did not adhere to his own high standards. He was starting to realize that he probably expected too much from most people. This was the largest project he had ever led; holding the line on quality was much easier with a smaller team. With so many code writers under his command, he wasn't always sure how to bring them all into line. In his year-ending message, he hinted darkly at dire consequences in the coming year if people did not show more discipline and attention to detail. "The [NT] system is complex enough that most bugs cost more than just the author valuable time," he wrote. "If you don't put [bugs] in, you don't have to find them and take them out!" He vowed that in 1992 he would have "much less . . . tolerance" for sloppy check-ins.

This threat sounded ominous, since Cutler already counted as a tough guy. How much tougher could he get?

8. DEATH MARCH

Johanne Caron slumped into a window seat, her straight, auburn hair dangling over her eyes, which narrowed when she smiled, giving a dangerous edge to her scrubbed, freckled face. Deeply set, her eyes were protected by high cheekbones. Her gaze furtive, she looked away from other passengers as she left the Northwest airplane in Montreal.

It was Christmas Eve 1991. Caron had made it home in time for the holiday, but barely. Her Montreal-born husband, who shied away from family gatherings, skipped the trip. Outside, snow fell heavily. Caron's father, who met his daughter at the airport, gathered her bags. He was eager to join the family party in the city. Caron awaited the arrival of her skis at the baggage area. The skis still hadn't arrived two hours later. She gave them up for lost, and they left.

Caron quickly fell under the spell of her parents. She spoke little about work and even less about her absent husband. The past six months had been the most grueling period in Caron's twenty-seven years. Thrilled by her job at Microsoft, she nevertheless at times found it too much to bear.

The return to her home town of Sherbrooke, a small city one hundred miles east of Montreal, drenched Caron in warm memories. As a child, she flip-flopped so often between French and English (she first spoke the latter at the age of six during the year her father spent studying at the Jet Propulsion Lab in Pasadena, California) that she grew disenchanted with both languages. She took refuge in mathematics, "where at least the language is the same, no matter where you are." She excelled, though she was never the best. At ten years of age she competed vigorously against her best girlfriend, a superior math student whom teachers viewed as the pacesetter. "Every time I almost caught up with her," Caron said, "she was done and going on to other problems."

Caron attended an all-girls Catholic high school. Mathematics was her forte, "my easiest subject no matter where I went to school. I always was one of the top students, so I pushed on math." Caron enrolled in the university in the town where her father, a physicist, taught. He urged Caron to work with people and not machines; perhaps she should gain a degree in physical education. Her mother, who had studied history in college and now worked for the municipality, told her: "Study something that will make you money."

Money meant independence. Following her mother's advice, Caron pursued computing. The machines scared her at first. "You go through the basement of the university, and there's this room with tables and terminals and everyone is just sitting there typing away and you don't know what's going on." She started typing herself but her screen stayed blank. Embarrassed, she realized her computer wasn't switched on. She couldn't find the switch. "I tried not to look stupid when I turned the the thing around. But it was obvious I was looking for the switch."

Her quiet determination, zest for problem solving and mental precision made her well suited for programming. It even helped her love life: She met her boyfriend Paul in a computer class. While Caron felt that he too closely resembled her overly logical father, she married him after a few months of dating.

When Paul took a job at Microsoft in the spring of 1991, Caron left Canada with him. They traveled by bicycle, in two months pedaling roughly three thousand miles from Montreal to Microsoft's campus. Then Caron, who held a master's degree in computer science, joined Microsoft as a temp, catching the tail end of the effort to make Windows programs run on OS/2. With Microsoft's withdrawal of support for OS/2, the effort was dropped, and many in the group found a home on NT.

On June 4 Leif Pederson, a Cutler lieutenant, asked Caron to adapt for NT a piece of Windows, called the program manager. This code set the way a user launched and organized applications and made it easy to turn NT on and off. Customers could tailor the program manager to their tastes, so that certain applications automatically opened when they logged on to NT.

The task of adapting the program manager was tricky. Caron inherited, in Pederson's words, "a gnarly piece of code" written in a prior, failed attempt. Caron also was constrained by the requirement that her code precisely duplicate the Windows program manager. Yet despite its seeming routine, her assignment was a plum; Caron had the chance of her young career to make her mark on a premier piece of software. To the customer, the program manager was among the most prominent pieces of NT. Besides grouping applications, Caron's code would set NT into motion and shut it down. In order to do so, her code would have to flawlessly close all running programs and decide when it was safe to shut off the PC.

Caron leaped at the chance to code the program manager. She'd never touched NT before, but she knew it was the hot thing at Microsoft. After Pederson welcomed her aboard, she called her parents with the news. "Oh my God, they're trusting me to do this!" she gushed. "I had better do this right. It's my chance to prove what I can do."

She felt awkward at first. In her group, which handled various aspects of NT's Windows personality, she was the lone woman. It showed. "I could tell the guys were used to having a team of only men. A guy would start to tell a joke, then suddenly stop, aware of my presence." Immersed in work, she knew nothing of the Hoppers women who had just launched the campaign against nude images.

Icons were Caron's first hurdle. These tiny pictures, which activated NT's features or the applications themselves, were a big part of the Windows program manager. It took her weeks simply to make a plain blue box stand as a poor substitute for each icon. Meanwhile, when Cutler complained that the Mips version of her code lacked even blue boxes, she had to catch up on that code. She spent two days in Cutler's office—he was elsewhere—working on his Mips PC, one of the few available that summer. Sitting in Cutler's office, only a month on the team, she found it easy to meet people. "Who are you?" they asked her. Pleased by the visibility the office gave her, she wondered about Cutler. A photograph on his desk, showing him holding an animal head at the end of a hunting trip, stuck with her. "I don't think I'm going to like this guy," she thought.

As her code took shape, Caron asked more and more questions of the team's old-timers, who'd written pieces of the kernel. The program manager sent messages to the kernel, which returned answers to Caron's code. To undo flaws in the program manager, she required intimate knowledge of the kernel's terrain. Sometimes when her code didn't work properly, she blamed a mistake in the kernel. Delivering the news wasn't easy, since under the team's loose organization she had to tell the offending code writer personally. She found Steve Wood to be the most irascible and condescending. From Wood's standpoint, young code writers almost always overlooked something, so he would turn their questions about his code into questions about *their* code. Caron ignored Wood the first few times he flipped her inquiries, but she finally confronted him one day. "I came here to talk with you about a problem in your code," she said. "Why are you switching all this around?" Then she stormed off.

Caron took the fight personally. She felt that Wood didn't respect her and that made her work harder and more carefully. The next time she queried Wood about his code, she covered all the angles in advance, "so he couldn't say, 'Yeah, what about this?'"

With work a kind of mental combat, she found relief in karate. She'd dabbled in it in Montreal and enrolled in a school near campus that taught the *shito ruy* style of Japanese karate, which stopped short of full contact. "I wasn't really talking to anyone, I didn't have any friends, and I was working long hours, so why not karate?" Caron explained. She enjoyed making the spare, formal movements of karate as well as handling the six-foot-long oak staff used in some of her sessions. By the time she left to visit her parents at Christmas, she attended karate classes four to five nights a week. In the office, she stepped lightly, reluctant to raise her voice. At karate, she abandoned her reserve while retaining a sense of order. It felt like writing a perfect piece of code.

After ten days with her family, Caron boarded the Northwest flight back to Seattle. With the start of a new year, she took stock of her life. She wondered about her marriage. She was too busy to spend much time with Paul and didn't miss him. Paul granted her independence. "He lets me be selfish," she said. But they moved in different orbits, she felt. Just finishing a big project, he looked forward to a fallow period. For at least another six months, she was in ship mode along with the rest of the NT team, the tension high and rising.

As the jet taxied on the runway in Montreal, Caron sat still, peering through the window for a last glance at Canadian soil. Then she took a deep breath and held it, feeling her lungs expand. The plane lifted, hurtling forward. She let out a breath, laid her head against the side of her seat and closed her eyes. Like a moth drawn to a flame, she was headed back into the fray.

Cutler, impatient for victory, began 1992 with large hopes. Three years had passed since he began his journey to create a next-generation operating system for PCs. To be sure, there were kinks to work out of NT, but Cutler thought, "Hey, we're on the final run."

The team would finish coding NT's features in February and release a final sample edition to applications writers in April. This edition also would stand as the first "beta," or test version, sent to hundreds of choice customers. If customers reacted favorably to the beta, Cutler imagined NT going on sale before the end of June 1992.

Once more NT's complexity mocked Cutler's plans. Having adopted Windows as its personality, NT now had to support a broader array of existing hardware, such as printers, monitors and keyboards, than Cutler or anyone else had originally expected. Code had to be written to direct each of these devices. The team had to produce some of this code, though it expected device makers to supply the rest.

At the same time important features took longer to finish than Cutler had expected. The feature most important to NT's future—its ability to run existing Windows applications—was nowhere near done. The file system was taking much longer than anticipated.

Stress results, a key measure of NT's health, were almost uniformly poor. Meanwhile, program managers still called for adding features to NT, distracting the attention of code writers. One grew so agitated that he began swinging a baseball bat he kept in his office whenever a program manager approached. Bit by bit the schedule slipped. As software pundit Fred Brooks once observed, "How does a project get to be a year late? . . . One day at a time."

In February Cutler acquiesced to the inevitable. He revised his schedule, pushing his code-complete date into March and then into April 1992. Then he decided the team should delay the release of the developers' version from April to July 1. This meant customers would not get their first taste of NT until the second half of 1992.

Paul Maritz and Bill Gates paid close attention to the team's slipping schedule. They were especially eager to release a polished edition of NT to applications writers. Without the support of these outsiders, the operating system was as good as dead. Microsoft, of course, would make sure that its own applications—Word, Excel, PowerPoint and the others—took advantage of NT. But Maritz and Gates ultimately wanted every popular program, whether it came from Microsoft or not, to run on NT.

To this end, Microsoft appealed to applications writers from other companies. The wooing began in April with a four-page letter to applications writers from Maritz, who invited them to attend a three-day conference on NT in San Francisco, from July 6 to July 8. Maritz expected about a thousand people to attend. He promised that the conference would help people plot "the next wave of applications development for Windows."

"Bill Gates will personally deliver the keynote address," the letter went on. "And you'll have a chance to hear from key NT developers, including David Cutler, Architect and Windows NT Development Director."

The retreating schedule upset Cutler. He hated missing deadlines: "I never take any deadline lightly, ever." In NT's case, he wanted to ship less, sooner. But those in favor of shipping more, later carried the day. Cutler did not look back. When a deadline was missed, he signed up for a new deadline as soon as he could and pushed on.

Even as one deadline after another faded from view, Cutler gained an unexpected boon: personal vindication. Digital Equipment, his former employer and current nemesis, agreed to become the first computer maker to buy NT for the purpose of porting, or adapting, it to computers powered by Digital's own microchip, called Alpha. The very people assigned to do the port were some of Cutler's old employees at Digital West.

Cutler exulted. "Digital's management ran me out of the company," he said, "and then a mere four years later they knocked on my door." Cutler saw the Mica operating system, whose cancellation by Digital prompted his departure, as the rough equivalent of NT. Always willing to refight old battles, he insisted, "Digital is now paying for something it could've had for free."

Cutler found Digital's embrace of NT "ironical," but his own nostalgia for his former employer was strong. Even now, after more than three years at Microsoft, he still rued the loss of the intimate community he had forged at Digital. He even believed "it would've been a whole lot easier if we'd done" NT at Digital.

But that was inconceivable. Digital feared that Mica would erode sales of computers controlled by its VMS program. And the company could never have sold an operating system to its computer rivals. With the industry embracing standard software, Microsoft was the ideal purveyor of NT. Cutler had saddled the right horse at the right time.

While embracing NT, Digital officially expressed no affection for Cutler, maintaining an eerie silence about him. But some Digital people privately agreed that Cutler's departure still rankled top executives and that Digital's adoption of NT was tantamount to admitting a mistake. "Driving away Cutler was one of the dumbest fucking things Digital ever did," one person said. "But we can't say we screwed up because some of the idiots responsible for that are still here."

A bad loser, Cutler won without grace, too. With a weakness for I-told-you-so, he rubbed Digital's nose in his triumph. "Digital is paying for something it could've had for free" became a team motto. Cutler even "saved" Digital time by laying the groundwork for its port of NT, but in so doing he tweaked his newfound ally by naming the directories of the program after pieces of Mica. "That'll piss them off," he told Wood, who egged him on.

In a rare exchange with the press, Cutler also crowed about humiliating Digital. At Gates's next meeting with Digital, an executive took him aside, then thrust at him a copy of an article containing Cutler's comments (which he had made, via e-mail, to a computer magazine). Gates had never seen the article, and his immediate reaction was to say that he hadn't hired Cutler for his charm. But after reading Cutler's slam, he thought, "Whew, this is bad," and promised to keep his software ace away from reporters.

For Cutler's fiftieth birthday on March 13, 1992, his friends and managers on the team threw a gala party at his house. The two-story home hugged a secluded stretch of Lake Washington, across the Evergreen Point Bridge from Seattle, in an exclusive village named Medina. Cutler had purchased the property six years before for nearly half a million dollars; it was worth four times that now. Just up the road Gates was building himself a palatial mansion. About eighty of Cutler's pals (Gates not among them) attended the party. Guests arrived to find an old Digital computer filling Cutler's living room. It was a Vax 780, one of the machines that ran the VMS software Cutler designed for Digital more than a decade earlier. Short and some others had purchased the old Vax for about a thousand dollars and kept it in Short's garage until the day of the party. While Cutler was away, Short stationed the computer in the atrium of his house. Even under a twenty-five-foot ceiling, the computer still looked big, standing five feet high, eight feet long and thirty inches deep. Short didn't power the machine because it could not run on household electricity. Instead he connected a terminal to a small MicroVax hidden inside the big computer, which made it look as if it really ran VMS. When Cutler walked in the door about seven that evening, he was stunned. His first reaction was to wonder how they'd gotten this big clunker to run.

Aside from the Vax stunt, the party had a decidedly raunchy edge. Invitees were asked not to bring any gifts, just dress in neon clothing. Booze was plentiful, and good taste was absent. One person came as a plastic penis, another as a vibrator. Some people brought gifts, after all. As Cutler had been half seriously talking about investing in a female roller derby team, someone arrived with several big-breasted dolls outfitted in roller derby gear. Lucovsky came with a framed piece of a wall that Cutler had destroyed recently in a fit of pique over a problem in a build. David Thompson and Leif Pederson passed out a newsletter, which included a baby picture of Cutler and excerpts from the news flashes penned years before by Darryl Rubin.

For the finale, a stripper showed up. Cutler hammed it up. A crowd gathered. The stripper handcuffed Cutler to a chair, then began taking her clothes off, undulating her body gently near Cutler's face. To the relief of the wives in attendance, the stripper kept her private parts covered.

With the July 1, 1992, deadline seemingly attainable, Cutler worked the lash. He implored his code writers to show greater attention to detail, though he relied on more than mere words. His cure for bad check-ins called for brute force. He himself would become a sentry for quality, reviewing as many of the seventy-five to one hundred daily check-ins as he could. "I don't see any other way of getting this product out the door," he told himself.

This meant camping in the Build Lab. On a project this large, it was unheard of for the chief designer to move in with the builders. But Cutler wished to be close to the action. Lucovsky, who had watched over the Build Lab for the first two releases, wanted a break. Cutler looked forward to taking his place. He led by example, and his presence in the Build Lab sent a message about the importance of quality code. No amount of rhetoric could equal the example of Cutler's actions. "If I'm in the Build Lab, that tells [the code writer]: I better not check in shit." It also meant that everyone on the team was equal in toil, so long as they produced. Power in a group, Cutler believed, "comes from what you accomplish," not from a title or talent. "The fact that I'm down in the Build Lab says this guy really wants [NT] built well, if he's willing to sit in the lab and do it. This provides a lot of focus."

And not just for the code writers. His presence vitalized the builders, lending discipline and a sense of importance to their effort. By the time Shannon and Duncan arrived in the morning, Cutler was sitting comfortably in the lab, reviewing check-ins and preparing fixes for the next build. He invariably sat in his favorite seat, a plush maroon swivel chair that skated across the hard, linoleum floor on its wheels. He liked to lean back with his hands behind his head as he looked over the code.

When the day's check-ins seemed bad, Cutler greeted the builders with the cry: "What the hell took you guys so long? Get in here!" After the builders manned their machines, he then began what Duncan called "driving." With the list of changes in his hand, Cutler methodically issued instructions. Said Duncan: "He's not giving us the list, he's basically saying, 'Go to this directory and sync this file.' He's saying, 'Pick up this file, do this, do that.' Before long everything is clicking; everything is working."

As the number of builds grew from a couple to a half dozen some weeks, the builders worked longer and longer hours. "I used to be the laziest guy on earth," Shannon said. No longer. At crunch time, the Build Lab stayed open seven days a week, from early morning until past midnight. Even at the busiest times, building was a hurry-up-and-wait process. To kill the tedium, they named their test machines after characters in the TV series *Twin Peaks* or mused about which actors would play leading roles in the movie of NT. Everyone agreed that Jack Nicholson should play Cutler.

When the builders needed outlets for their nervous energy, they practiced spinning basketballs on one finger or tossed baseballs against the wall. Seeing the builders careening about the lab one day, Cutler issued his familiar warning: If they ever broke a build, "Your ass is grass and I'm the lawn mower." But while the ball playing dented walls, it never harmed a build.

Lunchtime was often the worst part of the day. Just as the builders prepared to break for a meal somewhere, Cutler would leap to his feet, race to the door and order them to complete something before he returned from his squash match in an hour. That meant the builders either skipped lunch or ate at their computers. "We'd be afraid to ask him: Could we break for lunch?" Shannon said.

Even worse than missing lunch was the uncertainty over when the workday would end. "You couldn't plan for the evening," Shannon said. "We'd *think* we were all done for the day, then test the build and it wouldn't boot. We'd run around looking for the [programmer] whose [code] broke it. Dave would stay until [the build] was fixed, and we were expected to stay too." With the builders accepting from 150 to 200 changes to the build each day in the weeks leading to a release, late nights occurred with disappointing frequency.

The regimen hurt Shannon's social life. He befriended people easily, especially women. But as the project wore on, he grew more isolated from the outside world. His non-Microsoft friends tired of his predictable answer to every invitation: "I'm too busy." The worst part was that Shannon never knew when he'd leave the Build Lab. Once his girlfriend arrived in the lobby of Building Two at around midnight, expecting him any time. Shannon asked her to wait. Cutler was in the Build Lab, and Shannon wished to stay until he left. At 1:30 in the morning, Cutler showed no signs of leaving but asked: "Who is that pretty woman in the lobby?" When Shannon claimed her, Cutler looked at him quizzically and said, "Get out of here."

While Cutler pulled rank now and again, he helped out on even the grungiest build tasks. He saw himself as one of the guys. He could laugh at himself and let others poke fun at him. He was amused, for instance, when Shannon called him "Tom." It was an inside joke: On a recent ski trip, a friend of Shannon's had seen a "tumbling older man" (Tom for short) roll down an entire slope. It had been Cutler.

Loose and gregarious, Shannon played off Cutler's banter, at times gently needling the older man. When Cutler one day said he felt so comfortable in the Build Lab that it seemed "like just another room in his house," Shannon smiled, noting the remark. When he next saw Cutler in the men's bathroom, located down the hall from the Build Lab, he cracked, "Dave, is this another room in your house?"

Shannon's teasing went only so far. He considered Cutler a hero. Even Cutler's own contempt for heroes ("I don't look up to anybody," he said flatly) seemed heroic. Even shrill criticism from Cutler, while it stung badly, was taken as a badge of honor; it was rewarding simply to be noticed by him. "He only yells at people he likes," Shannon said.

The challenge was to survive Cutler's displays of rough affection. One defense was to tap his ample reservoir of anger. "If he gets mad at you," Shannon said, "shift the blame as fast as possible to someone else."

Shannon spoke from experience. One day he replaced his "safe" build, which played a crucial part in his day, with the newest build, which seemed to him "quite stable." His safe build had withstood tests. "It could've been built a week before or maybe even a few months before. You used it to boot [or launch, the PC], so you could download the current build for testing." On that day, Shannon downloaded the new build, which looked so good in testing that he deleted his "safe" build. He then took a late change from a code writer, but the change killed the build and Shannon's PC too.

Even after the code writer fixed the build, Shannon still couldn't apply the fix to his PC because it wouldn't boot. This provoked Cutler's fury, since it prevented Shannon (who had no backup PC) from testing the new build. Six hours passed before Shannon repaired his PC. Afterward Cutler asked him for the day's lesson. Shannon knew the answer Cutler wanted: "Never prematurely delete the safe copy." But rather than remind Cutler of his error, Shannon said, "Never take a fix from this guy," naming the code writer who made the late change.

"Yeah, that's right," Cutler replied. "I've got to talk to that guy." Forgetting Shannon, he strode off after the maligned code writer.

Cutler assaulted code writers with sufficient regularity that he seemed like a rumbling earthquake. "When people checked in shit, I'd get them on the phone and chew them out," he said. No wonder team members liked Microsoft's telephone system, which flashed the identity of any internal caller. At least they could gird themselves before taking a Cutler call.

A whisper of complaint from Cutler instantly turned some managers into jelly. This left room for merriment, of course. Some accused Cutler of grandstanding, feigning anger just to keep colleagues off guard; he occasionally fanned such speculation by actually admitting to this. Pranksters, meanwhile, staged mock shows of Cutler terrorism. Jim Horne, the worrywart who handled the user aspects of security, fell victim to one such trick. Two members in Horne's group told him that a piece of their code broke the day's build. They had checked in a big piece of code without testing it. Cutler wanted their heads, they said.

Horne, trembling, thought of Cutler's threat about the grass, the lawnmower and the ass—in this case, his ass. He stopped breathing, broke into a sweat, then turned green. His colleagues, fearful Horne might expire on the spot, told him of their joke. Horne was too drained to complain.

Code writers got even, usually by bullying the builders when Cutler was out of earshot. Duncan tried to stick to his build deadlines, but code writers pressed late changes on him all the time. Often they felt they had no choice but to steamroll Duncan. Their own bosses insisted on visible progress; the only real measure of their work was how well it performed in the build. Did it screw up some other part of NT? Missing a build deadline delayed answering this question by at least a day. So the code writers had a lot riding on whether Duncan or another builder agreed to accept a change once the build had commenced. "Our little group was given a lot of power," one builder said. "I don't know if we deserved it, but somebody had to play the role."

After months of saying yes to postdeadline fixes, Duncan began saying no. Sometimes he'd assent just to quiet a frantic code writer, then not make the fix.

Controlling the selfish insistence of the code writers ultimately proved futile. To stay on top of the Build Lab, Duncan found himself sleeping nights in his office. Even then, he found no refuge. Many nights code writers assailed him as he snoozed on the floor beneath his desk. "We have all these cowboy developers, just slinging code like crazy, calling out: 'We need another build! We need another build!'" Duncan grumbled. It was like a bad dream. Finally he hung a sign on his door while he slept: DO NOT DISTURB. I'M SLEEPING UNDER MY DESK.

Duncan was among those on the team whose nerves frayed in the drive to finish the release for applications writers. The victims called it a "death march." Spouses and friends constantly asked, why such long hours?

The reasons were many, if not always credible.

Cutler set a ferocious pace, which many felt compelled to match. While Cutler took his vacations and usually kept a daily noon squash date and a weekly massage, he worked abundantly. As milestones approached, he held a daily meeting (Saturdays and Sundays included) at which he hashed out issues with managers. An early riser, he vowed to face every challenge shoulder to shoulder with his troops, and he did. "Dave gets in at 6:00 a.m. He's there every weekend. He's in the trenches," said Duncan.

The July deadline, meanwhile, was immovable. Earlier deadlines had been self-imposed—and changed with the wave of a hand. Not so with the gathering in San Francisco. Hundreds more applications writers enrolled each week for the conference. Even though Microsoft booked more space, an overflow crowd seemed likely. As part of the $795 admission price, participants expected a copy of NT in their greeting packet (those programmers who couldn't attend the conference could still buy a copy of NT on a single compact disc for $69). All told, tens of thousands of copies of this test version of NT were likely to be sold. If the program wasn't ready and in reasonably good shape by the conference, Cutler and his team would suffer much embarrassment and NT's image might be tarnished forever.

And yet the team was understaffed by ordinary measures, even after counting the dozens of contractors hired by the team for specific and usually brief jobs. Everyone seemed to have more to do than was possible in a forty-hour week. This was by design. "Microsoft's theory is if it takes two people to do a job, hire one," Shannon explained. "It's a stated policy. I've seen it in memos. It's called the N-minus-one policy." In the abstract, the approach made good sense. For all the complaints about workers lacking initiative, most bosses disliked employees who did too much or broke with tradition or set their own priorities. At Microsoft most managers, finding themselves shorthanded, had no choice but to let their people run away from them. Smaller numbers of people, especially on a huge project such as NT, made communications between teammates easier. And it helped the bottom line. Microsoft earned twenty-five cents on every dollar of sales mainly because it offered hot products in a growing market, but the company also knew how to pinch pennies. The company kept salaries low, including Gates's own, and counted on its appreciating stock to recompense workers for the mountains of unpaid and unacknowledged overtime hours. Many employees felt that they received heftier stock grants by working both productively *and* long.

Writing software was time consuming. After years of downplaying its significance, many engineers now viewed programming as among the most complex human activities. Code writing was a solitary pursuit, but designing and fitting together diverse pieces demanded cooperation and compromise. One large team broke into many groups, and communication between and within groups required lots of back-and-forth. Electronic mail reduced but did not banish time-consuming face-to-face contact. The crucial tasks of finding and fixing bugs benefited from many minds. Code writers suffered frequent interruptions. Even the most disciplined spent at most half of their time coding and the rest writing memos, responding to questions, reviewing prior work and learning new skills. Code writing, of course, was the painstaking part of their day. Though simplified by tools, programming resisted automation. The programmer seemed to be a throwback to an earlier age of handicrafts, when each maker put a distinctive stamp on what were functionally the same products. Well rewarded, the programmer's work was judged harshly. "A computer is a merciless critic," Joseph Weizenbaum, a pioneering computer scientist, has observed. Designers are ranked by peers, but code writers ultimately are measured by a machine.

The very mystery of code, meanwhile, bedeviled even astute practitioners. It was far from certain why some programmers wrote better code than others. The best ones were at home with abstractions and saw problems in terms of symbols. They were either adept at formal mathematics and logic, or they instinctively grasped the principles of these disciplines. They enjoyed speaking the private language that only their computer really appreciated. The sheer number of lines of code written said nothing about its quality. The best programmers doggedly stuck with problems, driving toward a solution even if it interfered with ordinary pleasures. No matter the degree of their experience or competitive zeal, they acknowledged an element of serendipity in their work and tended to view themselves more as artists than craftsmen. They often hung around the keyboard waiting for inspiration much as a painter held fast to his studio. Testers, meanwhile, lived with the constant anxiety that, try as they might to expose all the hidden bugs, something bad lurked beneath the surface. Their only defense: Never stop testing.

The need to keep pace with peers was another pressure. The most successful people at Microsoft worked long hours. Those who didn't risked "being ostracized and cut off from the team," said Ellen Aycock, who quit the NT project at the end of 1991 to spend more time with her children. "The people who consciously decide to work forty hours are off the track. They're put on the sideline."

There were notable exceptions. A few respected team members avoided working weekends and most nights by cramming a huge amount of coding into five Herculean workdays. They succeeded by keeping their managers informed, hitting their deadlines and avoiding surprise setbacks. They benefited from the stubborn reality that some programmers might write ten times as much code as others, which freed them to work less. Thus, they were fresher to tackle intense tasks on short notice. "Working in a state of exhaustion," said one, "isn't very productive."

Then there were those who wasted time or failed to manage their time well. Code writers, like engineers generally, tend to get sidetracked by interesting but irrelevant conundrums. This perennial issue was compounded by the team's relative inexperience. For one in five members, Microsoft was his or her first job out of college; for the rest, NT was the project of a career. Many people couldn't or wouldn't pace themselves. Lacking anything better to do, they often hung around the office. Their friends were there, so why leave?

The computer itself exerted a strong hold on people, presenting a palatable alternative to human companionship. Many code writers agreed that their enthusiasm for computing bordered on obsession. More than a few spent vacations writing code or weekends doodling away at a half-baked program. This was sometimes merely a way for code writers to teach themselves about new tools or techniques. But often, a person could not resist programming. "It's an addiction. What else can I say?" said one team member.

The call of the computer took precedence over love or food at times. Bob Day, by general acclaim the most gifted tester on the team, enjoyed programming so much that even during the death march he kept alive a few personal projects, some of which aimed at improving Microsoft products outside his day job. Day's wife, Terri, often failed to separate her husband from the laptop computer he carried around the house. Day sometimes would arrive home from work after his half-hour commute and head straight to the spare bedroom, where he kept a new desktop PC. Other times, he would hide his programming from his wife, pretending to be doing something else. Then Terri would be reading a book or watching a movie or making a trip to the bathroom and suddenly realize that Day had slipped away to the spare bedroom. "Even if I can get fifteen minutes in, it's worth it," Day said.

Terri tried not to take personally her husband's attraction to computing, but she doubted herself and blamed the computer for her husband's inattention. "I felt hostility toward the computer," she said. "It was like the computer was the other woman. It really felt like that." On a Saturday afternoon she'd ask Day to go for a drive; he'd say he'd rather program. Then she'd say, "Bob, don't you have any other interests?" He'd answer no. Finally, she'd ask him, "Bob, why did you get married?" He'd say, "Because I love you."

Others played or created computer games or did both. Walt Moore's passion for playing computer games was infamous. But he played them during the day at work, when he was supposed to be writing graphics code. During the death march it seemed that Moore was a burnt-out case, incapable of rising to the occasion. Yet he still mustered the strength to play his electronic version of Pai Gow for hours on end; he was now able to play seventeen hundred hands without error. Moore took perverse pride in his prowess at games; colleagues considered him a victim of some strange disease, which they called "*Waltz*heimer's." Moore found the diagnosis funny. But some friends were saddened by his decline, wondering at the same time if perhaps their own finely honed skills could so quickly desert them. Observed one colleague, "It seemed like one minute Walt was essential and the next minute he was garbage."

A passion for computer games wasn't the kiss of death, however. Jim Horne, between bouts of frenzy over NT's security features, played computer games more purposefully than Moore. He wrote FreeCell, a logic puzzle in the form of a solitaire card game. Unlike most solitaire games, there was no luck involved after the first hand; all the cards were dealt face up at the start of the game. FreeCell was a hit; the marketeers agreed to add the game to the version of NT to be released to applications writers (the Windows program had gone out to customers with several games).

The ceaseless tapping at the keyboard, whether to write code or monkey with it, reflected the sheer fun some found in computing. Caron loved solving problems; she felt lost without a problem to solve. Wood reveled in the endless possibilities for ingenuity. Cutler, while he considered programming all business, found in it an extraordinary outlet for his perfectionism. Lucovsky marveled at the way the computer halted debates over competing approaches to code. As Gerald Weinberg noted in his study of programming, the practical effect of a piece of code was paramount. "At the very least we can put the program on the machine and see what comes out," he wrote in *The Psychology of Computer Programming*. "An artist can dismiss the opinions of a critic if they do not please him, but can a programmer dismiss the judgement of the computer?"

In a world of ambiguity and conflicting opinions, in which definitive answers were in short supply, the computer's power to separate between good (it works) and bad (it doesn't) software had a hypnotic appeal for code writers. It was hardly surprising, then, that the creation of programs—a message from a person to a machine—would appear to some as a sanctuary. Social psychologist Sherry Turkle has written: "Before the computer, the animals, mortal though not sentient, seemed our nearest neighbors in the known universe. Computers, with their interactivity, their psychology, with whatever fragments of intelligence they have, now bid for this place."

While the reasons for the long hours differed among team members, the effect during the death march was similar: strained relations with lovers and friends, spouses and children.

Darryl Havens, the Cutler crony who oversaw the design of NT's sprawling input-output piece, clashed with his fiancée, who complained that he lacked time for her. They attended weekly counseling sessions, at which Havens realized, "I'm married to my job." He and his fiancée talked of breaking up.

Caron, consumed by the rush to prove herself, gave less attention to her husband, Paul. Having married too young and impulsively, she felt that salvaging the relationship would be hard in the best of situations. And this was far from the best. She was immersed in her work yet thirsted for more. Making good progress on the program manager, she volunteered in early March 1992 to write an adjunct to her main code. Her boss considered assigning the piece, called the group editor, to someone else. But before he did, Caron finished it. "That shocked them," she said, feeling sassy for a change.

To add to her pressure, she took on another big task, creating the user profile. This piece defined and stored the various settings—screen colors, keyboard speed, network and printer connections and other personal preferences selected by a user. NT could store many user profiles, so that numerous people could share the same machine and yet instantly have their familiar preferences available. In the midst of this, testers and dog-food eaters banged away at her program manager, pestering her with problems. Since her code accounted for launching NT, she was among the first contacted when someone couldn't start the operating system. Her code often wasn't the problem, and she grew angry over false alarms. It reached the stage where, when criticized by a colleague, "I'd jump down their throat."

After her father learned of these confrontations, he offered, in late April, a plan for dealing "with those pain in the neck people." He explained: "You put fireworks into the display, with appropriate sound effects. Then flash a message that says: 'Welcome to the system that isn't quite done yet. If you break it, you pay for it.' This will have a thundering impact."

Caron would never consider playing a practical joke with the build. She instead sought relief in exercise. She supplemented her daily karate class with a few miles of running. She added miles until she ran a marathon. When chopping, kicking, jumping and running weren't enough, she swatted tennis balls at a wall until her anger ebbed. Meanwhile she saw less and less of her husband. She arose early and went to bed before 11:00 p.m., while he stayed awake into the night and slept late. The gulf between them expanded. Caron's marriage withered, and she let it. "I put all my energy in my job," she said. "I didn't even try to save the marriage."

Jonathan Manheim, the senior tester, and his wife, Leigh, wrestled with different pressures. She faced the twin challenges of raising children with little help from her husband and accepting her role as a housewife after years of holding a job. This was especially hard to take because her husband acted like a hippie in his younger days. "Now suddenly he and I are living this Ozzie and Harriet kind of life," Leigh said.

Only *their* life seemed even less eventful than that TV version of the 1950s family. Each weekday morning Manheim's alarm sounded at 6:30. Leigh, an early riser, awoke straightaway, while Manheim took a bit longer to shake off sleep. Leigh dressed and went to the kitchen. For breakfast Manheim ate half an English muffin, toasted, with cheese melted on top. Every day. It was as if he were on autopilot, Leigh felt. He also took orange juice and strong black coffee, but only in that order. It bothered Leigh that if for some reason he sipped the coffee before she served him the juice he then would refuse the juice. "It's too late," he would say. "I already had my coffee." By 8:00 a.m., he was gone.

In the midst of the death march, the Manheims purchased a larger home nearer Microsoft's campus. Leigh marveled at the house but the weight of the move fell squarely on her, and this stole from her joy. "Here I was with three kids and a big house to unpack and him gone all the time," she said. "My resentment started to build. I wanted him home to help." She also felt "the hardest part for me" was not bringing problems—with her or the kids—to Manheim's attention "because he's got enough to deal with. So I constantly felt like I can't really go to him with this [or that] problem because he's already got too much pressure."

Children simmered over their parents absences from home, too. As the death march worsened, code writer Gary Kimura often worked until 11:00 p.m. His young son and daughter, whom he'd last seen at breakfast, missed wishing him goodnight before they turned off the lights. With their mother's aid, the kids telephoned

Kimura one night. Kimura was too busy to answer the phone, so his spunky daughter left a taped message on the automated answering system. Before leaving that night, Kimura checked his messages. His daughter's voice startled him. "Daddy, we're going to bed now," she said. "Good night. We love you."

Kimura sank into his chair and thought, "Why am I here?" He was tempted to forward the message to Cutler, with a sneering note: "See what you're doing to me." But he didn't; the moment passed. Kimura's wife, who worked as an engineer at Boeing, took his absences calmly, partly because Kimura gave the kids breakfast each morning and prepared them for school. "If NT didn't take him away, something else would," she said of her husband. "He's that kind of guy." So the phone call from his children became a nightly ritual, a private game between Kimura and his family.

A child's desire wasn't always so easily satisfied. One Saturday morning Manheim dropped off his seven-year-old son at a soccer game. He was in a hurry to get to the office, since he needed to fight a terrible bug, a showstopper, that kept a popular drawing program from running right on NT. As he pulled his car to the side of the road, his son grudgingly opened the door and said, "I would throw away all of my toys if you would be here after the game." The words hit Manheim "like a knife in my heart." He stayed with his son that day.

Many on the team sought to resolve the contradictions of work and family by selling some of their Microsoft shares and flushing their lives with cash. The money—what it bought and what it stood for—was a balm for the workaday aches. Some bought security. Lou Perazzoli eschewed a new house and even a new car for himself. Instead he socked away enough to pay for college expenses for his two daughters and an early retirement for him and his wife.

Others went on shopping sprees. In the year leading to the July deadline, one code writer bought a mansion a half hour's drive from work, a vacation home in Vail and four new cars: Saab and Porsche convertibles, a Voyager van and a Honda Accord. He paid cash for the cars—nearly $150,000 in all. "For me spending money is a release," he said. But before long he wanted another—a Lotus Esprit, a sports car even pricier than his Porsche. He installed a tennis court on his estate but bemoaned his lack of playing time. Another highly successful code writer lived alone in a sumptuous home on Lake Washington but slept in his office so often that he called himself a "homeless person."

Some questioned the value of the prosperity wrought by their tie to Microsoft. "The company provides really well for us," said Leigh Manheim. Yet she felt uneasy: "It's like the old saying: Be careful what you wish for. That's how I feel sometimes. Through his job Jonathan and I have had our lives transformed—from renting a tiny cottage in California and scraping by—to reaching this whole other income level. Now we've got all the trappings of success. In a way I'm thinking to myself, 'Well, this is the American dream. We got it! And fairly overnight, too.' But there *are* sacrifices to be made. It's been very hard on our marriage, very hard to live with. But would it be any different if Jonathan worked for another large corporation? When a company has you, they want you. They want a big piece of you. And then it's very hard to have a personal life."

It was no help that Cutler's own feelings toward family were peculiar. "DaveC's four priorities are work, play, friends, family, in that order," said one colleague. Cutler had a steady girlfriend, an engineer at Digital, who had no children and appeared willing to forgo motherhood. Although sharing a house with him, she seemed to accept that twice-divorced Cutler did not wish to marry again, or "strike out for a third time," as he said. Cutler rarely saw his two sons and daughter. Now in their twenties, the children had grown up in the East, with Cutler seeing them mainly during summer vacations from school. "I guess I admire people that did better at raising families than I did," he said. Yet this didn't show. He rarely offered encouragement to coworkers grappling with family issues. He preferred to avoid the subject, perhaps out of shame. "I don't think I did a very good job as a father," he said. "I was so dedicated to all the work I was doing. I didn't leave a lot of time for family."

The line between work and personal life, which many on the team struggled mightily to maintain during the death march, vanished entirely for Eric Fogelin. In 1985 he and his girlfriend drove around the country aimlessly. Running low on cash, he stopped in Seattle. Since he held a bachelor's in computer science from the University of Massachusetts, he visited Microsoft and was enlisted into its cadre of lowly customer support personnel. This was the glorified title given people who answered the telephone, fielding obvious questions (and some stumpers) from purchasers of Microsoft's programs. To excel at this unglamorous task required immense knowledge of the tedious and lengthy instructions on making a particular program do a certain thing. While hardly a launchpad for greatness, the routine chatter with customers fired Fogelin's enthusiasm. In explaining to others the intricacies of packaged software, he found his life's passion.

After a time, Fogelin shifted into writing and editing manuals. Often lampooned, these texts, if studied with a fanaticism ordinarily reserved for the Bible, revealed a multitude of secrets. A strong manual made a program more useful; since most manuals were terrible, good ones stood out. The typical customer rarely appreciated a manual's craftsmanship; he or she eschewed instructions in the rush to get a program going. But specialists in a program devoured any and all documentation. This was especially true for operating programs. DOS, which came packaged with a manual, spawned a cottage industry of how-to books. Independent publishers might someday explicate the workings of NT, but until then both applications writers and ordinary users would depend on Microsoft's documentation.

As a work in progress, NT posed special difficulties for Fogelin, who had been chosen in late 1990 to lead the group producing manuals on the operating program. For the July release he wanted to issue an encyclopedic account of NT's innards, but "that's hard to do when the program isn't finished." He hired a platoon of freelance writers to describe the various pieces of NT, editing their work and, along with a few staffers, stitching together the end result. He even wrote some of the manual himself.

Early in the push, Fogelin was a whirlwind, doing the jobs of three people and ready to take on more. His colleagues marveled at his capacity for toil. With Microsoft roughly doubling its sales and profits annually, a zealous worker such as Fogelin rarely saw a stop sign or breathed the stale smell of bureaucracy. Though he took care of only a tiny part of one of the world's biggest software projects, Fogelin held so much authority—and received so little scrutiny—that "it felt like I had my own small business."

This made Fogelin happy. Then one morning he awoke in terror. He rattled off the books he'd promised that his group would deliver in time for the July conference. There were four reference books, a separate guide to designing applications, seven books on various programming tools and a single volume on general coding techniques—thirteen books in all.

Fogelin panicked. He feared he'd miss the deadline, which was of course unthinkable. Applications writers might tolerate sundry glitches in NT itself, but without documentation they were lost. Fogelin girded himself. "I don't have to be a one-man army," he thought. Though it ran against the grain, he asked for help. His boss agreed, spreading the work around.

Fogelin had learned an important and simple lesson: "How to ask for help."

In the final push for the July release, however, he found little chance to practice his new skill. He worked every day during the month of June, some days for as long as twenty hours. He took most of his meals at Microsoft; the cafeterias on campus served breakfast and lunch, and a special meal was prepared for those working late on NT in Building Two. Since he lived on an island about ninety minutes away, requiring a ferry ride to and from work, Fogelin never went home for thirty days during the height of the push. He slept on a cheap green cot he'd bought. It was nothing more than a thin piece of canvas stretched over a narrow metal frame. By day it stood upright near his desk, a sturdy reminder of the forfeiture of creature comforts for the soul of a computer program.

Exhausted, his mind addled from too little sleep, Fogelin at least knew his cherished manuals would go out with the July release.

Kimura and Tom Miller knew no such thing about NTFS. Having won a reprieve from the feature chopping block, they raced furiously to hammer their file system into solid shape.

By the end of January, NTFS was still too crude even to turn over to Somasegar and his fellow testers. This was partly because Kimura, Miller and Brian Andrew, also working on the code, still spent a part of their time maintaining the two older file systems.

Another drag was the continuing debate over the specifications for NTFS. Incredibly, the program managers still had questions about the handling of long and short file names. One riddle was whether to allow a customer to change an automatically created short name for DOS files. The managers argued for the flexibility. Miller protested, digging in his heels. The technical cost of this freedom was too great. Customers would simply have to stick with the short names NT gave them.

Another persistent complaint: NTFS was slower by some measures than the older DOS and OS/2 file systems. Miller and Kimura had promised they could achieve at least equal performance, but then what did their critics expect? Kimura reminded them: "To make it recoverable will cost you performance." This was inherently true, since the file system was creating essentially a duplicate copy of every operation. A safeguard against failure, it still chewed up computer cycles.

Then things started to look up. On February 14, 1992, the group passed its first key milestone. It was possible to write code for NTFS using NT. "This is the acid test for all file systems," Kimura said. A few days later, the group felt the file system was good enough for testing.

Somasegar attacked the code at once. He was thrilled to work on a new file system "from day one." Ordinarily he would first functionally test the file system—making sure it did in isolation what it advertised. But because of the late start, he decided to test at the same time the way the file system interacted with the rest of NT. The first test he ran on NTFS was Tilt, the favorite of his that opened and closed files all night long. In a minute, the file system crashed.

This was an ominous sign. Within a few days, Somasegar found so many serious bugs that he politely returned NTFS to its code writers. He felt guilty about it. "Tom and Gary are a great team, and I've learned a lot from these guys," he thought. Yet he also told himself: "If we want a full-fledged file system for the [release to applications writers] we should've started earlier."

But there was no turning back. A week later, Somasegar received a stronger version of NTFS, and testing resumed. Then on March

20, Kimura proudly added NTFS to the official build. "Then we started getting bug reports left and right," Kimura said.

It was hard to convince colleagues to use the file system at first. It was risky; a person could lose a day's work in a flash. Cutler wouldn't try it. Then Miller and Kimura sent out mail pleading with people to treat NTFS as dog food. Cutler still held back, but a few people tried it.

At the same time, the testers worked over NTFS. Scores of bugs were found. Kimura, Miller and Andrew felt overwhelmed. "Once the testers start going you can't shut them off," Kimura said. "They will flood you and bury you with things to fix. And it all has to be fixed now." An especially ardent tester was "the bane of our existence," Kimura felt. "He runs these tests that I'm surprised anyone could ever pass." Kimura once called him "obstinate."

Bugs were routine, of course, but the trio also grappled with unexpected design problems. It was late in the game for that, but there it was. The goals of the file system were aggressive. Both ensuring against the loss of data and accommodating the old file systems placed a heavy burden on them. Fresh riddles emerged with unnerving frequency. One especially vexing one: How to sort files alphabetically in such a way as to account for the differences between English and dozens of other languages? After trying different schemes, they chose to store within NT the alphabetical ordering of each language, so the file system could literally check for the right way to order files in a specific language.

By early May, Perazzoli, their boss, had his hands full keeping Cutler and Maritz at bay. While they agreed that the design of the file system was elegant, they were frustrated by the slow progress. The work took "much longer than it ought to have taken," Maritz insisted. Miller and Kimura were good, "but they weren't supermen."

Perazzoli defended his men, saying they faced a killing work load. "They didn't underestimate NTFS," he argued. "They underestimated the amount of time it took to care for the other file systems." This was a substantial obligation, which effectively turned Miller and Kimura into repairmen, always on call. "When almost *anything* goes wrong with NT, its easy to blame the file system," conceded one critic. "So they couldn't just shut the door and work on NTFS. Those constant interruptions were nerve-racking."

Kimura was finally able to shift most of the maintenance work to a fourth programmer, who'd helped all along with the old file systems. The question then became: How the hell are they going to get the job done with three people?

Throwing more people at the problem wasn't an option, Perazzoli decided. The knowledge shared by Miller, Kimura and Andrew was so arcane that adding two or three newcomers to the group might actually halt progress altogether. "It probably will make them even later," Perazzoli believed. The veterans would spend so much time tutoring the novices that they would lose track of their work. And by the time the new hires learned enough really to help, the group would have missed the deadline anyway. "For the same reason," Perazzoli said, "your wife's not going to have a baby in three months if you give her two more people."

Even so, some teammates felt NTFS "might never get done." From Perazzoli's viewpoint, his code writers were stuck. In early May, he told them that if they missed the July 1 deadline, their file system would be dropped from the product. Uncomfortable laying into people, Perazzoli unleashed what—coming from him—passed for a tirade. "Get those bugs fixed," he intoned. Kimura responded testily: "We're working on it."

And as hard as they could. Miller especially was swept up in the race. "I always felt paranoid we weren't going to finish," he said. He spent so much time at work that he neglected his domestic life. He stopped opening his mail. Bills piled up. One April night, he arrived home to find his house without water, his supplier, the city of Bellevue, had cut him off for nonpayment of bills. It was absurd. He owned a fifty-thousand-dollar car and had a small fortune in Microsoft stock, yet his house had no water. A month later, he almost lost his electricity for a day, also for not paying his bill. He called the electric company a few hours before the cutoff, agreeing to deliver a check immediately in person. All this left his wife, a bank executive, mystified. She wanted to handle paying the bills, but Miller steadfastly retained this duty. He used an electronic bill-paying program, which his wife had not yet mastered. He crowed about the program's virtues. With just the press of a key, a payment traveled from his checking account to a creditor. "It's great—as long as you remember to do it," he said.

In the first week of June, the group finally stopped work on features and began fixing bug after bug in the hope of getting NTFS stable enough to win admittance into the July release. At about the same time, Cutler began eating NTFS with his daily dog food. Cutler's scrutiny of the file system seemed to make everyone more aware of the importance of shaping it up. Reports of bugs surged. They were not always the fault of the file system. Often, someone writing another piece of NT misunderstood the file system and thus created a glitch. Perazzoli himself spawned "a whole stack of bugs" when he wrongly assumed that Miller would synchronize the calls made between the file system and memory manager. Miller had assumed Perazzoli would do that. As a result, the fit between these two big pieces of NT was poor.

Awash in bugs, Kimura felt them begin to "all blur together."

NT's reliability improved despite the slow maturation of NTFS. The team now consisted of nearly 250 people, including dozens of full-time temporaries hired to push the product over the hump. Each night, the latest build was stress-tested on about 120 Intel PCs and 80 Mips PCs. In the final month before the deadline, stress results improved steadily as the team turned to fixing bugs exclusively. Scores were fixed a day, with the changes quickly patched into a fresh build. The numbers told the story. On June 3, half the Intel PCs and two-thirds of the Mips PCs passed the barrage of tests given the latest build. A week later, the percentages rose to 68 and 79 percent, respectively. On June 15, Cutler announced the start of "the final countdown" of the release. "We have promised a stable system. . . . We must deliver!" he wrote the team. The trends looked good. One week before the deadline, the newest build passed stress on 91 percent of Intel PCs, a performance that exceeded the release criteria by six percentage points. But the build passed stress on only 75 percent of the Mips PCs, below the acceptable level. With another week of building and testing, the stress results rose to 94 and 85 percent, respectively.

On June 29, a week before the San Francisco gathering, Cutler chose a build for release. The deadline had been met handily. No sample version of a Microsoft operating system had ever achieved such high quality. Cutler was satisfied. That afternoon he sent a message to the team, saying the latest version of NT "represents a significant achievement that you all can be proud of":

Over the last two months you all have been working hard to finish planned work, fix bugs and improve the quality and reliability of Windows NT. Over this last weekend we ran a record number of systems at record levels of uptime with the highest level of stress ever. We had few failures. This is a testament to your work and the quality of the system. Thank you for your effort under very stressful circumstances.

As you know, we did not reach the level of functionality we had planned for this release and must look on to the coming months to finish that functionality, fix the remaining bugs, increase performance and reduce size where possible. Our target final release date remains the end of the year.

The team still had a long way to go to meet the year-end deadline. The new file system was included in the applications release, but its condition was shaky. Miller and Kimura were overjoyed that applications writers would see NTFS. But then Perazzoli felt compelled to issue a disclaimer about the file system in the "release notes" to applications writers. Users of NTFS should segregate their files from the rest of NT in order to guard against failure. Moreover, they should "not store critical data" on NTFS files. These warnings left Miller and Kimura "crestfallen and embarrassed," Perazzoli said. "It was like I had just told them that all the work they'd done for the past year was terrible and they'd have to rewrite it all."

Another disappointment: Microsoft could not flatly promise that current Windows and DOS programs would run on NT. Only about thirty-five out of seventy high-profile Windows programs ran reasonably well. As the release notes put it, NT users "should not expect" their current DOS and Windows applications "to run perfectly" because compatibility "has not been thoroughly tested or proven in [customer] situations."

On balance, however, the team approached San Francisco on a rising note. Nearly everyone believed the final push to finish NT would follow the conference. The past six months had been difficult for many on the team; pulling together the various strands of NT had nearly broken them. Yet, despite Cutler's lash, they had retained their spirit and sense of initiative.

The conference offered a welcome respite in the team's breakneck schedule. A few dozen programmers planned to attend the conference; it was something of an honor to receive an invitation from Maritz. Most team members would deliver speeches about some arcane aspect of NT. But the real draw was the chance to mingle with people who would write applications that took advantage of NT's powers. The team was well aware that interest in the conference had stunned Microsoft, which kept adding more and more rooms to accommodate the expected crowd at San Francisco's convention center. After being closeted in Microsoft's Building Two for so many years, the team was ready for the glare of the limelight. After all, in many ways this was NT's coming-out party. Some of those on the team who could not travel to San Francisco, for whatever the reason, were bitterly disappointed. Patrick Haluptzok, the graphics coder, was invited to address the conference but declined because his wife, Chenoa, was expecting a baby any day. Though he knew he should stay close to home, Haluptzok resented missing the conference. "Millions of people will use our code, and that makes everything we do seem so important," he said. "I wanted to be there for the start of it all."

On his way to NT's debut in San Francisco, Cutler took a three-day detour for his own celebration. He went to the Russell Racing School at the Laguna Seca Raceway outside Monterey. About a dozen teammates joined him, including Wood, Rob Short, Lucovsky and Darryl Havens. They went to relax. "We're so hyper," one said, "we relax by driving race cars."

Only Havens had raced cars on a professional track before, though most people in the group owned sports cars (Cutler drove a purple Porsche 928 with a 320-horsepower engine). Shannon, who owned a red Miata, also attended the school. The class fee stretched his budget, but the chance to hang out with the project's giants made it worth the money. Cutler's romantic companion, Deborah Girdler, also came along. She shared Cutler's taste for the outdoors and adventure, often joining him on trips with NT people. This was the first time either had raced cars.

Steve Wood had found the school and arranged for the three-day class. At a cost of $1,895 a head for the class alone, with no refunds in event of rain, the school took a liberal attitude toward applicants: It took "anyone! No experience is required." The students drove Formula Fords, open-cockpit, rear-engined cars modeled after the slightly larger ones raced in the Indy 500. The school provided driving suits and helmets and, after some training, allowed students to race complete laps, which were timed. Drivers even could pass other cars, though not on curves.

Cutler had a blast. His head in a helmet, every part of his body was covered with some protective garb. Inside his twelve-hundred-pound car, both his shoulders were holstered; a lap belt restrained his waist; another kept his legs in place. On the track a truck drove ahead, flashing the proper gear for each curve, so the shifts occurred at the right speed. Cutler could visualize the layout in his mind, the way to aim for the tree on curve 8a or shift into the steep twist on turn 2.

There were no actual races in this initial class, and mostly Cutler checked his competitive zeal. But once Cutler passed Shannon, flipping him the bird. Shannon decided to pass Cutler. He followed him for two laps, looking for his chance. Then Cutler braked hard into a curve, surprising Shannon, whose car was suddenly on top of Cutler's. To avoid a smashup, Shannon locked his front wheels, sending his car careening off the track and onto the dirt, kicking it up. He tasted the dirt in his mouth. It was all over him.

The gang went straight from the racetrack to the Moscone Convention Center, where 4,800 applications writers (three times the original expectations) converged. On the opening morning Gates hailed the coming of NT and proudly pointed to the shrink-wrapped compact disc containing the program. It was the largest conference ever staged for applications writers by Microsoft, and—despite NT's shortcomings—Gates was swept up in the excitement of this "hell of an event." "I know it's our dog food, but I was eating it," he said.

Next Maritz gave his speech, summarizing the various aspects of NT. He seemed tense and preoccupied. He disliked public speaking. Earlier in the year Gates had made him chief of the company's entire operating programs business, putting Steve Ballmer in charge of sales. The promotion gave Maritz formal and actual authority over Cutler and the entire NT project. Still, he avoided confrontations, preferring to wait until Cutler came to see the benefits of Maritz's views. Increasingly Cutler and his inner circle viewed Maritz as a powerhouse and not an empty suit. "He's critical to the project," said Short. "He got into the project a little bit at a time. Slowly he blended his way in until it was obvious who was running the show: Him."

The classic field general, Maritz amazed people with his ability to, as Short put it, "get to any level of detail he wants." Calm and sardonic, he had stomach enough for the foul smell of the infantry. After his speech Maritz bumped into Wood, who enjoyed tweaking both friend and foe. Wood gravely asked if Maritz had heard about Cutler's catastrophic car accident. Maritz knew that Cutler had escaped unharmed from racing class; he wasn't amused by Wood's joke.

Later, Cutler delivered a wooden, hour-long lecture on the guts of NT. Ill at ease before the big crowd, he squinted into the lights, droning on about one or another utterly opaque concept. His gifts were best expressed in the heat of the moment, but here he merely parroted his carefully reviewed presentation and showed none of his trademark fire.

Cutler felt no more at home off the podium than on it. He was easy to find. At the company's insistence, every NT code writer wore a bright red polo shirt. Dutifully wearing the special shirt, Cutler shone among the stars. Applications writers followed him all over. A few asked for his autograph. For most prima donna code writers, this would have been a joy. Taking a page from Hollywood, the computer industry held frequent meetings, at which technical luminaries strutted about like stars attending the Academy Awards presentation. Cutler avoided these sessions. In a field engulfed in self-promotion, he acted like a hermit.

So it was at the conference. True to his promise to Maritz, he answered questions from applications writers. He was proud to do so, but it was hard. When he stopped to answer a question from one person, others flocked to him, eager to hear his explanations or merely to brush against him. Cutler felt caged. "I couldn't walk anywhere," he said. "People even followed me into the bathroom."

9. BUGGED

When the San Francisco conference ended on July 8, 1992, and the applications writers stopped cheering, Paul Maritz faced a sobering day after. NT was surely the foundation for Microsoft's next generation of software, but it was still "too big and too slow," Maritz believed. "It wasn't usable," not by typical customers, anyway. *PC Week* agreed. After evaluating NT on three of its own computers, the computer magazine opined that NT "is a product only a developer [of programs] could love, as no end user would tolerate its current limitations."

The bugaboos were size and performance. These twin yardsticks of PC software each carried an "overhead" cost. In a certain sense, choosing an operating system was similar to buying a car. Besides the purchase price, there was a cost of ownership. The size of an operating system largely determined the amount of memory required by the computer. Just as some cars guzzled gas, some operating systems consumed large amounts of memory. Operating systems also varied by the speed in which they carried out ordinary operations, such as opening a file, saving a document or making a calculation. Obviously faster was better. Nobody liked waiting for a computer to do its thing.

Regarding both size and performance, customer preferences were clear. They wanted software that gave speedy results on inexpensive hardware and got great mileage out of memory. On both counts, NT so far failed to meet the admittedly aggressive sights Gates had set for it three years before.

This put Maritz in an awkward position. "There's a huge amount of the company's investment in this project, and we're not meeting our targets." He kept calm. It helped that Gates did too. Ordinarily, when a project was badly off mark, Gates rained insipid criticism on the team leaders. But NT was no ordinary program. Gates knew that Cutler would go berserk if he got wind of the dark feelings hovering about his team's effort. So Gates bit his tongue. Others at Microsoft did not. They understood that NT was a memory hog and a performance slug, and their advice flowed freely. Maritz scrambled to "filter that stuff from reaching Dave" and igniting a conflagration. The last thing Maritz wanted was for Cutler's troops to become demoralized just as they faced their stiffest test.

In times of crisis, Maritz stayed the course. He was not mercurial like Gates or Steve Ballmer. Since he brought an exacting and grim seriousness to his tasks in the best of times, he found this same demeanor effective in the worst of times. When he spoke with Cutler about NT's health a few days after returning from San Francisco, he was crisp and familiar. But his message was severe: Push back the finish date three months to early April 1993. Complete NT's features from July to mid-October 1992. Then from mid-October through mid-December make NT speedier and smaller. Better to "eat the bad news" now, Maritz said, than to face a disaster in six months.

While Cutler well knew that NT was too big and too slow, he resisted pushing back the end date. He gave Maritz his customary reason: A program as complex and powerful as NT—so sprawling that "one mind can't comprehend it all"—can be polished and improved "forever." Besides, NT was about as good as he expected. Maybe if Microsoft had not saddled him with so many neophytes, he reasoned, he would have posted better results. Not that anything was wrong with NT that time would not heal. Poor performance was a common failing of most new programs. The annals of software amply showed this; nearly every landmark system, from IBM's 360 to the various flavors of Unix to Microsoft's Windows, was released in an immature state and evolved over time to win broader acceptance. Indeed, people *expected* the first commercial release of a new program to contain flaws of all sorts. As Fred Brooks wrote in *The Mythical Man-Month*, his meditation on the perils of programming, "In most projects, the first system built is barely usable. It may be too slow, too big, awkward to use, or all three."

Cutler took the situation in stride. He had midwifed the birth of big operating systems before, so he knew it took no special feat to find shortcomings in NT at this stage. Moreover, NT's current condition was consistent with Cutler's philosophy of code construction. "Always do the job right, get it reliable and then worry about performance" was his view. "Add more polish as you go along," he said. "That's what I like."

As sensible as this sounded, Cutler's principle begged the crucial question of timing. When should performance work begin? With hindsight, the team probably waited too long to start the tricky job of making their code faster. This was true of graphics, the file system and networking. "We should have started our performance work sooner," said David Thompson.

The guzzling of memory spawned remorse too. For many months, Cutler and Perazzoli, the team's memory guru, believed that Gates's public goal of eight megabytes as NT's memory minimum was impossible to achieve without crippling the program's utility. Perazzoli thought NT would require twice as much memory, or sixteen megabytes, in order to satisfy the typical customer. At the time, most PCs came with four megabytes of memory, just one quarter of the memory needed to readily support NT. Adding memory was technically simple—the chips plugged into a board inside a PC—but costly. Besides the labor, the memory chips could cost as much as five hundred dollars, or perhaps as much as the entire PC was worth. The risk was that many people might ignore NT because it required an expensive rehabilitation of their PC.

Before the San Francisco conference, Perazzoli even asked Maritz point-blank, "What's more important? Features or size?" His answer: features. The team couldn't retreat on features because NT "wasn't going to be measured against DOS," Maritz insisted, but against the standards set by the OS/2 and Unix operating systems. "If NT requires sixteen megs," he told Perazzoli, "that's the price you pay."

But did the price have to be so high? Perazzoli now regretted not paying closer attention to the amount of memory consumed by the team's code. Nearly two years before, when the team greatly expanded to take on the challenge of giving NT a Windows personality, he considered creating a system that tracked the memory required for each addition or change in NT. He figured it might take a couple of weeks to incorporate this memory tracker into the check-in routine. He also briefly entertained a more severe approach at holding down memory use, whereby "anytime people wanted to use memory, they'd have to tell me what they were using it for. I would track the memory they used." In the end he decided against either imposition. "We hire good people, so why should we have to spend the time tracking memory usage?" he concluded.

It turned out that many code writers virtually ignored the memory implications of their code. They were "clobbering memory, running away with it," Perazzoli said. Of course, human frailty was only part of the problem; even closely tracking memory usage would not have solved it. Basically, NT consumed more memory than Gates wanted because the program did more things than he or anyone else initially envisioned.

While Cutler took the criticisms of NT very personally, his confidence was unshaken. He saw himself as an unabashed success. Both professionally and financially, he had it made. Whether NT shipped or not, whether it was a bomb or a triumph, he was set for life. Money meant a lot to him, a poor kid who made it *his* way. "You can never have enough money," he once said. He had earned a small fortune at Digital, but his original Microsoft options were now worth far more, given the astonishing sevenfold increase in the company's stock value in the less than four years since his arrival. As a tangible sign of his wealth, Cutler was closing on the purchase of a second home in the elite town of Medina. His present residence, a short jog to the north on the same street, bordered Lake Washington but was close enough to the bridge spanning the lake that the sound of passing cars was an irritant. Cutler's new property included a thirty-thousand-square-foot lot and 125 feet of lakefront. For a purchase price of $2.5 million he acquired the choice property and the privilege of knocking down the house on the site. He would replace it with a house more to his liking.

Delays kill morale. By August 1992 it had been nearly four years since Cutler and his gang arrived at Microsoft from Digital, and two years since the horde of Microsofties joined the team following the decision to mesh Windows with NT. Most people on the team had expected the operating system to be finished by now. Instead, they faced many more months of tedious programming and testing in order to finish certain features and improve NT's speed and reliability.

The prospect of a continued push without a clear finish line depressed some on the 250-person team. A few people departed. Jim Horne, his work on security largely done, left to join another part of Microsoft. Mitchell Duncan finally escaped from the Build Lab, transferring out of the project. And Kent Diamond, manager of the graphics group, quit. "Walking away in the middle of the project is not the right thing to do," he felt. But with the project running late, "I thought I had stuck around for twice what I signed up for. In many ways, I fulfilled my moral obligation." Diamond and his wife, Sue, were wealthy enough to do whatever they wanted for a spell. "We had taken so much from society, it was time to give something back," he said. The couple joined a relief organization in Africa.

Diamond's resignation set off a chain reaction in the graphics group. Fifteen minutes later Patrick Haluptzok sat in the office of Leif Pederson asking for the job of leading the graphics group. Pederson smiled weakly. "I'll consider it," he said, though he had no intention of doing so because of Haluptzok's inexperience.

Haluptzok wasn't the only one who cheered Diamond's exit. Steve Wood and Mark Lucovsky, two vocal critics of graphics, felt that under Diamond "the guys in the group did less than a professional job. That they didn't put the effort in other people did. They checked in stuff that wasn't ready. They didn't fix their bugs. They made tons of promises and didn't keep them. So [we] felt personally insulted." Cutler, meanwhile, placed much of this blame squarely on Diamond: "He really hurt the group. He was always shielding these guys, protecting them. We wanted them to be more aggressive; more responsive to the need to get stuff done; more ambitious in signing up to do things. With Kent in the middle, it was always, 'Jeez, we can't do this or that.'"

Pederson thought some of these claims unfair; critics didn't consider the unexpected difficulties facing graphics, particularly when it came to precisely matching the visual appearance of Windows, even down to mistakes built into the program's arithmetic. Besides, graphics was shorthanded. Whitmer had tended to badly underestimate the size of jobs, unwittingly saddling a few colleagues with Herculean tasks. They needed a helping hand. "You can't get water from a stone," Pederson insisted.

Yet Pederson was no fan of Diamond, whom he thought lacked a can-do attitude. He had recently talked with Robert Muglia, the chief program manager, about replacing Diamond. But Pederson had delayed. A cautious manager, he was squeezed between Cutler above and his troops below. He suffered the embarrassments of trying to explain to Cutler the actions of his zany group, while at the same time trying to figure out what Diamond, Whitmer & Co. were really up to. He often wanted to start fresh, clear the decks, but he feared "there wasn't a better alternative [than Diamond]. We were on a tight schedule. Why make a change when it wasn't clear another leader would pan out? That didn't seem reasonable." Now Pederson had no choice but to gamble on a new leader. From now on, he decided, graphics would toe Cutler's line, or else. Haluptzok noted the shift. "With Kent gone, Leif wasn't going to put up with shit any more," he said.

This was bad news for Walt Moore. Pederson asked him to find a job elsewhere at Microsoft. This won Pederson no gratitude from Moore's colleagues, who took a protective attitude toward him. Whitmer, for instance, felt that Moore deserved better treatment, though he and others agreed that the company had carried him for some time despite his "Waltzheimer's" disease.

Pederson's belief that graphics needed a new technical guru also upset Whitmer, who had long played that role. The implication was that under Whitmer's direction the group had lost its technical edge. He wanted to lead the group in its performance-tuning stage. He felt he was up to the task, with the help of Paul Butzi and a few others.

Whitmer's passion for NT had ebbed unmistakably. His breadth of interests and facility for abstractions pulled him in various directions. A torrid love affair with a biochemist was another distraction, especially since his lover lived in Turkey and spoke no English. Whitmer had met her in the summer of 1991, when he spent two months in Berlin studying German; she was in his class. "We spoke to each other in German," he said. "It was all we had."

After Whitmer returned home they exchanged letters, but the affair faced long odds. She was a practicing Muslim, and her parents violently opposed her relationship with an American, even a very rich one. In February 1992 they agreed to suspend their affair "to see what would happen." For a month they did not write to each other. Whitmer found his mind wandering at work. "I thought about her every day," he said. "Every few hours I'd look up and say, 'Shit, I miss her.'" Now he eagerly awaited the end of the project; as soon as NT shipped he planned to travel to Izmir, Turkey's third largest city, and resume his courtship. This visit he would woo both his beloved and her parents.

With Diamond gone, Whitmer lost his shield and came under attack. In late August, Cutler asked Patrick Haluptzok about Whitmer's progress on switching some C code into assembly language to make it faster. Whitmer had "checked out" this code from the master build some days before, and Cutler wondered what was taking him so long. Edgy about the need for performance improvements in NT, he wanted code writers to make their revisions as quickly as possible so that testing of the changes could commence promptly. What was the holdup? Eager to help Cutler, Haluptzok offered to finish revising the code himself. Cutler approved, then hollered this advice: "Don't take a week to do something that should take a half hour!" Dropping everything, Haluptzok checked out the same code as Whitmer and started on the same task. In failing to tell Whitmer, he breached code writer etiquette.

Two days later Whitmer learned of the situation and reamed Haluptzok for backstabbing. "I call it brown-nosing when you're so eager to do something quick for DaveC that you're willing to step on somebody's toes and impede [his] work," Whitmer wrote. "Working with the [graphics] team is ten times more important than making brownie points with Dave." As to Haluptzok's feeling that Cutler's word was law, Whitmer retorted: If "God told you to check in the files, I still expect you to come back and say, 'Chuck, God himself just told me to check in the files, so you'd better talk to him if you don't want me to."

Until Diamond left, Whitmer presumed he'd command the effort to improve graphics performance. With the arrival of Michael Abrash, all bets were off. Tall and wiry, Abrash was thirty-five years old, married and the father of a school-age child. He had brown hair, a tan complexion, a long neck, small darting eyes and a hawk nose. He had the mind of a forager.

Muglia found Abrash while pursuing freelance code writers to help the team quickly create display drivers—a dire need partly because of Moore's burnout. Display drivers, which controlled how—and how quickly—something appeared on the screen, were key to improving performance. Abrash was a whiz at writing them. Over the past decade he'd created several video games for PCs and produced a variety of graphics software packages. He'd authored a book on writing fast assembly code for an early Intel microprocessor and over the past two years had published a column on graphics programming for the esteemed (by code writers) *Dr. Dobb's Journal.*

In the insular community of device-driver coders, Abrash was a sort of celebrity. His columns often began with a chatty vignette from his personal life, crafted to underscore a point about programming. He began a piece about how best to apply "linked lists," a simple approach to code writing, with a tale about youthful inexperience: "It wasn't until ninth grade that I had my first real girlfriend. Okay, maybe I was a little socially retarded as a kid, but hey, show me a good programmer who wasn't; it goes with the territory." At Microsoft, Abrash's reputation preceded him. Jonathan Manheim, the senior tester, felt "in awe of Mike because of his background. I'd read his writings and thought it was an incredible coup when we got him."

Like many of the best PC programmers, Abrash was self-taught and displayed an independence that comes from mastering a field on one's own. He praised the value of a "flexible mind" and declared that becoming a code-writing guru was "more a matter of learning than being taught." While experience was the path to wisdom, certain habits of mind helped enormously. "Assume nothing. I can't emphasize this strongly enough," he advised in his book on code writing. When improving performance, for instance, "do your best to improve the code and then *measure* the improvement," he insisted. "If you don't measure the performance, you're just guessing, and if you're guessing, you're not very likely to write top-notch code." The road to success, however, was often crooked; leaps of intuition, rather than inexorable logic, frequently produced answers. "You don't solve certain problems by sitting there thinking about them," he said. "You go along and all of a sudden an answer comes into your mind."

Educated in Massachusetts, Abrash had spent several years in California's crowded Silicon Valley, until he decided he could work for West Coast high-tech companies while living in his beloved New England. So he moved to Burlington, Vermont. This wasn't impractical because Abrash was writing his own pieces of code as part of small teams. He sent his work electronically to his employer, with the aid of a computer modem, a device that converted the computer's bits into pulses a phone line then transmitted. Questions about his work were sent to him in the same way. When hired to write device drivers for Microsoft, Abrash hoped to retain this arrangement. But it wasn't practical; the NT team was so large that face-to-face conversations were crucial. So Abrash started flying to Seattle for a week at a time. Then Muglia pushed him to make a firmer tie to the project, offering to move his family to Seattle. Abrash resisted at first, but in July 1992 his wife and child visited the city and liked it enough to stay. "We were tired of being apart," he said. Besides, he sensed he was in the right place at the right time; he was fresh, bringing a relief pitcher's vitality to the tense late-innings of the project. This made it more likely he'd shine.

Abrash's enthusiasm for Microsoft stood in stark contrast to the studied cynicism that informed Whitmer's sensibility. Chaperoned by his boss Pederson, Abrash met Gates for the first time at a "new hire" dinner held at the Space Needle on the site of Seattle's Fairgrounds. Even as the number of Microsoft employees shot past ten thousand, Gates kept a hand in hiring and actually met many new employees at periodic "getting to know you" sessions. Though Gates was easily irritated and lacked charm, he could thrill newcomers. When introduced to Gates at the dinner, Abrash politely mentioned he worked on NT graphics, expecting Gates to quickly move on to a coworker. Instead, Gates grew excited. "What can we do about performance?" he asked. Within minutes Abrash was neck-deep in technicalities. Gates hung with him every step of the way. After a half hour, Abrash was "amazed the way Gates asked the right questions. It's like he's one of us."

Pederson, who stood by listening to the exchange, felt a huge weight lift from his shoulders. Finally he'd found someone to explain graphics to Gates. Patting Abrash on the back, he said, "You've just won the chance to give the group's next presentation to Bill." Indeed, the chance conversation was a good omen. Gates walked away thinking, "This guy knows his stuff."

Abrash talked a good game. His explanations reassured Pederson and Cutler, whose past fears about graphics were partly fueled by a lack of knowledge. Perazzoli also was impressed, seeing parallels between Abrash and Lucovsky. "Mike will go after anything. He knows his stuff so great," he said. "He's just like Mark."

Credit for landing Abrash went to Muglia, highlighting anew his knack for boosting the team. It rankled that he received scant praise from code writers, but the attitude flowed from Cutler. "Even now there's still a lot of tension between Dave and Muglia," one colleague said. "Dave doesn't show him much respect because Muglia always wants to do things without seeming to know what it costs timewise. Yet Muglia gets tremendous respect around the company." Maritz held Muglia in especially high regard, viewing him as just a rung below Cutler in importance.

This made it all the more difficult for Maritz when, in early October 1992, he asked Muglia to join the Cairo team, which had vague plans for a follow-on to NT. Formed in early 1991, Cairo badly needed the sort of product definition that Muglia had given to Cutler's team. Yet Maritz considered it "a huge, risky decision" to remove one of NT's three top managers (Cutler and Moshe Dunie were the other two). This was partly because Muglia's management duties would fall heavily on Dunie, who would oversee all aspects of the project outside of Cutler's core area of code building. Maritz also felt guilty about shifting Muglia just as the team verged on victory. The move was bound to deflate even as buoyant a personality as Muglia. "It's like taking someone away from his wife right before his baby is born and putting him in some other mess," Maritz thought. "The guy has to start all over again."

Indeed, Muglia didn't want to join Cairo at first. He shared with Cutler a vague sense that the project would not "amount to anything." Cairo's approach was risky; it perhaps called for too large a leap by forcing individuals to greatly change their way of using PCs. Instead of working with several familiar applications, a Cairo customer would deal directly with data. Gates called this having "information at your fingertips." Though it was an untested concept, Gates was as passionate about it as he was about putting NT on many different types of computers. But unlike NT, which was nearly done, Cairo seemed closer to science fiction.

At Maritz's insistence, Muglia visited Cairo chief Jim Allchin who described his program as a new way of controlling a PC that sat on an NT base. The pitch left Muglia unconvinced. He wanted to stick with NT until after its completion. In his mind, he ticked off the reasons why he should not switch to Cairo, then saw Maritz. After listening politely for a few minutes, Maritz spoke about Cairo's importance to the company's future and changed Muglia's attitude. It wasn't all persuasion; Maritz made it plain that Muglia's departure from NT was "inevitable."

Muglia was sad. He would miss out on the birth of a new operating system. For the next few days he was numb, looking at things as if for the last time.

The crush of work made it hard for Muglia to dwell on his future. Within one week, on October 12, 1992, the team planned to finish the first sample version of NT to be released to potential customers. This was the team's first true "beta." Software companies had a tradition of supplying beta versions of forthcoming products to important customers who might then critique the program. Often companies issued just one beta, but Microsoft planned at least two beta releases for NT.

When the beta shipped on October 12, Muglia felt remorse. "You never feel good about a beta," he believed. "You know there are bugs."

The beta was impressive for its reliability. NT scored well on stress tests, which grew in difficulty as the operating system evolved. Key features looked good. The file system, a useful barometer for the project's overall progress, was rounding into shape. Tom Miller and Gary Kimura had "redeemed themselves," said one critic. "I have to eat my words now. NTFS is pretty much what they promised."

Similar gains were made in other parts of NT, setting the stage for the crash effort at improving performance. In a memo on October 13, 1992, Cutler wrote: "We have approximately 2,000 bugs in the backlog, our performance is not what we want it to be and our size is not small enough. These will be major pushes in the coming months." If all went well, the team would release a second and final beta in January 1993 and then be done with NT in March: "While we can breathe a sigh of relief for the next couple of days, we must also start to look forward to beta 2 and the final release."

Cutler tried to set the pace, taking on the task of speeding up text output for the Mips version of NT. Text output was a key measure of a PC's performance. Most people use a computer for writing, so they can quickly grow impatient with a machine that creates text sluggishly. The operating program accounted for an important part of text speed. This particular piece of code, chosen by Cutler for revision, was produced by Whitmer's team. "It needed to be faster, and I was pretty upset that nobody was paying attention to it," Cutler said. "So I did a little research on how to do that. I mean, I'd never done any of that before, at all. I found out how it ran the system."

Cutler had assailed Whitmer about resorting to assembly code too readily (because it was specific to a processor and thus reduced the portability of NT). But Cutler himself relied on assembly code to make text appear on screen faster. He did a splendid job. Abrash gushed later that Cutler was "the best assembly code writer I ever met."

Haluptzok welcomed Cutler's sudden involvement in the guts of graphics. "This gets people going," he said, and it gave the several young graphics programmers the chance to view Cutler as a role model. Haluptzok noticed his teammates' rising enthusiasm. There was a feeling: "We gotta be like Dave. We gotta do it. We can't just talk about it. We gotta get it done."

Pederson, meanwhile, felt that Cutler "set a good example" with the text work. "It helped to solve a problem. What doesn't go over so big is when people whine about problems but don't have solutions."

Many members of the team worked on performance, but a few stood out. Of these Joe Linn was among the most devoted specialists in speed. A stocky thirty-eight-year-old, he shaved his face ultraclose and cropped his black hair short. Before coming to Microsoft, he'd spent years writing classified code for the Institute for Defense Analyses, a military think tank. Code speed meant everything to him; he wanted to "beat everybody on every test."

Linn himself moved deliberately, at times languorously. He was soft-spoken, patient and courteous to the point of formality. This seemed quaint at a company where good manners were often seen as a sign of weakness. But he also had an air of danger about him. Linn was a brown belt in karate, a sport he shared with his wife, Cathy Jo (she worked on Cairo and attended karate classes with Johanne Caron; the two women were running partners and best friends).

Linn took a hard, quantitative approach to performance. He concentrated on the speed with which data in a file were stored on a storage disk. Without accurate baseline measurements, he was lost (as were so many people who tried performance work). It took him months to get his baselines. Then he compared the speeds of the NT code against DOS and OS/2 on specific actions such as the amount of data each sent to storage in a single shipment. These comparisons identified slow actions, which he then analyzed, choosing to revise stable code first. "If the darn thing doesn't work because of bugs, its pretty hard to do performance work," he explained.

Since the file system heavily influenced the overall speed of NT, Linn naturally scrutinized it. He did this without sentimentality toward Miller and Kimura. He worked for a different boss and thought it "isn't good to get too cozy" with the code writers. He expected to find shortcomings in their file system, if only because NT's performance generally was poor. On investigation Linn found that NTFS compared poorly with the older file systems on such commonplace tasks as storing new information in documents and retrieving it. The magnitude of the difference was "alarming." He asked himself: "Are we slower because of something inherent or because we screwed up?"

Linn concluded that Miller had unwittingly created an awful bottleneck in recording data to the disk drive, the PC's principal storage device. The problem was an unintended side effect of Miller's zeal for reliability. Miller had sought to reduce the number of times his file system moved data from a PC's temporary cache memory into permanent storage in a hard-disk drive. He wished to do so because it took a relatively long time for data to be placed into the hard disk (because this device was electromechanical; a spot on a spinning disk had to be found and secured each time the file system "wrote" to the disk).

Miller relied on a fairly commonplace technique called "lazy writing." Lazy writing held the data in temporary cache memory in order to reduce the number of times the file system wrote to the disk. Unlike disk memory, which stayed intact for years, cache memory was wiped clean whenever the PC lost power suddenly or was turned off. However, writing to cache happened very fast because the process was wholly electronic. The lazy writer, then, worked on a simple principle. When enough data piled up in the cache, the lazy writer shipped a batch to permanent disk storage. These transfers resulted in fewer disk shipments and that meant a faster file system.

Lazy writing could lessen reliability, however. When the lazy writer made its periodic dump, something could accidentally happen to wipe out the data. To protect against the loss of accumulated data, Miller made it impossible for NT's file system to write anything anywhere else, even to temporary cache memory, when the lazy writer was ready to move its payload to permanent memory. Miller's safeguard, however, slowed the file system by a factor of twenty in some cases.

Over a few months, Linn persuaded Miller to modify the safeguard so that files could be opened, altered and stored more quickly. At first Miller resisted, but then he hit upon an efficient solution by creating a small test that essentially asked the file system whether at a specific instant it was okay to suspend his safeguard. If it was, the file system could store data temporarily even as the lazy writer dumped its load.

Linn made many other suggestions, though most were "small tweaks that gave us good payoffs." His modesty made it easier for Miller to accept advice. That some of Linn's insights were stunning also melted barriers. Sometimes Miller slapped his head and cursed aloud because an improvement by Linn was so simple that he couldn't imagine why he hadn't thought of it himself. Such was the value of a fresh look. "We knew the code so well," Miller said, "it made sense to us—even when maybe it shouldn't have. Whereas Linn looked with a critical eye."

Abrash also benefited from coming in from the outside. He was an adept programmer; one coworker described him as "arguably the strongest Intel programmer on the face of the earth." With a flair for explaining how to improve code speed, Abrash quickly identified problems, crafted nifty solutions and happily shared his ideas. His impromptu explanations were finely wrought, reflecting an unusual self-awareness about his craft. Most code writers were like gifted athletes; they learned by doing and could not explain their actions. They just did it. This method, while fine for getting started, often hampered efforts at making code faster, which required unblinking self-analysis. "The secret to optimizing speed" he said, "is to ask yourself, 'What does this code actually need to do? What's the least work I can do to solve this problem?'"

All too often, programmers could not answer these questions. "Under pressure or working with unfamiliar things, you tend to be satisfied with approximations; you don't actually understand everything that's going on," Abrash said. "You say, 'Okay. I don't know exactly *how* this subroutine [a piece of code that performs a specific action] works, but it does work. So I don't want to mess with it.'"

Asking radical questions about a piece of code often led nowhere. But sometimes the benefits were big. This was the case when Abrash considered ways to increase the speed of a crucial device driver, the piece of code that controlled an increasingly popular PC graphics adapter, which displayed on a computer screen 256 colors in so-called Super VGA format.

The team was glad just to have the driver at all, because originally plans called for NT to support just the 16-color VGA adapter (ceding to hardware makers and others the responsibility for making NT work with other monitors). But after Abrash joined full-time, he decided NT must offer a Super VGA driver. "If we didn't provide one," he felt, "that would hurt our credibility." He asked a rookie to write it. With Abrash's guidance, he built the driver in six weeks. It arrived remarkably free of bugs, too.

Abrash refused to stand pat. A Super VGA monitor usually drew two pixels, or dots of color, at once. For several years, he'd thought about a "trick" that might increase that to eight pixels at once. Now he wanted to try it.

But there was a hitch. Abrash was advised to do nothing to improve the performance of the new display driver, since it was already a late addition to the product. It still had to be tested, after all. Better to stabilize the new driver than to risk introducing bugs into the code with changes.

Abrash brushed aside this sensible advice, saying he'd attempt the improvements on his own time, at night. That way, if he failed, no one could argue that the attempt detracted from other work. He went ahead, sketching out his trick in code. It amounted to sidestepping the normal behavior of the Super VGA hardware and creating special circumstances that triggered the acceleration of 256-color drawing. Then he revised the code that controlled the creation of text on screen so that it took advantage of the ability to flash eight pixels at once.

Suddenly NT's text appeared on screen plenty fast. And finally— finally—the graphics group had something to crow about. People long had complained about the group's sluggish gains in speed. They had all but given up hope of dramatic improvements. Then, as one teammate said, "a miracle happened: Mike Abrash."

The effort to improve performance highlighted tensions between groups of code writers. When code was criticized for poor performance, people scrambled to apportion blame. One of the worst outbursts of finger-pointing pitted Therese Stowell and Steve Wood against Whitmer and Butzi.

The issue was text speed. Why were characters formed so slowly on NT? This question arose repeatedly because creating text was the most common activity on a PC. The graphics group bore much responsibility for this, but Butzi argued that certain base elements of NT contributed to the problem. He singled out the console code written by Therese Stowell.

Butzi brought his case with undue certainty. "It's your code that's slow," he told Stowell.

She reacted with grim predictability. "No, your code is slow, and you don't know anything about the console," she said.

The two agreed at least to meet again. Then Stowell conceded that her code could improve. Butzi, joined this time by Whitmer, seemed to Stowell to view her concession as an excuse to attack her while avoiding a discussion of his own code's shortcomings.

Stowell was furious. She complained to Wood, who was like her big brother. The mere mention of Whitmer could send Wood into a rage. Defending Stowell, Wood sent a flaming e-mail to Whitmer and Butzi. "This is fucking bullshit," was his message. "You guys have been jerking Therese around. If you want her to look at the console, you better look at your own problems too."

Wood's diatribe greatly upset Whitmer. It was the hypocrisy that bothered him most: Wood himself was famous for clashing with other programmers, who often accused Wood of applying a double standard when it came to his own mistakes. Feeling wounded, Whitmer thought seriously about resigning on the spot. Among the wealthiest code writers on the team, he continued to work at Microsoft for the personal challenge. Whatever his failings, he'd held together graphics through years when no one else, certainly not Cutler, understood the black art his gang practiced. So why such hostility toward him? It darkened his mood.

Stowell wasn't thrilled either. When angry, she could flash a bone-chilling look of disapproval. "I hated Paul (Butzi) and Whitmer," she said. "I felt they were ganging up on me. And they were *lazy*. They were pointing the finger at me instead of trying to figure out what *they* did wrong."

The dispute simmered until teammates suggested that both sides cooperate on a series of evaluations, or benchmarks. Aimed at deciding who was responsible for what part of text speed, the benchmarks showed that Stowell and Butzi carried roughly equal responsibility. With the animus contained, improvements in the text speed flowed rapidly. Afterward both sides felt their code improved, though at the expense of their egos.

The standoff between Stowell and Butzi highlighted the significance of personal conflicts in technical culture. Conflict over ideals and style loomed large—they were the lifeblood of innovation. Because code writers relied on logic and mathematics in their designs, they downplayed the role of personality in their technical decisions. But the sense of inevitability, ascribed to all seminal inventions, is an illusion. There are invariably many ways to achieve roughly the same technical ends. Technical choices are often highly personal. While shaped by commercial considerations, technical decisions also reflect human values and psychology.

Cutler saw the benefit of allowing personal differences over technology to play themselves out. He rarely stifled conflicts. Usually, he followed the dictum of one of the century's finest research managers, E. R. Piore, the U.S. Navy's most perspicacious chief scientist, who said: "Conflict introduces life in the laboratory. When there's no conflict, a lab is no good."

Technical jousts, however, were not confined to the NT team. The unexpected size and sluggish performance of NT was a subject of broader concern within Microsoft; after all, this was the company's next-generation operating program, its platform for the twenty-first century. With Microsoft's future hanging in the balance, it seemed entirely proper that people outside the group step forward with suggestions. To do so, however, was to risk triggering Cutler's wrath—a prospect that sufficiently discouraged most people from sticking their necks out.

But not Rick Rashid, chief of Microsoft's newly formed "advanced research" lab (essentially a think tank for software). Rashid was perhaps the nation's leading academic expert on operating systems. He had never built a commercial program, but his experimental systems were influential. His best-known program was Mach, which gained much attention in the late 1980s because in theory it supported many types of hardware and multiprocessor computers as well as conventional single-processor machines. Rashid explained the "key notions" behind his approach:

> The fact is you could build a system with a relatively small number of basic abstractions. That those abstractions could be made to work together. That you could build a system to be machine independent [portable] and not pay a performance penalty. And finally, that you could rely on layers of [code] on top of a basic kernel without having to pay as much of a penalty as had been paid in the past.

That Mach, as Rashid described it, bore an uncanny resemblance to Windows NT was no accident. Cutler modeled some of his own approach on Mach. He was not alone in this. Steve Jobs, the cofounder of Apple Computer Inc., also became smitten with Mach and Rashid a few years after he left Apple in 1985. By then Jobs had founded Next Inc., which as its name implied sought to duplicate Apple's success only with far more powerful computers. Jobs chose Mach as the basis for his Next operating program. While a series of blunders doomed Next, its Mach-inspired software received critical acclaim (though it attracted a tiny following because it wasn't portable; fans were forced to purchase PCs available only from Next) even as Cutler's team strove to complete NT.

Jobs had tried to hire Rashid, then a computer science professor at Carnegie-Mellon University, but Rashid turned him down. He was reluctant to join the hurly-burly life of a corporation. His Mach research had been almost wholly funded by government grants; an agency of the Pentagon, his principal backer, saw Mach as crucial to unleashing the vast power of multiprocessor computers, inherently cheap machines that would someday replace pricey supercomputers as the backbone of the nation's military and intelligence-gathering networks. Besides, Rashid was an academic purist. He seemed sincerely devoted to pursuing knowledge about software for its own sake. This was rare, even among academics, because software was such a remunerative field that the brightest researchers found themselves inexorably pulled into commerce: The money was too good.

After two decades in academic computing, Rashid entered the marketplace, but on his own terms. As Microsoft chief of advanced research, he had no responsibility for new products. His staff, which would in time exceed fifty researchers, were really closer to faculty. Their concerns were usually five to twenty years out, long-term by Microsoft's yardstick. This meant, of course, that Rashid led a relatively cloistered life at the company. This suited him fine.

On his arrival at Microsoft in September 1991, Rashid met with people on the NT team to "make sure that some things we'd learned with Mach were passed on." He realized "it wasn't exactly my job" to monitor NT, but he was curious about it. Himself a creator of operating systems, Rashid looked at Cutler "the way one painter might appreciate another's work, or the way musicians like to listen to each other or see how they do it."

Rashid's appreciation soon turned to criticism. By then, the team was preparing to begin its performance push. Rashid slyly gained a copy of a current build of NT, without Cutler's knowing it. Next he and a few researchers tinkered with the program, then revised parts of NT's kernel to make fewer demands on a computer's internal memory. Rashid employed a technique called paging, which made a computer's internal memory, or temporary storage area, seem bigger than it really was. It did so by using the hard disk, ordinarily the place for permanent storage, as sort of ersatz short-term memory. Paging worked on the principle that every program set aside for itself more memory than it usually needed at any one time. A program reserved enough memory to race through the most memory-intensive moments. These moments, however, took place only once in awhile; at other times a program had a comfort zone. Paging used this idle memory by essentially shelving inactive parts of a program. Paging, however, cut performance because the process of sending and retrieving data to and from permanent storage took longer than doing the same with temporary storage.

NT already relied on paging for its high-level pieces; it took advantage, for instance, of a feature in advanced chips that made it appear as if a PC had unlimited memory. But Cutler had decided years before to forgo paging NT's kernel because it seemed too risky. Rashid, however, showed it was practical to page the kernel, or at least some of it.

The second leg of Rashid's effort centered on gaining more accurate measures of NT's performance. An operating system largely did one thing after another; actions only seemed to occur all at once because they happened so fast. The computer, at bottom, responded to a series of instructions. The fewer the instructions, the faster the program. Measuring instructions was tricky. Rashid's people created a few tools that counted the number of instructions between one event and another. They also devised a tool, which they nicknamed Leggo, which analyzed the flow of instructions and rearranged code to improve speed. Rashid was impressed with Leggo, which essentially did the work of a code writer only more uniformly and automatically. He urged the NT team to adopt it.

Cutler was peeved by Rashid's initiative; he wanted Rashid to leave him alone. He defended his decision to eschew pageability, arguing that Rashid was naive about the potential risks to NT's reliability. He rejected the Leggo tool, also citing its uncertain effects on code.

Robert Muglia, privy to the exchange, found Cutler's reaction predictable, and he branded Rashid's handling of the matter (but not his advice) inept. "Rick's approach was doomed to failure," Muglia said. "He took Cutler's code, modified it and said, 'Here, this is better.' Of course, that pissed Dave off." In Muglia's view, this was a classic battle between the idealist and the pragmatist. "Rashid thought like a scientist. He thought about what's possible. He made the kernel pageable and said, 'Let's see what breaks.' Those things that break, we won't make pageable." By contrast, "Cutler weighed the situation as an engineer. He wanted to design the solution in advance—figure out beforehand what's pageable and what isn't—because that's how you achieve robustness."

Rashid made no apology for the skirmish. "The frank reality of doing [operating] systems development is that you've got to be able to take the heat from other people looking at what you do," he said, adding: Before doing such work, "Check your ego at the door."

In truth, nobody worried about Rashid's etiquette. Of all people, Cutler *deserved* indelicate treatment. Other Microsoft leaders viewed him as a bully. One senior executive usually responded to a Cutler complaint with the succinct statement, "Fuck Dave." When asked why, the executive excused his boorishness with the reply, "Cutler tells me to fuck off all the time."

The goal was to improve NT, everyone agreed. By that measure, Rashid's clandestine intervention helped. It sent Cutler a clear message: Make NT faster or others will. Cutler listened. While rejecting specific advice, he couldn't ignore the general point. Rashid's critique "provided the necessary incentive for Dave to say 'Goddammit, I can do this better,'" Maritz said.

After waffling, Cutler agreed to make as many parts of the kernel pageable as could stand it (though he refused to use any of the code offered by Rashid's people). This meant rewriting parts of his own code.

In the midst of this, Cutler battled against the distractions that bedeviled the refinement phase of lengthy projects. With the making of NT approaching the status of a marathon by software standards, he had to distinguish between antics that eased tension and those that just wasted time. One day he noticed a lengthy and passionate e-mail exchange on the NTDEV bulletin board, about the correct usage of the words "who" and "whom." There seemed to be some concern over the laxity in the way these words were tossed about by team members. The mail enraged Cutler. This was not the sort of question he wanted discussed now. So he ordered a halt to the grammatical debate. "Get this off the ntdev," he wrote, "or I'll come over and walk through your wall." The code writers complied at once; Cutler "never saw another word" on the subject of grammar. As usual, Cutler's bark was so effective he didn't need to bite.

Cutler had plenty of reasons for barking. With NT scheduled to ship by April 1993, rewriting pieces of the program seemed an odd way to wrap up. Usually when a large project was this deep in ship mode, code writers were restricted to making just small changes and fixing bugs, with the emphasis on the latter. But for various reasons many people were rewriting pieces of NT. A few were even rewriting pieces of their own life.

Johanne Caron felt whipsawed between code revisions and bug fixing. On November 10, 1992, her own code looked so good her boss lent her to another group in order to help fix *their* bugs. Two days later, a feature called the registry shattered Caron's buoyant mood. The registry was an outgrowth of the upheaval in security, which a year ago had set back the project. As part of the security plan, the registry was created to provide a library of vital statistics about individual PCs on the network. The main goal was to make it easy to customize PCs on a network from a remote location. In practice this meant that a network administrator could alter a PC's software preferences from afar. The code for the registry was long overdue; the code's developer was well known as a slow starter who usually finished strong. The odds were he'd deliver the goods, but well behind schedule. Because the registry had long tentacles into many pieces of NT, the delay aggravated many people.

Now it was Caron's turn to feel the registry blues. The impending arrival of the registry upset her well-crafted user profile editor, the code that allowed a person to tailor NT to his or her own tastes. Visual aspects of NT such as icon size, the color of the electronic desktop and the speed of the mouse button could be personalized. Because of the registry's design, a flaw surfaced in the profile editor. It was no longer possible for two users of the same machine to maintain different profiles. This was an appealing feature, since it obviated the need for those who shared a PC to fiddle with its basic visual controls every time they used it.

Caron was loath to drop it, but that was Pederson's advice. He said, "Don't fight it. Leave it. Stick with bug fixing." She couldn't. She'd worked too hard on the profile editor to abandon it now. She told Pederson she'd fix the bugs and repair her code too. She began hoping she could revise user profile. Get in, get out—fast. After five awful days, she realized that revisions were insufficient. She must thoroughly rewrite her code.

She felt like breaking something. If only she could stop time. It was as if her red Miata were barreling into a big truck, only it was too late to do anything other than cover her face and take the blow. How sad to see her profile editor disabled, yet sadder still to suffer this setback in the same week that she separated from her husband Paul.

She felt little toward her husband; that was the problem. It was easier to imagine her marriage gone than to watch it vanish. And it was easier still to joke about her situation. Microsoft "should probably pay for divorce lawyers," she cracked.

At the same time, people harassed her about fixing bugs. They were not even *her* bugs. This seemed perversely cruel; she actually had to laugh to chase away tears. Of course she wasn't fixing bugs. Not while her marriage imploded. Yesterday, she and Paul talked of filing papers for a legal separation. The night before, she had had a nightmare: She dreamed that her boss gave her a bad review for not promptly fixing other people's bugs.

She asked her group leader for aid. He explained to the leader of the other group that he should call on someone else for bug fixing. He agreed. Caron was giddy with relief. The next day, November 18, she began rewriting user profile so that it worked with the registry and possessed her cherished feature. Over the next eighteen days she felt closer to her user profile than anybody or anything. A colleague wasn't surprised at the high quality of her work, coming at a time of personal trauma. "Her code was a savior for Johanne," he said. "Work is the best prescription for pain."

Caron finished the revision on December 5. It worked. She felt right and whole, the way she had last summer after running a blistering marathon.

Bill Gates entered the conference room off the lobby near his office and sat down at the head of a long, narrow table. Maritz sat closest to him. He was joined by the senior leaders of the project: Cutler, Dunie, Perazzoli, Thompson, Pederson. A few others, Abrash and Darryl Havens included, waited in the wings.

It was December 16, 1992, nearly six months since Gates had last assayed the project's health. Everyone was anxious and wished for a flawless presentation. "A Billg review is an extremely motivating factor," said Dunie. The team knew the consequences of appearing unprepared (or, worse, ignorant). Gates often took special delight in punching holes in others' ideas. Sometimes, he felt sufficient disgust to throw away a team's work because it fell short of his goals. The company's first database program, under development for more than two years, had just recently been shelved at Gates's behest.

No one in the room thought Gates would spike NT. If anything, Microsoft's chief was eager to see the program in customer's hands. This, however, hardly meant he would signal the project's last lap. Maritz had told them that Gates still had reservations about the size and speed of NT. The thrust of the meeting was to allay Gates's "too big, too slow" worries. It would not be easy. Gates had harbored such doubts about NT for more than two years. The risk now was that he'd insist the team write new code to improve performance. This would delay the completion of NT for months and, as Dunie noted, "could introduce errors into it and sacrifice robustness."

Gates arrived at the meeting certain of his ultimate intentions. He wanted "to ship this thing." NT was crucial to the company's future; the program was its best defense against rivals and the foundation for giving PC owners the kind of security and reliability now offered only with much more expensive computers. Moreover, NT was a big step toward the ultimate piece of software: a program that could run any application on any machine. To launch this new age in computing, Gates was willing to compromise. Indeed, he'd ceded his hope that NT would run well on a PC with just eight megabytes of memory. It now appeared that sixteen megabytes was probably the minimum that a PC needed in order for NT to perform adequately. Neither Cutler nor Perazzoli had the gumption to tell Gates flatly the bad news on memory, but over the summer he had gleaned the truth from Maritz.

The performance of NT was another matter. Gates would not compromise on that. If he did, customers would kill him. That Gates worried about customers seemed to surprise many people. Lately, he had come under fire for being a dictator who imposed standards on the computer industry that benefited Microsoft's diverse product line while driving competitors to the brink of annihilation. The Federal Trade Commission, a U.S. regulatory agency, was investigating Microsoft for possible violations of laws aimed at limiting abusive monopolies. This pained Gates, who felt he was simply a victim of his great success. "I don't think the rich get much credit for anything," he said. His own experience, he felt, bore this out. Just a few years earlier, he had been celebrated as the scrappy entrepreneur who courageously carved a thriving business from the technological wilderness ignored by entrenched powers. Now he was a maligned bully who wanted to own the entire software universe; a greedy man who thumbed his nose at both customers and competitors.

Which was the real Bill Gates? The richest American by virtue of his roughly seven billion dollars in Microsoft stock, Gates was an object of envy and awe, paranoia and adulation. These strong emotions made a balanced assessment of his actions impossible. Anyway, the choice between saint or sinner was an illusion; these were cartoon images of Gates. The real Gates resembled a big-city political boss; more Richard Daley than Rockefeller. This was because his power depended on both exploiting and nurturing a chain of dependents, everyone from applications writers to PC makers to customers. So it was with NT. Gates knew that a faster-acting personal computer was desired by everyone who relied on these machines. To many people, the memory of an era when computers took days to answer a question was all too fresh. Who could complain about the quality of software when every year computers made programs run faster? The faster, the better. If Gates had a master, it was speed. He knew Windows programs had to run relatively fast on NT, or else customers might ignore its impressive achievements and steadfastly stick with running the same Windows programs on DOS. Or, even worse, customers might choose OS/2, sold by archenemy IBM. Though no popular applications were specifically designed for OS/2, IBM had come up with a neat way of salvaging this dead platform. They were creating a future version of OS/2 that would run Windows programs just as fast (or perhaps faster) than they ran on DOS. "Now we're clearly in competition with OS/2," Gates thought. And while OS/2 offered large networks of PCs only a shadow of NT's features, it was more powerful than DOS.

Gates opened the meeting, impatient for performance data. This surprised no one. "We all knew Billg cares a lot about performance," Dunie said. "There was no secret about that." Coming into the meeting, Dunie hoped the team's progress over the past two months would impress Gates. In his mind the best measure of performance was how quickly Windows applications, on NT, completed familiar actions: opening and closing, scrolling, recalculating and so on. In this regard Dunie was optimistic. Applications speed had sharply increased recently. One application ran three times faster now. Still, none of the Windows applications ran as fast on NT as they did on DOS.

Gates seized on this failing. The blame fell mainly on the graphics group, he felt. It wasn't entirely Whitmer's fault. Gates kicked himself for long ago encouraging Whitmer to write his code in C++. He now realized graphics "paid a painful price" for resorting to a language that lacked important tools.

On the bright side, Abrash fielded Gates's queries with poise and clarity. Gates struggled to keep a lid on his temper because "we were at the point in the project where we're not supposed to be talking about the code in this way." Abrash's "very good answers" made it easier for Gates to check his dark impulses. He was impressed at how fast Abrash, a newcomer, had grasped the essential issues. Since Gates "trusted" Abrash, he told him, "Here's a list of things to improve. Go ahead and change the code."

There was still more to discuss about performance. The report on NT's file system puzzled him. It should be faster. Gates "was surprised there was a problem," since Cutler's team had so much experience in this area. Havens, the resident expert on input and output, defended the work of Miller and Kimura, saying they had not worked long on improving performance. "There's no cause for concern," Havens told Gates. He promised the file system would soon perform at the speeds Gates considered acceptable.

But Gates wouldn't let go. He wanted to know *why* NT was this slow. Havens's explanation didn't help. Gates thought people were confused.

Gates's scrutiny offended Havens. He started shouting. Gates took the show of anger in stride, keeping cool but sounding snide. Havens resented Gates's tone. "Yes, he's brilliant but he can't bullshit us," Havens said. "We know more than he does about what we're doing."

Cutler, angry with Gates for giving Havens such a hard time, stepped in. "They'll get there," he said, referring to Miller and Kimura.

The promise didn't seem to help. Havens left feeling that Gates was "very skeptical" about the team reaching performance targets.

The meeting ended with Cutler agreeing to another month of performance work. This was fine with Maritz, who came into the meeting willing to let the ship date slip if it meant making the performance closer to Gates's target. Dunie, who tended to housekeeping details, immediately scheduled a followup meeting with Gates, to be held in about six weeks.

The Havens blowup left things on a sour note, however. This was partly because Gates had become a stranger to the team, making his criticism hard to take. They worked so hard, and Gates seemed only to notice their flaws. He never sent anyone, from Cutler on down, a note of encouragement. Perazzoli was bewildered. "I kept waiting for him to get more involved. It never happened," he said. Worse, Gates seemed aloof to Perazzoli. "He didn't care as much about NT as we thought he should."

This inattention fueled resentment against Gates. Many Microsoft employees looked on Gates as a father figure; even members of the NT team, while less needy of his approval, saw him in this light. When he got a whiff of the team's disappointment after the meeting, Gates was troubled. "I wish I could've spent more time with those guys," he said. But he had his reasons for keeping a respectful distance. This was partly the result of the gulf between him and Cutler. They had never forged a personal bond, and Gates steered clear of situations where he and Cutler might clash. He also didn't want to waste Cutler's time. Or his own, which he rationed more carefully now than in the past.

This made sense. By the end of 1992 Gates was among the most celebrated figures in global business, with an unparalleled reputation as a technological seer. He was often sought for interviews and public appearances. Meanwhile, Microsoft itself had grown quite large. Sales nearly exceeded one billion dollars every three months, and the company, which had 250 employees ten years before, now had more than 10,000. Gates had a lot to keep track of. While he kept a hand in the company's operations, he spent most of his time pursuing the *next big thing*. Just as he'd immersed himself in NT at the outset, assembling key people and clarifying goals, he now did the same for a half dozen other major projects the public would not see for a few years at least.

All this meant that Gates had far less time to spend with his old Microsoft cronies than he once had. Of these insiders, only Ballmer still saw Gates frequently. "Time with Bill is now *the* currency at Microsoft," one pal said. "It's a symbol of what and who is important."

By that measure, Gates's agreement to see the team's other leaders again so soon after the stormy performance meeting illustrated NT's prominence. When he met the team again on February 1, 1993, Maritz felt NT had finally "turned the corner." While Windows programs still ran more slowly on NT than on DOS, the difference was small enough to satisfy Gates.

Havens crowed with delight when recounting for Gates the improvements made by Miller and Kimura. He reminded Gates that he'd predicted this. "I told you not to worry, I meant for you not to worry, so you didn't need to worry," he declared. Gates kept silent.

After listening to the others, Gates blessed the shipment of NT. "I felt featurewise and even performancewise, hey, there was no reason to hold this thing up," Gates said. "They knew the criteria and they could drive [shipment] knowing I wasn't going to ask for any additional" speed or features.

Cutler or Dunie didn't break into cheers. To start with they agreed to keep six people on performance for a little while longer. Then there was still the relentless push against the bugs that pockmarked NT. Just a week before, on Super Bowl Sunday, Dunie had arranged to feed a broadcast of the championship professional football game into the lobby of Building Two in order to encourage team members to visit the office and fix bugs. He rented a large-screen TV for the occasion; the team rewarded him by fixing fifty bugs as they watched the Dallas Cowboys thrash the Buffalo Bills. But Gates didn't need to meet with them again. When it came to eradicating bugs and selecting improving performance further, he trusted the team's leaders: "These are guys with incredibly high standards." Whenever Maritz, Dunie and Cutler felt NT was ready, they could release it. Gates would abide by their decision.

The three men already had settled on a schedule for the final days of the project. Entitled "Windows NT 1.0 Ship Plan," the memo called for a ship date of May 10, 1993, and carefully described the milestones over the next five months:

Jan. 24	Last performance check-in for beta 2
Jan. 31	Stress results in excess of 85%
Feb. 15	Builds achieve beta quality; stress exceeds 90%
Feb. 28	Beta 2 released to Sony for disc making
Feb. 28 to March 21	"Very selective" performance checkins approved by Cutler personally and pretested on private builds
March 28	Zero priority one and priority two bugs; stress exceeds 94%
April 30 to May 10	Final testing
May 10	Release to manufacturing

The May 10 date was crucial because it would give Microsoft time to manufacture and ship hundreds of thousands of copies of the English-language version of NT to software dealers by May 26. On that day, Gates planned to introduce NT officially while attending the year's biggest Windows trade show in Atlanta (German, French and Spanish versions of NT were scheduled for release within three to four weeks of the U.S. edition). The introduction was to be a public-relations assault, carefully orchestrated to ensure Microsoft the maximum publicity for its newest program. It was hoped that the sea of media attention, the result of Gates's endorsement of NT as the future of Microsoft, would spur sales. If for some reason NT were not available in May or soon afterward, the influential trade press and skittish corporate customers might ignite a wave of paranoia about the program's health. Both journalists and customers had watched as too many programs, hyped beyond credibility, never saw daylight for reasons of management ineptitude or the vagaries of software construction. Just a few days before, *Computerworld*, a respected weekly, had set off doubts about NT when it published a front-page article predicting that the team would either miss its deadline or meet it through the drastic move of scaling back features. The report shocked the team. Perazzoli felt compelled to cite the article in a memo to his stable of code writers as proof that "we can not overemphasize how important it is that we meet our ship plan."

At the same time, it was dangerous to rush the introduction of NT. If released with too many flaws, the program might never recover from the damage to its reputation. While customers expected blemishes on the first version of a program, they bristled at being treated as guinea pigs. Microsoft knew well the viciousness of this reaction. The company had just released its first home-grown database program, after years of false starts, only to be accused of selling the bug-riddled program prematurely. Though a big seller because of its bargain price, the program's reputation for reliability took a big hit as the company scrambled to track down the numerous bug reports.

Of course, Maritz, Cutler and Dunie had plenty of time to decide the right balance between shipping ASAP and polishing their product. Regarding this question, the key milestone was the release of the second beta. The very ambitions of NT dictated the need for a second beta; less complex programs often stood pat with one. The team wanted to issue a second beta because, after so many speed-enhancing and other revisions, NT was significantly different from the first beta. At the moment, the chances of staying on schedule looked good, especially since the team could miss the February 28th date by as much as a couple of weeks and still stay roughly on plan.

The imminent arrival of NT had turned the computer industry on its ear. After outsiders took stock of the first beta, expectations for NT grew. While easy to nitpick over flaws, some heralded the program as a grand achievement likely to alter the destinies of scores of computer and software companies. Those rivals most at risk—IBM, Sun Microsystems and Novell, to name the three biggest—girded themselves against the onslaught. First Boston, a securities firm that advised investors on the industry's outlook, captured the mood on February 15, 1993, calling NT the "most aggressive new piece of software ever."

Eight days later, Maritz called a rare all-team meeting. His timing was good. The team was wearing down; many needed reassurance that their project was indeed valuable to Microsoft and that it would end soon. The delays in finishing were hard to take; team members were starting to fear that the project might just keep slipping later and later into 1993. A sameness already had entered their lives, the builds blurring into one another, one bug becoming indistinguishable from the next. Facing NT each day reminded some people of the new movie *Groundhog Day*, whose central character kept reliving the same day over and over again—until he got it right.

Indeed, team members felt they had to get NT right before they could free themselves from this race. Maritz felt the team's frustration. At this stage software teams were often afflicted with a sort of cabin fever. After too much time cooped up with one another, it was hard to keep a common goal in plain view. Maritz reassured everyone that NT, despite the delays, still fitted nicely into Microsoft's plans. He discussed the project's latest schedule, then turned the meeting over to Cutler, who spoke of the need to halt work on new features. It was strangely difficult to make programmers stop adding things. As Cutler feared, every new delay prompted someone to ask whether there was time now to add his or her pet feature. To deflect these requests, managers had asked their more disciplined programmers to compile lists of features they wanted in the *next* version of NT.

Then Cutler issued an urgent plea. "We're almost there," he told the team. "We can't give up now." This was just what his wavering troops needed to hear. A handful had worked on the project for more than four years, with the bulk of the group putting in nearly three years' time. In an industry in which whole product lines sometimes turned over in eighteen months, three years was a long time to spend with the same project. The temptation to quit was growing, especially since some people on the team would have to find jobs elsewhere in Microsoft or, at the very least, new roles on the team following the completion of NT. Cutler was fighting a rearguard action against the specter of defections. As Patrick Haluptzok put it: "Dave made it clear that he wants everybody to finish what they started on NT. If you drop out now, you're basically shitting on everyone else."

Cutler aimed to keep the team intent on finishing, not thinking about the future. As usual, he made his point through his own actions. The very next day, he seized a chance to remind people of the importance of fixing bugs. It started with an all-hands memo from Jonathan Manheim. His group, which usually tested applications running on NT, had the job of porting to NT a program called WinChat, which was part of Microsoft's Windows for Workgroups product. WinChat was a variant on electronic mail; it allowed two or more people to type messages back and forth as if they spoke on the telephone. These "interactive" conversations were quite popular and illustrated the benefits of a computer network. It was important to test WinChat because NT was supposed to incorporate all Windows networking features. In his memo, Manheim was informing the team that they could use WinChat if they wanted. While his group was testing WinChat, others using it might also turn up problems.

Manheim's announcement bothered Cutler. He felt WinChat would distract people from bug fixing. He didn't want it used. "This isn't a fun app. It is a waste of time," he wrote to Manheim. "VMS had this program 10 years ago. It was a waste of time then and it is a waste of time now. Anyone I see wasting their time with [WinChat] is apt to get some verbal abuse." Copies of the message went to five others on the team, including Dunie, Manheim's boss.

Cutler's mail sounded like a threat to Manheim, who thought Cutler had no right to rebuke him so harshly and publicly. Not when he was doing his job, not after all he'd been through. NT wasn't going to cost him his marriage, but a few months ago he imagined himself joining the ranks of the divorced. Now he and his wife Leigh felt closer than they had in a long time. She was still home with the kids and alone a lot, because of his long hours, but she accepted her situation. She even learned to use a PC for the first time. She'd taken a computer class and, after a few lessons, cracked open the world that so obsessed her husband. Each day their marriage seemed more likely to survive NT. And Manheim knew he would survive with or without the project.

He was in no mood to let Cutler's insult pass unchallenged. After thinking about his response for ten minutes, he nervously tapped out a message to Cutler. Using Winchat "is not a waste of time," Manheim wrote, his anger rising. "It's part of the product that will be used by the customers and if it's trash we'll get shit for it. [Win-

Chat] came in late and we need to get the testing on it to make sure it's of good quality, just like the rest of the system."

"If you really feel it's a waste of time, it shouldn't be in the product and I shouldn't be busting my balls as I have been over the last few weeks trying to get it to work. Come walk through my walls if you want to or piss on my feet or whatever it is you do, but your mail was very discouraging. I'm just trying to do my job."

Manheim zapped the message to Cutler, ran his hands through his hair, took a deep breath and sat still. He started to hum "Backstreets," an old Bruce Springsteen song he liked to hear when he felt low. He waited. Maybe he would clean out his desk, start calling friends around the company about a job on another project. He half expected Cutler to burst through his office wall and rip his shirt off in anger. Manheim went on fretting like that for a couple of hours, and then the little beep sounded, marking the arrival of an e-mail. It was from Cutler. Manheim broke into a broad smile. The message was as close to an apology as Cutler, who never really apologized, ever dished out:

Testing [WinChat] is fine if we have to ship it. In fact you are right, we must test it if we ship it. That doesn't change my opnion that it's an app that will waste people's time. Yes, this is something that got added at the end that shouldn't have. I have direct experience with this kind of application at Digital. It is easy to get everyone to sit around and type at each other rather than fixing the bugs they should be fixing. If I had my way we would not ship this app. But then we wouldn't be compatible with Win 3.1 and we have to do that.

I know you are doing your job and you shouldn't feel discouraged. I just don't want to see everyone playing with the app rather than fixing bugs.

Fixing bugs. It was nearly all Cutler thought about now. Whatever failing prompted Cutler to mistreat people, his capacity for blocking out the ordinary distractions of life was his road to excellence. People rarely achieved greatness because they were too blinded by daily routine even to try anything extraordinary. For Cutler mediocrity was a failure of will, not talent. Now he willed that everyone on the team see one thing and only that. Bugs.

Bugs were the backdrop of the code writer's life. A comma in the wrong place. An "if" where there should be a "then." An erroneous call from one piece of the program to another. Each could instantly cause a seizure, the collapse of a finely wrought abstraction into a puddle of ones and zeroes. Only human, software was born to fail. If not catastrophically, then aesthetically. Every software captain knew this. Still, the possibility of perfection tempted Cutler like the image of a pristine world where the king of code can tame a splendid creature.

Of course, Cutler's idealism was leavened by the feeling that code writing was a kind of death sentence. Talk of perfection was gallows humor.

10. SHOWSTOPPER

The mournful voice of blues singer Nina Simone drowned out conversation in the Build Lab:

> *I want a little sugar in my bowl.*
> *I want a little sweetness down in my soul.*
> *I could stand some loving, Oh so bad.*
> *I feel so funny, I feel so sad.*

Cutler swung out of his swivel chair and strode over to the compact disc player. "What the hell is this?" he asked Kyle Shannon.

"I guess Simone is too sophisticated for Dave," Shannon thought. "Struck out again." He'd been trying for weeks to find music Cutler liked. Admittedly, it was too much to expect him to enjoy recorded bird songs, a Shannon favorite. And then there was Shannon's habit of playing a song over and over. A few days earlier, the builders had listened to Illinois Jacquet's big band play the swinging song "Tickle Toes" for hours. "We kept it on repeat until people went nuts," Shannon said. A programmer visiting the lab finally yanked the disc from the player and tossed it against the wall.

Cutler had never tried *that*, but he plainly disliked the Build Lab's music. He'd listened to plenty, too. It was late February 1993, and scores of bug fixes flowed into the Build Lab daily. In less than two weeks, the team would ship the final beta version of NT to thousands of customers. Following another six weeks of testing, the team would finish NT in early May and the project would end. Shannon could hardly contain himself. After so many hours under the fluorescent lights of the white-walled lab, the idea of a vacation, somewhere, anywhere, excited him.

Cutler camped in the Build Lab now, scrutinizing the check-ins, so Shannon wanted him to be comfortable. After further musical experiments, he finally hit on a sound that pleased Cutler. It was a raucous album by the rock group Journey. One morning Shannon slapped on Journey, and heavy metal sounds filled the lab. Cutler started bobbing his head, humming to the cacophony. Shannon smiled. Nodding gratefully, Cutler promised to share with the builders a couple of his own favorite albums.

He didn't have any favorite albums, but he saw a chance to relieve tension. That night he asked his companion, Deborah Girdler, to visit a CD store and buy something "really bad." She returned with two discs: Jim Nabors (star of the 1960s TV series *Gomer Pyle, U.S.M.C.*) singing gospel tunes and the fantasy characters Alvin and the Chipmunks singing children's songs. Perfect, Cutler thought.

The next day Cutler treated the builders to Nabors singing "In the Sweet Bye and Bye," "Onward Christian Soldiers" and other hymns. When Cutler sang along, everyone cringed; it was hard to tell which was more loathesome—Nabors gone gospel or Cutler gone musical. No one cheered when Cutler asked to hear the Nabors disc over and over again, day after day.

Before long Shannon and the builders regretted ever awakening Cutler's musicality. They finally hid the Nabors disc on the floor under a desk. When Cutler asked for it, Shannon invariably said, "It's in my car." Cutler, who caught the lie, laughed and laughed.

Cutler's bond with the builders sent a strong message. It endowed the builders with a cachet extending beyond the team's borders. Outsiders, who thought of Cutler as a brutal man, marveled that the builders could survive close encounters with him. Much of the credit for the sunny relations between Cutler and the builders belonged to Arden White, who had taken over stewardship of the lab from Mitch Duncan six months before. White was tight-lipped

and cautious, but his dark, narrow eyes betrayed a taste for mischief. A Midwesterner, White had studied computing at Southern
Illinois University, run the school's computer lab and then joined
Microsoft as an NT tester. In August 1992, he had agreed to manage
the Build Lab.

Under White's stewardship the lab gained crispness and organization. (Security, for instance, was so lax that on first arrival White
learned the combination to the lab's electronic door lock while over-
hearing the conversation of two code writers walking ahead of him in
the hall.) Tighter, brighter management was essential now that the
frequency of builds had greatly increased. Ever since New Year's,
White's group turned out on average a build a day, seven days a week.
Changes in each build usually were limited to bug fixes. Check-ins
now assumed a ritualized pattern. A code writer, having fixed a bug
and tested the replacement code, personally visited the Build Lab
and, if the builders were indeed accepting changes, wrote a quick
summary of the fix on a white board next to the lab's main door.

New builds arrived in the morning now; one of White's first actions was to shift the release from late afternoon. The old way was
hell for testers, who felt compelled to launch their tests before leaving for the night. When the build ran late, as it often did, it was
evening before testers sank their teeth into fresh code. Cutler resisted building in the morning, fearing that he'd come in one day and
find a build to be unusable. White personally vouchsafed that this
would not happen. It almost never did.

White understood that the Build Lab was more than a servant. It
was "the first line of testing for each build." As a former tester, he realized the value of presenting code writers with what he called "re-
produceable cases." Often bug hunters spent hours simply aligning
their equipment to create the exact conditions under which a certain bug appeared. A tester could win big points by simply recording precisely the conditions in force when he exposed a bug in the
first place. The sheer size of the build imposed a similar need for
exactness in building itself. Shannon recalled his early days building
NT from a single file of code. Now a half dozen builders wrestled
with more than forty thousand files, which contained millions of
lines of code. Creating NT from this raw material "is sort of like

making maple syrup," White explained. "The sap in the tree is pretty thin. You do a lot of boiling, so it can take several gallons of sap," which he likened to the source files, "to get a little of the thick syrup" of the operating program itself. An entire build took nineteen hours; through a combination of improvements, White hoped to shave seven hours from the process.

At first the weight of responsibility almost crushed White. When he worked as a tester, he had been so anxious that he suffered from chest pains. After joining the Build Lab, the chest pains stopped but his stomach erupted. Rolaids was the only thing that helped. The switch to the Build Lab heightened his anxiety. He felt overwhelmed during his first six months. He couldn't relax. He worked long hours; a lot of a builder's day was spent waiting and watching. The builders coped by juggling (a favorite activity of White's), tossing about a basketball or squeezing on a hand exerciser (a Shannon trademark). Even with these distractions, building NT became hypnotic. At times White felt "like a deer looking into a bright light." Even away from work, he seemed burdened. While swimming, he felt his muscles seize when something reminded him of the Build Lab. At home his wife was pregnant with their first child, and they were about to move into a new house, but it was hard to think ahead. He was just glad that the baby was due in July. "We're going to ship NT, then ship the baby," he said, smiling. "It's the perfect thing."

But White wondered how he'd survive from here to there. He constantly felt behind. Shannon told him some things could wait ("Mañana, mañana," he said). White knew this was just an empty cliché. The urgency, of course, partly stemmed from Cutler's habit of taking over the Build Lab. The first time White walked through the door and saw Cutler comfortably seated in the lab, he called out to Shannon, "Hey, what's *he* doing here?" Cutler swung his eyes from the screen, looked at White and said ominously, "This is just another room in my house." White was speechless.

White won Cutler's respect fitfully. In casual conversation he noted that he once wrote six thousand lines of code for a compiler class at Purdue. "That was a group project, right?" Cutler piped in.

"No, that was me alone," White said.

"Man, we've got the wrong guys writing compilers," Cutler said.

The builders' enthusiasm also reflected well on White. He lifted morale by letting them know "I was willing to do any of their jobs because what they did was important." He spent so much time in the lab that he never unpacked the boxes in his office or hung his framed pictures on the wall. He also solved an annoying problem concerning updated versions of NT shared with Digital and other computer makers who planned to outfit machines with the operating program. Certain tools, essential to the build but purchased from other companies, had to be removed before the team released a snapshot of NT to the hardware companies. Microsoft had the right to use these tools only internally. It took the builders ten days, however, to prepare the hardware build without them. White reduced the amount of time by two-thirds.

His evident accomplishments won White praise. At the daily 9:00 a.m. meeting, which brought together about two dozen of the team's managers in Room 2103, he drew encouraging looks by informing everyone of the build's current condition. The state of the build, which reflected the quality of the latest bug fixes, often dictated the mood of the meeting. White obsessively monitored the build and gave off a trace of that noxious quality that makes children call certain classmates teacher's pets. But he muddied his good-boy image by tweaking Cutler, who each morning sat in the same chair at the head of a long rectangular table. No one else cared where they sat, but Cutler plainly wished to occupy the power position in the room. Since this table had only one head (the other end was occupied by a big TV), Cutler invariably went to this spot. One day he found White in his chair and said, "You're sitting in my fucking chair."

"No, no," White answered. "Your fucking chair is in the Build Lab. This chair is mine."

Cutler was ready the next time White pulled his chair trick. He pulled up alongside White in a chair and pushed him aside. White, who felt Cutler enjoyed intimidating people with his gruff demeanor, decided against a game of bumper chairs. He retreated.

The 9:00 a.m. meeting was not just an occasion for ego strutting and pranks. It was the pulse of the project. At the meeting, stress results were reviewed and decisions were made about which bugs to fix. The latter was a crucial decision as the team raced toward the second beta, earmarked for 15,000 customers. The risk of introducing errors into tested code meant it wasn't prudent to fix *every* bug; neither was it possible to muster enough people to do so. This forced managers to debate the importance of any bug that *seemed* nettlesome. These debates had spawned a taxonomy of bugs. Showstoppers were the worst; they stopped the show, meaning that they forced the delay in a release. "Priority one" bugs were the next worst in severity; generally, a sample version of NT contained hundreds of these bugs. "Priority two" bugs were even less important and sometimes numbered in the thousands.

Unfortunately, the significance of a bug wasn't always clear-cut. Obviously, a bug that crashed NT required fixing. But most showstopper and priority one bugs were more subtle in their maliciousness. A certain Windows application appeared flawless on screen, yet carried an imperfection discernible only in printing: The space between the lines was slightly different when it ran on NT as opposed to DOS (this resulted in the text on a page breaking at a different point). This space was supposed to be identical whether the Windows application ran on DOS or NT. Further complicating things, NT supported hundreds of different printers from dozens of manufacturers; this flaw might surface on only a few of the printers or even just one. Was it worth mucking about in NT, at the risk of introducing an unrelated error, simply to fix a cosmetic flaw?

Or as Mark Lucovsky, with his gift for uttering blunt truths, observed: "Is it a problem we fix? Is it a problem we postpone? Is it a problem we work around?"

Such questions could be considered at length, drawing the opinions of a programmer, a tester and maybe a few managers. At the time NT contained hundreds of bugs that were intriguing enough to provoke heated discussions. Lucovsky, who was the team's Rush Limbaugh when it came to making vicious cracks, called those managers "old ladies" when they neurotically weighed the classification of a certain bug. Lucovsky argued that some decisions were better left to the line people because the "old ladies" were ignorant of the specific circumstances surrounding a bug.

The daily meetings were overrated, a ritual aimed as much at calming the frayed nerves of the team's leaders as anything else. More important in some ways was the dog-food diet, imposed by Cutler two years before. While distasteful, this forced code writers to contain the bug problem by fixing many bugs as they went along; the team had slain an astounding thirty thousand bugs over the past year alone. Only through such effort had the bug problem been kept in hand. Cutler's leadership in fighting bugs was perhaps his signal contribution to the project. Most of his technical ideas were borrowed, either from his own past efforts or from others. Indeed, he seemed hostile to innovations at times precisely because their unfamiliarity bred errors. Yet he understood a truth about gigantic programs that no one else fully appreciated: The potential for disaster meant that code writers must approach their jobs with a belief that any lapse could irreparably harm them, if not now then someday. This mental toughness was appropriate. Bug fighting was a fearsome activity. While performance improvements were surgical strikes, delivered from afar, fixing bugs resembled bloody hand-to-hand combat.

Bugs were inevitable; they were born of flaws harbored by every human being. To avoid bugs altogether, "one must perform perfectly," and people never did. On the "woes of the craft" of code writing, computer scientist Frederick Brooks has written: "If one character, one pause, of the incantation is not strictly in proper form, the magic doesn't work. Human beings are not accustomed to being perfect, and few areas of human activity demand it. Adjustment to the requirement for perfection is, I think, the most difficult part of learning to program."

The total bug count was closely watched by Cutler and his lieutenants in the same way casualty figures are studied in war. "Every morning we look at the bug count," said David Thompson, the networking leader. "If the count increases for too long, we are doomed." Thompson wasn't exaggerating for effect. Even seasoned code writers could not dismiss the possibility of being trapped in something akin to an infinite loop, wherein fixes spawned their own bugs. It had happened to others. The history of software was littered with projects, large and small, that had been abandoned in disgust, destroying careers. As a result, hard-boiled technical leaders such as Thompson fell to speaking about bugs in hushed, quasi-religious tones. His was the language of humility and of a recognition that this opponent was an elemental force best met on its own terms. Bugs were the most noxious element of any large program, Thompson insisted, because "they are *the* piece of the problem that is largely invisible. You don't know how many bugs you'll have."

Or when to declare a program good enough. On February 28, the day planned for the beta 2 release, the team was still saddled with forty-five showstoppers. That was too many to warrant a release; even though each one of the bugs might surface only once in a long while, taken together they represented a real hazard. The team took a week to reduce the showstoppers to twelve, then another four days to reach zero, which was the requirement in order to release beta 2. By then it was Sunday, March 7. That night, with the beta set to ship to Sony for duplication in the morning, a tester discovered an apparent showstopper. He sent an e-mail to his boss about the problem, and the message languished until 2:00 a.m. Monday morning. When the boss read it, he immediately called the tester, who woke up the person who wrote the code in the first place. Working through the night, they finally concluded that the glitch was linked to a flaw in the tester's PC.

In another part of Building Two, Jonathan Manheim went through the same drill with a few other testers. He wanted to know why WordPerfect's newest Windows word processor would not print. Printing poorly was bad; not printing at all was terrible. This was a showstopper. Manheim spent all night in his office searching for a fix. When the 9:00 a.m. meeting occurred the next morning, he still had no fix.

But enough was enough. Cutler and Dunie agreed to ship beta 2, flaws and all.

With the March 8, 1993 release of beta 2, the team was on target for a final release of NT on May 10. But in the ensuing weeks, the number of showstopper and priority one bugs rose sharply. Within six days, 263 such bugs surfaced. By April 9 the number of serious bugs rose to a worrisome 448. Cutler and Dunie decided to issue an updated beta to a select group of one hundred customers whose use of NT would augment the team's own tests. "The beta test was a key yardstick of system quality," Dunie said. "Given the large number of changes since the April beta, it was clear that we need another beta to verify quality."

Three days later, on April 12, the team shifted to a period of controlled check-ins, which generally made it possible for the team to drastically knock down the bug count. The builders reinforced the need for caution by imposing a five-dollar "fine" on any programmer who submitted a bad fix.

"Starting today we are only taking showstopper bug fixes, so the build group has erased all fixes that were on the white board," Shannon declared in a memo describing the new procedures. "If you have a bug fix that has been approved, please come down to the lab and write it on the board. How do you get a bug fix approved? Simple, talk to your lead." Shannon closed with a reminder: "We (the build group) will do our best to take the fixes as fast as you can check them in. Remember check-ins that don't compile, or cause the system not to boot will cost us all valuable time (and you $5)."

Over the next ten days, the team fixed every showstopper bug on its way to the beta update. But 361 priority one bugs remained, along with a whopping two thousand less important glitches. On April 23 Cutler killed the hope of the project coming to a swift end. Calling the level of bugs "bad news," he informed the team:

> We all want to ship a solid system with zero [priority one] bugs. We all also know that it takes time to fix all the bugs and we can't do that by May 10th. So we have decided to give ourselves some additional time to fix bugs and further stabilize [NT]. Our target for manufacturing is now June 7th.
>
> I want to meet this date and I know that you all do too. It is going to require another hard effort on everyone's part.

Separately he wrote the team: "This is the best system we have produced to date, however we can't afford to let up on our drive to the final release."

Cutler sought to combat the morale-killing effect of his announcement to extend the target date by repeating an exuberant slogan he'd adopted in recent months. "Remember, these are the good, ole days," he declared. "It may not seem like it now, but you will look back on this someday and marvel at what we accomplished. I know we can do it, so let's do it."

After reading Cutler's memo, Shannon cracked: "If these are the good old days, we're in big trouble."

Caron agreed. She couldn't imagine ever feeling nostalgic about these days. She was having trouble sleeping. And skipping her karate classes. All because of bugs. The push was on for each person on the team to reach "zero bugs," meaning no showstoppers or priority ones in their code. Cutler decided to give blue polo shirts, with the words Zero Bug Club stitched into the fabric, to those who made it. Cutler or a lieutenant passed out the garments to deserving code writers each Friday afternoon, when the team gathered in the lobby for beer and chips. The shirts stood as a badge of distinction; those who wore them were an elite; their celebrity was meant not only to prod people into correcting their lingering coding errors but to shame the laggards too.

Bugs upset Caron; they were a reproach. Her code had too many flaws. Or was she flawed? Caron and her ten thousand lines of code had merged into one, or so it seemed.

A quiet, hard worker, Caron had a flair for fixing bugs creatively. Though a careful programmer, her pieces of NT, the user profile and program manager, cooperated with so many other pieces of NT that unanticipated errors were relatively large. In her group of eight code writers, she had the most bugs, entering the month of May with a dozen. A few in the group already had their shirts; they wanted to help, but fixing other people's bugs was difficult. "I didn't know her code well enough to help her," said Caron's closest friend on the team. Another colleague generously devoted a weekend to fixing one of her bugs, only to discover later that the fix wasn't good. Caron solved the problem in an hour.

It was routine for a code writer to fix his or her own bugs. Testers sometimes cobbled together a fix, but fixes flowed most smoothly when they came from the code's creator. "When you build the framework yourself, you have a better idea of the assumptions," one programmer explained. "As an outsider, sure you can read the code comments, but you have no idea what the person was uneasy about. A fix that should take ten seconds takes a half a day."

So Caron wrestled with her bugs alone. One teammate, who knew she had the most bugs in the group, greeted her each morning with the taunt, "How many bugs you have left?" His needling hurt. She despised this guy but contained her emotions. When teased, she dryly asked the guy about a flaw in his code.

It wasn't as if Caron were a patsy. Rather, she was seen as a woman warrior, her reputation cemented following a run-in with Cutler a few weeks before. Caron rarely spoke with Cutler and found his tough-guy antics more campy than menacing. "He strikes me as a big teddy bear," she said. Hers was an idiosyncratic reading of Cutler, but it had the benefit of freeing her from feelings of anxiety when she faced him. One Saturday evening Cutler sat in the Build Lab, and Caron entered to deliver a bug fix. Cutler promptly chided her for not supplying it earlier in the day, so that it could be subjected to stress testing sooner. He asked her what possibly could have delayed her? "I was at karate class kicking butt," she shot back. Startled, Cutler replied weakly, "Okay." When news of the showdown spread, colleagues dubbed Caron "Karate Girl."

Still the bugs kept hitting Caron. Maybe a phone call or a visit from Esti Mintz, the tester assigned to her code. Or maybe an e-mail, which was cleaner. Astonishment and curiosity at the arrival of a new bug slowly gave way to irritation and befuddlement as Caron realized that "I can't rest until a bug is fixed." Sometimes she could dispatch a bug within a day. Such was the case on May 3, when Mintz handed her a priority one in the morning. The bug afflicted her program manager; instead of the icon for a DOS application appearing in a small window, it consumed the whole screen. Within a half hour Caron realized her mistake; through the misplacement of a few words she had unwittingly told her program manager to do the wrong thing. By one in the afternoon, she was confident enough to submit the fix to the builders.

The fixes flowed. A week later Caron stood on the threshold of "zero bugs." On Sunday, May 9, she had cleared two bugs, leaving one remaining—a killer that had hung around for weeks—bug number 569. It arose when certain databases were installed on NT. Normally

Caron's code created a separate group for new programs. But her code failed to do so with these databases, instead acting as if a new group already existed. As she fell asleep that night she imagined herself fixing this bug, then triumphantly strutting around the halls of Building Two wearing the "zero bug" T-shirt. Just one more fix.

She awoke the next morning at her usual time, 5:30 a.m., and quickly donned her exercise outfit: purple tights, a tank top, a green headband and running shoes. She tied back her hair, then stuffed a set of clothes in a white-and-blue striped denim bag. At ten minutes to six, she got into her Miata, top up, and drove a few miles on Highway 520, which passes Microsoft's campus. At the 51st Street exit, she turned off for the Pro Club, the company's official health club. Her workout was brisk. She attended an exercise class with three dozen others. Two women set the pace. Every five minutes, Caron switched activities: treadmill, stationary bike, rowing machine, Stairmaster, dumbbells. The class ended at 7:15. Another fifteen minutes for a shower, then the quick drive to Building Two.

Her heart raced as she climbed up the steep stairway to the second floor, where she had an office in Room 2032. She opened her door, switched on the light, flicked on her Compaq 486 PC and scanned her electronic mail. She always read her mail before launching into work. Messages piled up overnight; sometimes forty or fifty pieces of mail awaited her in the morning. It wasn't always easy to absorb this blizzard of information, but today she was searching for something specific. Oops, there it was. Two messages from Esti. She threw back her head as she read Esti's notes. Her stomach tightened. Two new bugs. The day's hope of qualifying for a T-shirt vanished.

Much of May was like that: persistent bugs. She'd fix one and another would appear. On May 23, she had thirteen; then she whittled the bugs down to five by May 26. That day she watched a broadcast feed of Gates delivering a benediction over NT. Before a rapt crowd, he promised the program would arrive in stores within sixty days.

Sixty days! The number stopped Caron. That meant late July. We're supposed to be done by June 7, she thought. But Gates had just told the world to expect NT a month later, which meant the team would massage the program until at least the middle of July.

She staggered back to her office and looked blankly at her computer. There goes another summer, she told herself.

Two days later, Cutler put a depressing coda on the revelation from Gates. In a memo entitled "Taking Stock," Cutler confessed: "I wish I could tell you exactly the day when we are going to ship, but I can't. We just have to keep working to improve the quality of the system. . . . When the system meets the ship criteria we will ship it and feel proud that we held it out until it was ready."

And so Caron pushed on. For the next two weeks she struggled with a half dozen bugs on any given day, then on June 9 wiped out all but one. The next day, a Thursday, she killed the last bug. She'd made it. She danced in the hall, raising her arms, shaking her behind. She called everyone she knew. "Zero bugs!" she crowed.

At the beer bash the next day, Leif Pederson, who oversaw Caron's group, stood on the receptionist's desk in the lobby of Building Two and held up a bug-club shirt. Somebody in the crowd whistled. Pederson shouted, "Johanne," and she moved toward him. Smiling, he tossed her a shirt. A cheer went up from the packed lobby. She grabbed the shirt and raised it above her head. Standing before her colleagues, she shouted, "At last!" It was all she could muster. Looking down, her hair covering her eyes, she suddenly tugged at her loose scruffy clothes. "Oh my God," she thought, "I can't believe what I'm wearing!"

Bugs were not the only uncertainty facing the team. Compatibility remained a big hurdle. Ever since the project was redefined nearly three years before, through the marriage of Cutler's dream with the market necessity of Windows, Cutler had held his breath, hoping that his team could enable NT to run DOS and Windows programs. Much of the responsibility for compatibility fell to Matthew Felton, the son of the influential British software pioneer and one of the team's technical leaders. If Cutler imbued NT with a soul, Felton and his fellow Windows programmers gave the operating system a reason to live. Indeed, Windows on NT was the linchpin of Gates's grand strategy for Microsoft. The ability to carry into the future thousands of applications from the past placed NT in a class of its own in the brief history of personal computing. But the Windows personality enabled NT to keep one foot in the past. This was the great departure. Computer makers previously had forced customers to adopt an abandon-ship attitude to their past applications software. To achieve a higher level of performance, customers were asked to leave everything behind (they could still use their old software if they were willing to essentially sacrifice the innovations in their new ship). Microsoft itself had essentially made this pitch when it initially introduced OS/2 in 1987. The failure of OS/2 left a deep impression on Gates; it gave him a better sense of the shock of the new, of just how much innovation the mass of PC owners could accept at once. Customers wanted to carry the past into the future, so NT must support old applications.

Achieving this support was a matter of *when*, not *if*. The notion of a general model, standing between NT and the world of Windows programs, was conceptually sound; indeed, it was the only logical way to accomplish the goal. Besides, NT was designed to take advantage of just such a general model. But tests of the model exposed weaknesses and strained relations between Felton's code writers and the testers assigned to them.

The compatibility testers were led by Jeff Brown, a short, bearded twenty-nine-year-old. Brown was a graduate of Brigham Young University, where he majored in political science. While in college he bought a personal computer, IBM's ill-fated PC Junior. On graduating he took a job with an insurance underwriter in Seattle, helping to oversee the company's computer system. Then in 1987, he responded to an advertisement placed by Microsoft inviting applications from computer enthusiasts who spoke a foreign language (he was fluent in German). Microsoft hired Brown as a contract employee, testing foreign-language versions of Microsoft's own Windows applications. Six months later he became a full-time worker. In June 1991 he switched to NT from the last remnants of the OS/2 project, where he worked on getting Windows programs to run on OS/2.

Rough-edged and workmanlike, Brown was the polar opposite of the smooth, sophisticated Felton. After being asked to test Felton's compatibility code, Brown went three months without meeting Felton. The separation might have been a blessing. At this time "the developers [of code] thought the testers were idiots, and the testers thought the developers were assholes," said one neutral party. "This wasn't a recipe for making rapid progress."

The conflict stemmed from the differing priorities of the two sides. Intent on refining their general model, programmers didn't want to distract themselves by fixing bugs. Meanwhile, testers wanted to test. This was a pointless activity when they saw the same bugs week after week. "It was frustrating," Brown said. "It's hard to continue to motivate people when they're seeing the same problems over and over again. And all the while, the bug backlog continues to grow." To relax, Brown took up Japanese swordsmanship as a hobby. Once a week he donned body armor, lifted a bamboo sword and began hacking at an opponent. It wasn't artful, "but at least I could take out my frustrations."

Relations between testers and code writers remained stiff until David Weld broke the logjam. Astute about the politics of organizations, Weld, the program manager, assembled the two groups in the same room for the first time. He appealed to them to think as a unit. He followed up his speech by regularly bringing testers and code writers together for freewheeling discussions. It helped. Before long the testers felt part of the family, and the code writers "were slaves to the bugs," as one put it.

Bob Day then made a breakthrough that dispelled the remaining doubts about the value of testers to Felton's group. Day had found a way around a problem that threatened to stall progress toward compatibility. Since Felton's compatibility model was not yet good enough to keep many Windows applications running for very long, how could the general model be tested in order to expose its specific shortcomings and thus find ways to improve it? To solve this problem, Day invented a software recorder that made a copy of every "call" made by a Windows application to the underlying operating system. The record of the calls made by, say, Microsoft's Excel spreadsheet, gave a specific target to a code writer. To prove its mettle, Felton's model simply had to duplicate the recording of the call.

To understand how Day's recorder worked, consider "MoveWindow," one of about nine hundred calls made by a Windows application. This particular call directs the movement of a window from one place on the computer screen to another (the window can contain, say, a document or a picture or a collection of icons). To make this happen properly, the call is given certain mathematical values that represent the destination of the window and its width and height. It is these values, embedded in the structure of the call "MoveWindow," that Day's tool recorded.

The hardest part of recording calls, Day found, was recording them all. After two minutes of activity, Excel had made five hundred thousand distinct calls. These had to be grabbed in proper sequence and retained for study later on. Indeed, Day's recorder grabbed so many calls so quickly that his final hurdle was to find enough storage space in a PC. He finally licked that problem, too.

Even with Day's tool, Felton's group lagged behind the rest of the team. The version of NT released at the San Francisco conference in July 1992 lacked the compatibility feature. Soon afterward the group finished its general model, but "we were playing catch up," Weld said. The trouble was that Windows applications hewed to no strict rules. Often a popular program relied on idiosyncratic means to call DOS; NT's model must somehow reflect these idiosyncrasies. When the group had only about a dozen applications working, "we always had this vision that we'd trained NT to run these apps alone," Weld said. "Because they ran perfectly, but [an unfamiliar] app wouldn't run out of the box."

Weld helped to overcome this by asking scores of applications writers for information about the tricks they'd employed in their Windows programs. The responses showed a pattern. "While many of the apps had their own unique problems, they definitely shared commonalities," Day said.

In October 1992 Felton's group broke into the clear. The model was good enough that about thirty-five of a target pool of seventy popular Windows programs ran very well on NT. Emboldened by the improvements, Weld rushed out to buy a copy of the new Windows version of Quattro Pro, a popular spreadsheet from Borland. When Weld installed it on NT, Quattro Pro quickly crashed, but with one fix to the model the program ran fine. Weld felt this was a turning point. In March 1993, Felton expanded the target pool of applications to two hundred. The list split evenly between "tier one" (the most important) and "tier two"; taken together, the tiers covered the most familiar programs. By early May, 80 percent of these ran without a hitch. Now Felton approached the team's goal for compatibility: Of the one hundred tier one applications, 93 percent must receive an excellent rating, while 80 percent of the tier two applications must be excellent. (Felton gave his group a nudge toward its goals by deleting a few applications from the list after "people got fed up with seeing them" listed as nonperformers.)

At a 9:00 a.m. meeting about that time, Weld declared that his group would prove to be the "dark horse" of the project. Everyone had assumed compatibility would hold up the shipment of NT. Weld insisted otherwise. While Cutler still harbored doubts—he called compatibility "a bear"—he relaxed visibly on hearing Weld's prediction.

Weld's optimism arose from two sources. The general model was improving rapidly. Weld knew this because of the steady progress in the performance of the second tier; Felton's group was doing little to accommodate these applications. Even Brown's testers were only hammering on the first-tier programs; those in the second tier were assigned willy-nilly to members of the team. So any improvements in performance of the tier two programs were due to refinements in the model.

The second reason for optimism was actually nothing to cheer about. In order to ensure that certain popular applications ran flawlessly, Felton approved the practice of writing into NT itself code he termed a compatibility "switch," or "flag." Bluntly put, these were workarounds; small hacks designed to accommodate the odd behavior of an application. This seemed like cheating, but applications such as Pagemaker were so widely used that the team had no choice but to follow this course. The danger, of course, was that the number of compatibility flags would grow too large. But this seemed unlikely; the group had resorted to about a dozen flags so far. Felton concluded the worst was past. "We're coasting to the finish line now," he thought.

And so was the team. On June 9 customers received another build of NT with much-improved Windows compatibility. Felton's group had now exceeded its ship criteria. Bugs were way down too. A week after the release, time enough for customers to report glitches, priority one bugs numbered less than 150, with showstoppers no more than one-third of the total.

On June 21 Cutler declared "the beginning of the final countdown for the release of NT." The journey was nearly over. "Things are looking better every day," he wrote.

It looked as if the project would end with a whimper. Cutler chose July 14 as the target date for release of the "golden master," the final version of NT. That was little more than three weeks away. "We can't afford to let down now in the final stretch," he reminded the team. "I can almost taste the release. I hope you can too."

Few issues remained. They attracted a frenzy of attention as many people found themselves relatively idle for the first time in years. Said one manager, "As the size and number of real issues shrank, on a given day there might be three important issues, and we would flock to them like vultures."

The daily 9:00 a.m. meeting now seemed like an example of managerial overkill. Steve Wood, for instance, found contemptible the lengthy debates over which bugs to fix. Invariably the decision was to fix virtually all of them. To Wood the meeting was a primer on "how to waste people's time. Most people in the room don't have a clue about whether to take this fix or not."

Still, the managers were entitled to ruminate. It seemed luxurious to lavish time on a small number of problems after feeling overwhelmed for so long. Things finally seemed in hand. Vacations were the surest sign of this. Microsoft paid for at least two weeks' vacation a year for its employees. The previous year Cutler and Dunie had made people cancel or postpone vacations. In May 1993, Cutler and Dunie, realizing NT would not ship until at least midsummer, decided not to forbid vacations. With less and less to do, some people vanished for a spell. Cutler led the way. On Monday July 5, he and about a dozen code writers returned to the race car school in Monterey, California. "A lot of people thought it was a good sign when Dave went away," said one teammate who stayed behind. "His leaving was like a vote of confidence." For three days he drove Mitsubishi Formula One cars, reaching speeds of nearly 150 miles per hour.

For code writers the final days saw an easy truce between work and play. They were discouraged from tampering with NT except to fix showstoppers, so there was little to do. But they stuck close to their offices, on call if needed. While they waited for action, most code writers assembled their ideas for future improvements and fixes to NT that were too risky or time-consuming to make now. These changes would be packaged together in the next major release of NT—dubbed Daytona—due out in the fall of 1994.

The penalty for impetuous fixes was grievous. One fix introduced an error that broke the build on forty machines. Cutler risked a similar disaster by changing the Mips version of NT in order to improve its performance; the breach of procedure so angered Lucovsky that he publicly chewed out his boss for setting a bad example. The only justifiable reason to alter NT at this stage, Lucovsky insisted, was to fix a showstopper. Such requests arose infrequently, but managers expected code writers to respond ferociously.

After getting her "zero bug" shirt, Caron went three days without a bug, then spent two days fixing one bug, then went five more days without a bug and then faced two bugs in one day. Tom Miller spent a day without making a fix on his file system, went home and worked an evening repairing the head in his boat. As he showered before bed, a tester summoned him back to the office to fix a bug. Miller worked through the night in order to make the fix, even though he had nothing on his plate for the rest of the week.

The winding down of the project gave some code writers a chance to indulge in sentimentality. The most notable example had an accidental birth. One day in June a Venetian-blind cord from the office of Bill McJohn, a programmer in Perazzoli's base group, fell into the hallway, making a circle on the carpeted floor. Then four pennies appeared inside the circle. More coins were added, and a rose and some gambling chips and then a Microsoft visitor's pass, which was an official-looking badge that snapped onto clothing. The badge caught McJohn's eye, and he resolved not to move the cord. He also added to the mosaic a candy wrapper and then a photograph of Cutler. It was a blowup of a small picture, so Cutler's face was fuzzy, making him look unearthly. Next, two candles appeared, stationed just outside the border of the Venetian-blind cord. Even unlit, the candles lent solemnity to the hodgepodge of trinkets surrounding Cutler's image.

No one moved a thing for weeks. Cutler walked by McJohn's office a few times a day yet never asked McJohn about it or disturbed the layout himself. Then one day he walked along the hall with Helen Custer, the technical writer who had followed him from Digital nearly five years before. As if seeing his picture surrounded by knickknacks for the first time, Cutler stopped and exclaimed, "What the hell is that supposed to be?"

"I think it's an altar to you, Dave," Custer said.

Cutler grunted and walked away.

The testers were too busy to build altars to real or imagined gods. This was their time to shine, and they were edgy. A lot still could go wrong. After all, the entire purpose of withholding NT from shipment now was to ferret out bugs. It was the fate of a tester never to really know what had been overlooked. More testing was the only logical antidote against worry. The more testing, the better.

The builders, meanwhile, were swamped. Building a test version of NT every day, sometimes twice a day, wore everyone down. There was hardly time to do anything else. Arden White fell so far behind in reading the dozens of mail messages he received each day that he even brought a laptop running NT to the hospital with him when his pregnant wife went into labor. His baby was born in between snatches of mail.

Dunie rode the testers and the builders hard. He urged them to wring more bugs from the program, setting out a clear ship criteria of no showstopper bugs; stress results of more than 95 percent; the successful completion of "heavy stress" on a network of 128 personal computers connected by NT; and ninety-three of the top one hundred DOS-Windows programs rated excellent, with the remaining seven ranked either good or acceptable.

On July 1 Dunie also gave another build (dubbed "a release candidate") to fifty customers. He asked every senior tester to adopt a few customers in order to stay in "close contact" with them. Although less than 5 percent of the bugs were found by customers, Dunie considered the problems uncovered to be significant because they "reflected the real world." Besides making bug reports, these elite customers were asked to vote on whether NT was ready for full release. The quick tally was an overwhelming yes. Still Dunie worried about how even the small number of showstopper fixes might affect NT. Due to the length of testing cycles in some areas, it could take two weeks to expose certain errors.

If a serious bug was found, Dunie expected test managers to react quickly. On Friday, July 9, Manheim began carrying a beeper. "I need to know immediately if you have found a showstopper. No exceptions," he told his testers.

Somasegar, one of the team's top testers and the one who had cut his teeth on NT's file system, didn't need a pager. Everyone knew where to find him; he left the office only a few hours at a snatch, usually during the middle of the night. In those final weeks he felt "like a sentry," always standing by. "If there's a problem, we can get on it right away."

His wife, Sandhya, was lonely without him. She had given birth to a daughter three months earlier and awaited the completion of NT. Somasegar had told her so often that the program was nearly done that she had stopped imagining the project's end. Her husband might be busy for another "month or two months or maybe forever," she fretted.

Having married Somasegar without ever visiting the United States, she was taken aback by how hard Americans worked and what this meant for a wife and family. She was twenty-four years old and might never live in India again. In her culture there was no tolerance for divorce. While feeling lost at times, she knew "we have to make this marriage work. We don't have an option." Her parents, who had arrived in February for a lengthy visit, were concerned about the amount of time their daughter spent alone. They were horrified by their son-in-law's hours; during their visit Somasegar had not even spent an entire evening with them or shown them around town. Sandhya's father joked that perhaps the only chance he'd get to really speak with Somasegar was when he called from the airport to say that he and his wife were leaving. Even after the birth of his child, Somasegar's work did not ease. He kept his normal pace. "A test guy should always have the same level of apprehension. Never get complacent," he said. This hardly seemed possible; he worked so hard that it was as if work met some craving he could not name. As July rolled on he still worked days, nights and weekends. He was away from home so much that he was a stranger to his infant child.

By July 9, 1993, stress results were sterling, an average of 95 percent for nearly two weeks. Showstoppers now numbered in the teens. Three days later about eighty customers received a second "release candidate" of NT. Using the program intensively, they quickly reported a few new showstoppers. The appearance of fresh errors in the code, undiscovered until now, was enough for Cutler and Dunie to push back the release date by a week or so; since Gates had given the team until late July to deliver the program, they might as well use the time.

On Thursday, July 15, Cutler began the move to a final release, announcing that NT would soon enter "escrow," during which time the program would be tested but not altered. "Tomorrow, we are going to get much harder core about approving bugs as showstoppers," he told the team. "The only thing that is a showstopper is something that would cause us to pull back the final bits from manufacturing." From now on, even serious bugs that arose in "obscure" circumstances would not be fixed until after NT's final release.

At 5:00 p.m. on Friday, July 16, the 509th build of NT (and the 170th of 1993) was put into escrow, which was expected to last at least five days. "What this means is that we have the final bits for the release," Cutler declared,

> but we want to continue to test and run on the system until next Wednesday before passing the final judgment. When considering the importance of a bug, it must be [so important] that we will stop shipment of NT and "pull back" the bits. Thus bugs that only affect one configuration or only occur under an obscure scenario will not be considered. So if you are raising a bug that is priority two or below, just mark it as postponed. And please don't raise priority one bugs that you know won't be fixed. We are only looking for disasters at this point.

The disasters were few. The next week the team fixed just a handful of showstoppers, and the completion of NT seemed assured.

On the morning of July 23, Cutler convened the project's final 9:00 a.m. meeting. As he sat with the team's leaders, he thought bittersweetly about "the end of another set of good ole days." He felt let down at the close of a project. NT had been his chance "to achieve something without outsiders getting in the way." There "was nothing like the feeling of being on track, knowing the direction you're heading without question." He would miss terribly the feeling of "having a purpose and the freedom to get the job done without management meddling." For a time at least, he would live without this sense of clarity that his job gave him.

Cutler kept his feelings to himself, listening as the talk turned to those bugs that could be postponed. Dunie described a bug that he didn't think ranked as a showstopper. It was a quirk exposed when the newest version of Pagemaker, a popular publishing program made by Aldus, tried to print under NT. An Aldus tester, reviewing the ten-day-old release candidate, had just reported that Pagemaker crashed when it tried to print a four-page test document that had a mix of fonts and graphics. The document, it seemed, erroneously exhausted the printer's memory, consuming forty megabytes of memory, a whole file cabinet rather than the tiny fraction it was supposed to use. When separated into individual pages, however, the document printed flawlessly. Dunie concluded the team could postpone fixing this. Though he felt bad about "blowing off a bug," this bug didn't rate.

Then Dunie described a showstopper involving the same Pagemaker 5 application. The fonts displayed under NT weren't accurate. Dunie was concerned that the bug had surfaced so late. It made him wonder, a problem like this showing up after all the testing. Five hours before, a code writer had fixed a glitch in nearby code on his second attempt. A few testers were on hand to make sure the fix worked. It had.

Dunie's tale drew nervous nods from Cutler and the others in the room. They agreed that ignoring the printing bug was okay. Everyone wanted the show to go on. NT must ship now, though no one seemed terribly excited about it. The team's official celebration was Monday; they should at least wait until then to wax proud. There was still the unknown; it made one afraid. For months Cutler had steeled himself against the flaws in NT, saying they were inevitable and that he'd never really be happy until NT carried no bugs at all. This, of course, was tantamount to confessing to a permanent unhappiness, since NT would always have blemishes. The program had more lines of code (5.6 million) than a 3,500-page unabridged dictionary had words. NT could never be perfect, only good enough. The meeting ended without a flourish. Nearly five years in the making, NT was good enough.

Or was it?

Paul Maritz held his breath. Now chief of Microsoft's entire operating-systems business, which accounted for roughly half of Microsoft's sales, Maritz was among Gates's most trusted and influential advisers. His belief in the ascendancy of Windows had prompted a sea change in Cutler's project. Now Maritz had the last word on NT's readiness. He asked manufacturing not to touch NT at least until Monday, no matter what. Even if NT was delivered on Friday, the mass duplication and packaging of the program was not to begin for at least forty-eight hours. Maritz wanted to avoid a rush at the end, though he did not tell Cutler of his caution, lest he provoke him. "You're constantly afraid of doing something stupid at the last minute," he said. "So I set aside a buffer."

Forty-eight hours was a big delay for manufacturing. Over the next few weeks, Microsoft would distribute hundreds of thousands of copies of NT around North America; ideally the first batch would be ready within six days, in time for Wall Street analysts, meeting with Gates, to receive a shrink-wrapped package of NT. Each NT package came with twenty-odd floppy disks because the product was so large. Simply obtaining enough disks took much time.

But Maritz had good reason for waiting. "There is always the bug you fix the night before," he said. "So I was just waiting to find out what it would be."

Like a stubborn brush fire, Dunie's doubts about Pagemaker persisted. Even as the 9:00 a.m. meeting broke up, a tester from Aldus arrived at Building Two. He'd found a new problem with the release candidate. Pagemaker 5 wouldn't print large documents on NT. It was a variant of the previous night's memory glitch, related to fonts.

Mysteriously, the amount of memory consumed by the document ballooned when NT sent it to the printer. It was still possible to print the document, but it took a very long time. Meanwhile, there was no problem when Pagemaker 5 ran on DOS. Dunie played devil's advocate with the Aldus tester. Won't customers just accept a slow print job? The tester convinced Dunie otherwise. Dunie walked back to his office, thinking he faced a showstopper. On his way he ran into Maritz, who was coming to tell him that he'd just received a promotion. Dunie was too caught up in the showstopper to pay much attention. He described the bug to Maritz, who agreed it should be fixed if possible, regardless of the effect on the schedule. NT might ship with the flaw, they agreed. But if it did, Aldus would be at least impressed with Microsoft's attempt to fix the bug. Microsoft lately had come under great criticism that it unfairly withheld information from rival software makers about the condition of its operating system in order to boost sales of its own applications. In the Pagemaker showstopper, Maritz saw a chance to show concern for a rival. His generosity was leavened by self-interest, however. Pagemaker was designed for powerful PCs, the sort of machines that could exploit the power of NT. It was important that Pagemaker run well on NT.

Based on the previous night's experience, Dunie knew this bug would not go quietly. Gilman Wong, a specialist in fonts, had worked from 3:00 a.m. until dawn earlier that morning on what was obviously a related glitch. Wong had joined graphics in July of 1990, when the group was still called the Undead. It was his first job after gaining a master's degree in electrical engineering from the University of Washington. Wong was viewed as a strong coder; his skills were burnished by an appreciation for the minute visual differences between typefaces and sizes. Haluptzok, who had ended up managing the font effort after the shakeup in graphics a year before, said Wong had "calibrated eyesight."

Like many people in graphics, Wong was eccentric. His weakness was stuffed animals. He kept eight in his office, not counting his inflatable stegosaurus. His favorite was a rabbit he called "smoky bunny" because it had survived a fire in Wong's college lab. The bunny now had a pencil stuck through its head and a transistor for an earring.

Dunie sensed that the key to this showstopper was somewhere in Wong's quirky mind. But Wong was asleep at home now, so Dunie turned to David Snipp, the team's printer expert.

Snipp's availability was a happy circumstance, since he'd spent most of the previous night awake, too, and had actually supplied the Pagemaker fix that Dunie spoke about at the morning meeting. Snipp was exhausted, but no matter what, he always looked at the bright side of things. One of the few smokers on the team, he found himself forced to smoke outside, in front of the team's building. Rather than whine, Snipp saw smoking outdoors as a boon, since printer glitches were so common that often people formed a line outside his door. Snipp also was one of a handful of people on the team who spent their vacations programming. He owned a software company in England, whose chief product was a program that automatically controlled the lighting employed during rock concerts. As soon as NT shipped, Snipp planned to spend a month in London sorting out his company's activities.

About noon on Friday Snipp ruled out printer code as the culprit. Dunie was crestfallen. More than most people, he took failure hard. Colleagues scored Dunie for lacking imagination, but he was superb at resolving sticky matters. He kept track of details and had a way of tuning everything out except the issue at hand. In this crisis, he only asked himself, "Am I doing everything possible to fix this problem?" It bothered him that the Pagemaker fiasco could have been avoided. A tester in Jonathan Manheim's group should have exposed it weeks ago. To prevent just this sort of lapse, Manheim had wisely created a buddy system between testers and critical applications, of which Pagemaker was one. He'd also asked a tester to watchdog printer problems. It turned out that the same tester was responsible both for Pagemaker and printing. That was fine—until the tester quit.

It happened a month before. The tester walked into Manheim's office and told him, "I can't do this any more. How do I resign?" Manheim was stunned. Resign? "You can't do this to me," he pleaded. The guy insisted. He had to leave; he was finished at Microsoft. To be sure, this wasn't a complete shock to Manheim, just the last act in an unmistakable case of burnout. The tester recently had bought a Laundromat—a Laundromat!—as an investment. It came with three employees, thirty-five washers and an equal number of driers. The tester's brother-in-law managed the Laundromat, though less well than the tester wished. "Never have family work for you," he muttered one day in the hall. Then the tester started leaving the office at odd times, telling Manheim that he had an urgent meeting with Laundromat employees or a washer on the blink.

Manheim tried to convince the tester to set aside the Laundromat. "You're just reacting against your situation here," Manheim told him. But the stress of NT made the guy yearn for simplicity. The Laundromat was his emotional life raft; it was the one place now where he was king. No unwanted deadlines, no angry colleagues, no code to write or test.

Despite Manheim's pleading, the tester refused to stay until the end of the project. "I really can't code any more because of my emotional state," he said. In quitting, he walked away from company stock options worth $250,000. Manheim made the tester promise to spend a week training a replacement, but the transition was rough. Besides, at this late stage a substitute might be more liability than aid.

If that had been the end of it, Dunie might have howled over the Laundromat affair. But it got worse. Manheim himself wasn't there either. He was on the island of Hawaii. Dunie could thank himself for that; earlier in the year, he and Cutler agreed that people could take their vacations. Manheim had planned his vacation for late July, at a time when no one thought they'd still be working on NT. Leigh Manheim had bet him five dollars he would not miss the end of the project. She happily lost the bet. This very day she and her husband were lying on a beach. In a few hours, as the sun went down, they would reenact their wedding vows, barefoot in the sand.

Dunie now pinned his hopes on the graphics group. By Friday afternoon Wong was back, revived and aided by Michael Abrash, the group's lead. At 6:30 p.m., Haluptzok stumbled in with another graphics coder; thinking the project had ended, the two had water-skied all afternoon. Haluptzok had only dropped by to check his e-mail and call his wife, Chenoa, to tell her he was on his way home.

Wong was happy to have the reinforcements. His mind was fuzzy. He was also beginning to think that the glitch lay in memory, which wasn't his strong suit. Pagemaker was asking NT for memory, receiving it, then wrongly trashing it. Almost immediately Haluptzok hit on what looked like the answer. "This must be the bug!" Wong shouted. "Great!" Haluptzok started to fold the fix into the code. Wong thought about leaving, but Snipp told him to stick around. Good advice. A few minutes later Wong realized that his colleague had found a bug, but not *his* bug. He felt scared; it was as if he'd sat down for a big exam and suddenly realized that he'd studied the wrong book. No, it was worse than that. "You're about to ship a product after five years, and there's a last-minute bug and it had to be mine," he thought.

Fortunately, Wong wasn't on his own. He and the other graphics coders, joined by Snipp and Dunie, piled into Leif Pederson's first-floor office. It was a tight fit. The office was nine by twelve feet, with dull gray carpet, off-white walls and overhead fluorescent lighting. Pederson's desk faced the door, about four paces away. A window behind him exposed a parking lot, rimmed with trees. On one wall hung a large white board on which the code writers sketched out their ideas for each other with markers.

This evening Pederson was the highest-ranking programmer in Building Two. Cutler and most of the other senior code writers had gone to a beach party thrown by a teammate. Pederson was invited, but since he oversaw graphics he stayed at work. There actually wasn't much for him to do except cheer-lead and order pizza—then more pizza. When the food arrived, Abrash was going over graphics code line by line with the debugger. Snipp and Wong swapped possible solutions. As he watched people eat pizza, discussing the bug between mouthfuls, Dunie let a crooked smile break onto his face. "What a sweet way to finish the project," he thought.

It went on that way for hours. Haluptzok was so absorbed in the drama he wouldn't leave Pederson's office and too embarrassed to call Chenoa from there and explain his tardiness. For hours, meanwhile, she had called her husband's office so many times she'd lost count, never getting an answer. Her fury grew. Lying in bed, she tried reading a book given to her by Haluptzok, who was always trying to explain to her the inner workings of Microsoft. The book was a biography of Bill Gates. As she read, she worried about her husband. "Is he in a car wreck or at a movie with his buddies?" she wondered. She hated not knowing where he was and felt angry with him for not calling. But it would be horrible, she thought, "if he was dead in a car wreck and I'm sitting here in the bedroom mad at him."

In Pederson's office Snipp leaned over to Wong sometime after 10:00 p.m. In his Cockney accent, he laughingly suggested that Pagemaker might be miscalculating the font size, thus explaining why it grabbed so much memory (because it acted as if the font were much bigger than it should be). Wong felt a light go on in his mind. He let out a whoop. Snipp was half right. There were two bugs, one in graphics, which in turn exposed the Pagemaker bug.

Wong took ten minutes to fix the graphics bug, which occurred because the existing code was reserving too little memory in order to store the fonts needed for printing. By reserving the proper amount of memory, four lines of code corrected the error:

```
prfnt->cache.pjAuxCacheMem =
(PBYTE)PVALLOCMEM(cjMaxBitmap + sizeof(GLYPHDATA));
prfnt->cache.cjAuxCacheMem =
(cjmaxBitmap + sizeof(GLYPHDATA));
```

While he waited for a compiler to turn his code into something the computer could read, Wong wondered, "If we go ahead and fix this, what will the impact be? Could my Pagemaker fix break a hundred other applications? Are we risking the entire stability of the system on this?"

The same questions crossed Dunie's mind. It was now around midnight. He telephoned Bob Day and Jeff Brown, both of whom had worked through the early hours of Friday morning. Day, a night owl who had no children, was awake and rushed in. Brown was asleep when his call came. His wife, eight months pregnant, answered the phone. Hearing Dunie's voice displeased her, and she handed the receiver to her husband. The call upset her. Brown had been awakened by Microsoft last night and now again tonight. The conception of their second child, due in August, had deliberately been delayed because the couple had thought NT would absolutely be out of their lives by now. How much were they supposed to give this company? As Brown hung up the phone and rose to dress, his wife said nothing and tried to fall asleep. Brown himself was furious about being called back. This was a bitter ending to the project, he felt. The past year was a blur. He felt he'd missed an entire year of his three-year-old daughter's life. "Can you put a price on that?" he asked himself. "Is a million dollars worth missing one-third of a kid's life?" But Brown wasn't the rebellious type. He took orders. "In this economy I can't afford to tell Microsoft to take a jump if I disagree with the company's policies or decisions," he said. "They pay the rent, so I do what they tell me to do."

Dunie called a third tester too. He arrived with his wife, who had driven him to the office, which was thirty miles from their home. Worried about his evident exhaustion—he'd worked through the prior night—she intended to drive him home too. Carrying a pillow and a blanket, she curled up on the floor of her husband's office while he went off to test.

By the time the testers arrived, Wong and Abrash had reviewed the fix three times, stepping through the code line by line with the debugger, watching it execute in assembly language (just to make sure there was no bug in the compiler that might distort the fix). They rewrote the code in a few places, making it more efficient. Then the testers put it through its paces.

Dunie, meanwhile, took aim at the second bug, the one that seemed to cause Pagemaker to grab too much memory. He thought he might better understand the glitch if he talked with Pagemaker's chief designer, whose name escaped him. It was now after 2:00 a.m.

"If we are awake, maybe it's okay to wake him, too," Dunie said. He wanted to telephone the designer, but neither Dunie nor Pederson recalled his name. They thought his name might be Ping or Wong or maybe both. They first searched for the Pings in the telephone directory for the city of Seattle, where Aldus had its offices. Then they tried the Wongs in the directory. Ken Gregg, a test manager, called a Wong and asked for Ping. He was greeted with a blizzard of Chinese. Wrong Wong, he realized.

Then Pederson remembered he had Wong's business card somewhere. He found it, but it only listed his work number. Pederson called it and left a message. Dunie, however, wasn't ready to stop the search. He thought Wong maybe lived in the general vicinity of Microsoft, across Lake Washington to the east of Seattle, where the burgeoning suburbs of Bellevue and Redmond lay. Perusing the Eastside telephone directory, he found a Ping Wong. He called and got an answering machine, which convinced him he had the right man this time. Dunie explained he had a showstopper involving Pagemaker and left Gregg's beeper number, since Microsoft's switchboard was closed.

By then, Abrash, Snipp, Gilman Wong and Haluptzok drifted off. The fix held so far. Haluptzok was in the mood to celebrate, until he arrived at home and found Chenoa awake. "Where have you been?" she shouted and withdrew from him. Haluptzok slunk into bed, quietly defending himself.

At Building Two, the testers fought exhaustion by gobbling doughnuts and candy bars. Besides launching their tests, they plotted various possibilities that might explain NT's troubles with Pagemaker. They kept the adrenaline flowing by posting one another on their results. During the waiting and watching, they found much amusement in a toy that Brown had brought to work. He called it the Word Box. Push a button and the box uttered ribald phrases in impeccable English. The testers broke into laughter when the box said, "Up Yours."

In the midst of this, the tester's wife awoke and found her husband. "Are you done?" she asked wearily. "Almost," he said. She went back to his office and returned to sleep.

At some point before dawn, activity ceased as testers collapsed on the floor in exhaustion or went home. Dunie left disappointed that there was no reply from Ping Wong.

Actually, Dunie's call had awakened Ping. His first reaction was to consider the call a prank. Dunie had hung up before he'd reached the phone. He called Microsoft's switchboard (no answer) and the beeper number, but something went awry because no one got paged. Ping went back to sleep mystified by the call, since "other than the drama, awakening me in the middle of the night won't achieve anything," he thought. "I don't think I'd trust myself or another engineer to think clearly in the middle of night." In the morning Ping called the only person he really knew at Microsoft, Snipp, and left his home number on Snipp's office answering machine. He also said that the bug was of Aldus's own making.

About 10:00 a.m. Saturday morning the Aldus tester who'd kicked off this affair arrived at Building Two with the good news that Ping was studying the situation. The bad news was that Aldus had found another showstopper bug (embedded in Pagemaker) that hampered printing on NT.

Dunie wanted to place responsibility for this new bug on Aldus alone, but he decided not to pass the buck. "To the person trying to use NT and Pagemaker together, it won't matter who caused the bug," he reasoned. "So let's fix it. Let's have a happy ending."

So the graphics group resumed work. This time Haluptzok and another programmer did most of the heavy lifting. About dinnertime a compatibility flag was inserted in NT in order to work around the Pagemaker flaw. But before allowing the code writers to leave, Dunie insisted they explain the fix to Bob Day on the telephone. Then Day decided to see the fix for himself in the office. With Dunie hunched behind him, Day tested not only the new code but anything near it. The code passed his tests.

At 10:00 p.m. Saturday night, the graphics programmers streamed out of Building Two, leaving a fresh crew of testers behind. Dunie went home. His nine-year-old son was still awake, waiting for him. They played a few games of tabletop soccer. Then his son went to bed, and Dunie listened to Beethoven's Ninth Symphony. He thought about the team, the sweet way everyone pulled together to handle the Pagemaker mess and Cutler's phrase, "the good ole days." Suddenly he felt sad; he would miss this time in his life, just as Cutler said.

Then Dunie took a hot shower. He went to bed, but he couldn't sleep. He kept waiting for the telephone to ring. He knew the tests could reveal another serious flaw in NT, and he fought the urge to relax.

After forty-one hours of uneventful testing, Windows NT was released to manufacturing at 2:30 p.m. on Monday, July 26.

Cutler was satisfied. Once more he had confounded his doubters and proved that a team, however unwieldy, could make order out of chaos. The past year had been hard. The team had fixed an astonishing thirty thousand bugs. With so many details to consider, Cutler was "surprised as many people survived as did because the stress level was extremely high." Now it was over—for everyone.

Alone in his office, Cutler sat down at his computer and began typing a message:

> NT is officially released to manufacturing!
>
> Let me state that again—NT is released!!!!!
>
> This has been a long hard effort. You have all done a great job.
>
> Thank you all for your contribution, especially in the final three months where we managed to fix upwards of 200 bugs per day without serious regressions. It took an unparalleled effort on everyone's part to accomplish this.
>
> We met or exceeded all ship criteria!

When he finished writing, he zapped the note across the computer network that tied every member of the team together. In an instant, he had touched them all.

EPILOGUE

Sandhya and her mother fried chapatis, a thin Indian bread, and vegetables for dinner. The smell of curry filled the kitchen. The phone rang. It was her husband, Somasegar. Three hours had passed since Cutler declared the departure of Windows NT, and Somasegar was nearly finished taking stock of the last rush of testing. He called to say he'd eat dinner with the family that night, for the first time in weeks.

Sandhya's heart leapt when she heard his voice.

"It's gone," he said.

Her face flushed. The ordeal was finally over. She felt a mixture of elation and relief and gripped the phone tightly in her hand as if to squeeze every last bit of happiness from this moment.

"Amma," she called to her mother. "It's gone!"

Her mother looked blankly, as if she'd heard this all before. "Is it *really* gone?" she asked.

A chilling thought flashed through Sandhya's mind. "Soma, amma wants to know, is it really gone?"

He was too tired to mock her question. NT was gone, he replied.

Her joy restored, Sandhya told her mother, "Yes, amma, it is really gone."

On the day NT shipped, team members and their families and friends grasped that a chapter in their lives had ended. People were glad but too drained to celebrate. Having deferred a dream for so long, they felt curiously empty on realizing it.

As the days passed and the distance from NT's release grew, emotions crystallized. Some people felt remorse over not insisting the product ship sooner; they cited the relative paucity of improvements in NT during the project's final three months and argued retrospectively for shipping in April or May. While this would have yielded a buggier first version of NT, the team would have tackled the work of improving NT's speed and reducing its size (the two most obvious shortcomings of the operating system) sooner.

Others felt bitter. Darryl Havens, a founding member of the team, blamed the project for the split with his fiancée. But the experience, while painful, impressed on him the need to impose firmer limits on his work load. He believed that many of his teammates had lost their innocence in the drive to complete NT and would never again accept long hours so uncritically. "We'll never work this hard again," he vowed. But some survivors of the project seemed eerily at peace, almost as if purified by their fiery trial. "I don't regret anything," said Johanne Caron.

While the team's reactions were muted, Bill Gates was gleeful. Impressed with the care taken in polishing NT, he sent the team a congratulatory note "on a super effort" and predicted that their work "will redefine . . . the expectations people have for operating systems." Others at Microsoft echoed these sentiments, marveling at the team's accomplishment. "No other project of this scale has ever been done at Microsoft," noted one senior executive. "You should be proud of your achievement. My hat is off to you."

Perhaps the most heartfelt of these paeans came from Jim Allchin, whose Cairo team was building a massive program on top of NT. He called NT: "A truly amazing accomplishment, probably the most ambitious project ever completed successfully in the world!" It was, he added, "clearly a fantastic team effort, requiring not only your untiring dedication, but the dedication of your families and loved ones . . . truly amazing."

Outsiders reacted more coolly. Cynics, who noted that the hardware required for NT was too expensive for most people, said the program's initials stood for "Not There." Even Microsoft sent out mixed signals, touting another program in development, code-named Chicago, as the likely successor to Windows, at least in the short run. Chicago merged together DOS and Windows, overcame their most glaring shortcomings and even boasted a few of NT's advanced features, such as the ability to process thirty-two bits of data at once. Many observers predicted that Chicago—due out in late 1994 or early 1995—would steal NT's thunder.

Customers were intrigued by NT but reluctant to buy large quantities of the program. For the first year, sales were roughly half of the one million copies that Gates had expected. Slower sales reflected a natural caution on the part of serious software buyers, who never trust the first version of any complicated piece of code. Yet by May 1994, enough customers were studying NT that *Information Week*, a respected computer journal, observed, "NT is finally starting to show signs of maturation and market acceptance that may yet make it the gangbuster product Bill Gates had hoped it would be."

Despite its relatively modest sales, NT had greatly altered the computer industry. Peddlers of the Unix operating system were so frightened by NT that for the first time they seriously tried to set aside their differences, to unify the fragmented Unix standard and even find ways to run Windows programs on it. Novell, Microsoft's archrival, was so afraid of NT that it purchased a major Unix supplier. Makers of microprocessors, meanwhile, flocked to NT. At first, the program ran on the Intel, Digital and Mips families of chips. But by fall 1993, IBM, Apple, Hewlett-Packard and Motorola began adapting NT to their own chips, too. After NT was just a few months on the market, plans were in place for it to work with virtually every major computer, putting it on a path toward becoming the first universal operating system.

Microsoft's rivals grasped the essential importance of NT: The program defined the shape of software to come. "NT is like a concept car," said one. "Maybe only a few people will ever drive it, but the car will be a showpiece for innovation and will influence the whole future of operating systems." At the very least, NT promised to serve as the foundation for a variety of ambitious Microsoft programs to be released throughout the 1990s—everything from video-on-demand software (a key part of the ballyhooed "information highway"), to future desktop operating systems, to the corporate information networks that in a few years would make swapping audio and video as easy as swapping text and graphics today.

Why did NT meet most of its goals and arrive, if not on schedule, at least in time to affect the competition? How did Cutler's team avoid the loss of purpose and initiative that often burdens large teams?

Because of its scale and ambitions, the making of NT says much about the greatest organizational challenge of these times: the management of complexity. In recent years some of the world's most powerful organizations have lost their way because they can no longer track and influence the countless variables and forces affecting their course. Since the 1960s, when the U.S. government unsuccessfully fought wars against poverty and North Vietnam, confidence in large public enterprises has ebbed. The breakup of the Soviet Union illustrated that totalitarian regimes also were not exempt from the disease of Bigness. In the private sector, the decline of once rock-solid industrial giants, such as General Motors and IBM, showed that no amount of wealth and power guarantees prosperity in the face of rapid technical change.

A quarter century since the first fissures were spotted in the edifice of Bigness, it is now fashionable to dismiss big organizations as dinosaurs, incapable of managing complexity. It is hard to argue against specific examples. But this does not mean that small organizations are by definition the answer to the challenge of complexity. While the entrepreneur and the lone genius are rightly celebrated as engines of creative destruction, "small is beautiful" is a false cure for the Bigness disease. The really grand dreams of humanity increasingly require immense resources and armies of skilled people; however nimble, small agencies are ill equipped to marshal the required people and resources. Nations, no less than corporations, are becoming more reliant on organizational expertise even as faith in large organizations vanishes.

The saga of NT is a compelling instance of how one organization balances order and chaos, rules and serendipity, innovation and tradition. This task is messy, irrational and often painful. Born of conflict, innovation is dangerous because it hastens change, which is the main source of an organization's instability in the first place.

Microsoft had marked advantages when it began building NT: a monopoly position in operating systems, vast wealth and proven expertise. Yet its success was no sure thing. Organizations in possession of such assets have failed time and again at big challenges. In periods of rapid change, power, wealth and expertise often perversely bind big organizations to the past. The reasons for the completion of Windows NT lie elsewhere.

The substance and style of Microsoft's leadership was a decisive factor. Cutler sustained a mythic realm for both himself and his followers, in which the ambiguities of life were transformed into black and white, good and evil. He renewed this break with ordinary reality every time he flouted convention in word or deed. No one had a hold on him, not even Gates, the richest American. Cutler divided the world into Us and Them. This opposition echoed the profound distinction between sacred and profane: We are clean; they are dirty. We are the chosen people; they are the scorned. We will succeed; they will fail.

Cutler's grasp of the psychological power of tribalism was buttressed by his practices. He lived his spare ethic. As player-coach, he promoted the goals of NT and moved the team closer to the finish line. By getting into the muck with his colleagues, he gained and kept great credibility, though at times he cruelly turned on those who crossed him. His anger, while sometimes a liability, at least showed how much he cared about his job and the outcome of the project. His devotion to duty, fierce stubbornness in the face of repeated setbacks and loud wish to do something stupendous made him an irresistible figure to many of those around him. Even his penchant for shunning management matters, while sometimes sowing confusion, struck many as statesmanlike. As he said, "I'm no empire builder."

Cutler's handlers were a big help. Paul Maritz protected Cutler from undue criticism and resisted the urge to reform him. He identified strategic and tactical issues that Cutler ignored. Maritz was Cutler's eyes and ears onto the market. When conditions changed, he married NT to Windows, which instantly pushed the project from the periphery to the center of Microsoft's future. And Maritz kept the peace by exacting from Cutler no ritual expressions of obedience. Nor did he insist on public credit for sorting out the project.

Gates, meanwhile, gave Cutler the resources to finish NT; at $150 million it was the most expensive PC program ever. Gates's knowledge of the marketplace enabled him to serve as a counterweight against Cutler's obsession with the inner workings of software. Gates also knew when *not* to interfere. It is fashionable to praise those chief executives who stay directly involved in their businesses; by this measure Gates scores high. But in his handling of NT, he evinced a new awareness of the limits of his authority. Too much involvement on the part of a chief executive holds its perils. At key times, Gates ceded authority to Maritz and Cutler in a way he had rarely done before on major projects. This reflected his awareness of the growing diversity of software. No one person—not even Gates—can maintain a deep knowledge of every aspect of this burgeoning field. From the start, Gates signaled his distance from NT when he hired Cutler and his Digital gang. This allowed Cutler to create his own company *within* Microsoft. While risky, this was probably the only way Cutler could be absorbed by Microsoft; had he joined alone, his severe criticisms of the company and his imperiousness would have doomed his chances of success by souring potential allies.

Strong, secure leadership brought the project only so far; effective teamwork was just as important. But it was teamwork of an uncommon kind. Most people think of teamwork as precluding individual expression. Teams might be fine for football clubs or armies, but in the creative realm the individual is preeminent. In this light, creative work is antithetical to teamwork, which depends on cooperation, conformity and compromise for the "good" of the group.

Perhaps this positive notion of teamwork is a casualty of the great divide between technical and humanistic cultures. In technical communities the team gives an individual's work its bedrock value; the complexity of the system is such that each single piece holds little meaning outside the whole. Teams retain and spread technical wisdom in much the same way that preliterate people preserve the folklore of a tribe. In both cases the wisdom is kept in people's heads. Indeed, there are many similarities in the way members of technical teams and preliterate tribes communicate. Technical advance is now so rapid that printed matter is outdated in a stunningly short time. Fields of knowledge are so specialized and change so fast today that no manuals or textbooks can reliably describe central practices. Code writers thus must depend heavily on teammates for know-how and measures of progress.

But teamwork does not necessarily require the surrender of individuality. The NT team included many stridently opinionated people. Without violating the mores of the team, they broke old rules and made new ones in response to shifting circumstances. They felt free to criticize their managers or seek the advice of people who had no formal responsibility for their work. They rarely asked permission before taking important initiatives that they believed would improve NT. And they unapologetically ignored those prohibitions that seemed nonsensical.

Many technical teams, while encouraging conflict, spawn bureaucracies. To protect themselves against incorrect decisions, they form committees to weigh important matters. These committees spawn subcommittees, and before long a straightforward proposal is subject to a lengthy review by people who aren't actually doing the work. The NT team never fell prey to this stultifying process. The team's one regular meeting occurred each morning, and usually only managers attended. Meetings of the entire team were rare. Most technical discussions unfolded casually, and code writers usually held sway over their work. Outside review came only sporadically.

To be sure, the NT team had its flaws. At times more deliberation would have helped. Work was sometimes wasted because managers were too busy to coordinate the various pieces under their purview. There were too many false starts, too many dead ends explored, too much confusion and duplication. Tension between the team's needs and an individual's desires sometimes seemed pointless, no more than a display of ego bashing. And too few people asked whether an alternative existed to neglecting their families, their loved ones and themselves. Managers turned a blind eye to the psychological wounds suffered by their people and exacerbated the situation by not hiring more people to help finish the job. This kept expenses down but raised the psychic toll. If this was not cruel, it was shortsighted. It fueled the widespread feeling among team members that they must make big money now because at their breakneck pace they might not last much longer on the job.

With the release of NT, some team members naturally moved on. Jonathan Manheim left to manage the Chicago project's test group. Kyle Shannon, bidding farewell to the Build Lab, took a job helping Microsoft to sell computer makers on NT. Lee Smith, the team's highest-ranking woman, left to pursue amateur rowing full time. Chuck Whitmer quit graphics and traveled to Turkey, where he convinced his lover's family to sanction a marriage. The newlyweds then split their time between Europe and Turkey while she finished her doctoral studies.

A few others were forced out of Microsoft, as Walt Moore (now programming for a company run by his brother) had been a year before. Gates boasted to colleagues that every year he wanted Microsoft to fire the weakest 5 percent of its programmers. He thought this would prevent the company from growing moldy with age. But the forced departures, coming on the heels of such an arduous project, seemed distasteful to some of those who remained. "If we don't complain about these people, we could be next," said one team member who felt Microsoft was sending an ominous message to its better code writers: Fall down on the job and you're out. While he hardly endorsed poor work, this team member argued that there were many understandable reasons why a solid programmer might slip for awhile. "They told us *all* not to worry about the future. And this is our reward."

The bulk of the team stuck around for the sequel to NT, joining Cairo, Allchin's project. Cairo was ready to crystallize the techniques that hopefully would realize Gates's dream of "information at your fingertips." Cairo's code would sit atop NT, so it would naturally benefit from the talents and experience of NT's creators. It made sense to Maritz, chief of Microsoft's operating-systems division, to bring the two teams together.

But a finished Cairo program wasn't expected until late 1995 at the earliest. By fall 1994 Microsoft planned to release Daytona, the streamlined and speedier version of the original NT. Cutler wished to begin work immediately on Daytona because he was so troubled by NT's "too big, too slow" image that he wanted to place the full weight of his veteran tribe on the problem of trimming the memory requirements and increasing the speed of his program. While proud of NT, Cutler was disappointed in it, too. "Every first release of an operating system is a compromise," he said. "So it is with NT."

To ensure significant improvements to NT, Cutler wished to hold his team together for another six months to a year. But Maritz feared that maintaining two separate teams (NT and Cairo) would hamper progress on Cairo, which was still struggling for an identity. With a single team, work could proceed on the Daytona release of NT, but more people could tackle Cairo.

Even before NT shipped, Maritz decided in favor of a single team with Allchin as its head. Cutler would run Daytona—the largest group on the combined team—but answer to Allchin. A rival of Cutler's was chosen by Allchin to oversee all Cairo coding.

Cutler fumed about the decision. The end of a project was always a difficult time for him. He always pushed to outdo himself, never lingering for long over his achievements and eschewing any examination of his motives and psychology. "My motivation is I like to do this stuff. I just like to do this stuff," he said. "I like to get [my code] done and see it work." Rather than monumental, his concept was Sisyphean. He dared not speculate about the benefit of his labors for society. Nor did he concern himself with his place in the history of technology. He only looked forward, abolishing the past as he went on. "This isn't the end," he said. "Ten years from now we'll be designing another system, and everyone will be sitting around bemoaning that it will have to be compatible with NT. That will happen."

Fearing Cutler's resignation, Gates made a personal plea to keep him at Microsoft. He and Cutler had spent scant time together in recent years, so Gates wanted to make explicit how much he valued Cutler's contribution. "It was an opportunity for me to learn from him what he found frustrating," Gates said. "And I made absolutely clear to him what a great job he'd done and how important I thought it was for him to stick around."

Cutler was grateful for the compliments, but unswayed. The euphoria over Cairo was misplaced, he believed. Why rush Cairo? Completing it would be "an awful lot of work" and would detract from "providing NT all of the polish" Cutler felt it needed. A proud father, Cutler wanted to help his child grow up. In the few weeks since sales of NT began, the computer magazines had attacked the program with the familiar refrain: too big, too slow. Cutler couldn't accept making Cairo a higher priority than the Daytona release of NT. He decided to quit.

When he learned of Cutler's intentions, Lou Perazzoli assumed his familiar role. He sought to moderate Cutler's impulses. Perazzoli was Cutler's most trusted lieutenant, and perhaps the lone member of the team confident and knowledgeable enough to change his mind. Perazzoli took the merger with Cairo in stride. Even without Cutler, "life would go on," he realized. Others would step forward in his place. Yet it seemed senseless for Cutler to depart. Perazzoli told this to Maritz, arguing that "we can survive without Cutler but he's a doer and we need more people who can get things done." Now Perazzoli told Cutler he was "an idiot" to quit. "Just give it six months, and [the plan for Cairo] will collapse under its own weight," he said. When Cairo fell behind schedule, Cutler would gain the chance to polish NT after all.

Cutler was not persuaded by Perazzoli's reasoning. In late July he flew to Ireland for a vacation. When he returned a week later, he still had not decided whether to stay or leave Microsoft. By now, Gates fretted over the possibility of Cutler's departure. Wasn't there a way to keep the NT and Cairo teams separate? Maritz nixed the option. Making one final stab at retaining Cutler, Gates met with him and explained there were "damn good engineering reasons" for merging the NT and Cairo teams under Allchin.

That did it. Cutler relented. He felt the hunger of the chase again and the willingness to "make a pretty big compromise." He agreed to stay at Microsoft and work on both Daytona and Cairo. As for

Allchin's position as chief, Cutler considered this a formality. He thought he was the linchpin of the new team. "I personally don't think there is any way [Microsoft] can pull off Cairo without me," he said.

Cutler was proved right. In March 1994, Allchin—distressed by slow progress on Cairo—gave Cutler authority over all Cairo code. It was the "good ole days" all over again.

A NOTE ON SOURCES

All of the quotations in this book are from author interviews or memos by participants except the following:

The quotation on pages 10–11 of chapter 1, beginning, "What about the poor programmer?" is from a lecture by E. W. Dijkstra to the Association of Computing Machinery, August 14, 1972.

The quotation on page 12 of chapter 1, beginning, "Now anyone with a logical mind and the desire could learn to program a computer," is from Stan Augarten, *Bit by Bit: An Illustrated History of Computers* (1984).

The quotation on page 17 of chapter 1, "guiding, arguing, fidgeting and creating the computer strategies that [turned Digital into] IBM's strongest challenger," is from Glenn Rifkin and George Harrar, *The Ultimate Entrepreneur: The Story of Ken Olsen and Digital Equipment Corp.* (1990), p. 41.

The quotation on page 18 of chapter 1, beginning, "They started out quietly, with fifteen minute overviews of the agenda," is from Rifkin and Harrar, p. 140.

The quotation by Gates on page 24 of chapter 2, "being a philosophical, depressed guy, trying to figure out what I was doing with my life," is from Michael W. Miller, "How 2 Computer Nuts Transformed Industry Before Messy Breakup," *The Wall Street Journal*, Aug. 27, 1986.

The quotation on page 31 of chapter 2, "a crazy idea," is from Julie Pitta, "Microsoft's Other Boy Genius," *Forbes*, Aug. 2, 1993.

The quotation on page 96 of chapter 5, beginning "the castor oil of programming," is from Gerald M. Weinberg, *The Psychology of Computer Programming* (1971), p. 262.

The quotation on page 249 of chapter 10, beginning "If one character, one pause, of the incantation is not strictly in proper form," is from Frederick P. Brooks, *The Mythical Man-Month: Essays on Software Engineering* (1975), p. 8.

The following people were interviewed for this book:

Michael Abrash	Bob Day
Jim Allchin	Terri Day
Brian Andrew	Kent Diamond
Ellen Aycock	Mitch Duncan
John Balciunas	Moshe Dunie
Steve Ballmer	Matthew Felton
Gordon Bell	Thomas Fenwick
Julie Bennett	Eric Fogelin
Jeff Brown	Asmus Freytag
Paul Butzi	William Gates
Johanne Caron	Michael Glass
Steve Cathcart	Rob Glazer
Chuck Chan	Ben Goetter
Larry Churches	Roger Gourd
Mark Cligget	Ken Gregg
Christine Comaford	Chenoa Haluptzok
Helen Custer	Patrick Haluptzok
Arleta Cutler	Ralf Harteneck
Bonnie Cutler	Darryl Havens
David Cutler	Jeff Havens

Roger Heinen

Dan Hinsley

Orson Hoeksema

Jim Horne

Jane Howell

Naveen Jain

Jawad Kahki

Nadine Kano

Jim Kelly

Gary Kimura

Rikki Kirzner

Eric Kutter

Jon Lazarus

Chuck Lenzmeier

Val Lenzmeier

Gordon Letwin

Joe Linn

Dominic Livedoti

Keith Logan

Cindy Lucovsky

Mark Lucovsky

Scott Ludwig

Jonathan Manheim

Leigh Manheim

Paul Maritz

Don McLaren

Tom Miller

Robert Miller

Walt Moore

Robert Muglia

Nathan Myhrvold

Peter Neuport

Mike O'Leary

Kirk Olynyk

Larry Osterman

Valorie Osterman

John Parchem

Stu Parsell

Leif Pederson

Lou Perazzoli

Roel Pieper

Trevor Porter

Rick Rashid

Bob Rinne

Steve Rowe

Darryl Rubin

Eric Schmidt

Benn Schrieber

Andrew Schulman

Kyle Shannon

Lin Shaw

Rob Short

Donald Sidoroff

Brad Silverberg

Charles Simonyi

Lee Smith

David Snipp

S. Somasegar

Sandhya Somasegar

John Spencer

Larry Spencer

Greg Stepanets

Carl Stork

Therese Stowell

David Thompson

David Treadwell

Andre Vachon

Brian Valentine

Cliff Van Dyke

Dwayne Walker

Bonnie (Cutler) Ward

Colin Watson

Manny Weiser

David Weld

Arden White
Susan Whitkoph
Chuck Whitmer
Chris Williams
Bryan Willman
Lon Willoughby
Callie Wilson

Ann Winblad
Catherine Wissink
Gilman Wong
Ping Wong
Steve Wood
Mark Zbikowski

ACKNOWLEDGMENTS

My account of the birth of a computer program stems from a front-page article I wrote for *The Wall Street Journal*. Were it not for the encouragement I received from my *Journal* colleagues, I could not have written this book. I wish to thank especially G. Christian Hill, San Francisco bureau chief; John Brecher, page one editor; and Paul Steiger, managing editor.

In researching this book I was helped by many Microsoft employees and their families. All these people unconditionally shared their lives with me, answering questions about professional and personal matters. I owe each of them my deepest gratitude. In "A Note on Sources," I provide a complete list of those interviewed. Every interview with a Microsoft employee occurred "for attribution," meaning I am free to identify the speaker if I wish. (In the text, when I choose not to attribute a quote, it is almost always for reasons of style.) A promise of anonymity covers small parts of a few interviews with team members.

Microsoft Corp. neither sanctioned, reviewed nor approved the contents of this book. At my request, Paul Maritz, the senior executive in charge of NT, promised in a memo to Microsoft employees that no punitive action would be taken against anyone who assisted me. This assurance relieved the anxiety of numerous current and former employees who wished to see a chronicle of their labors.

For their uncommon sensitivity, respect and good cheer, I thank Moshe Dunie, Lou Perazzoli and Helen Custer. While I am solely responsible for this book, their patient explanations enriched my knowledge.

During the editing of this book, Sandhya Somasegar was killed instantly in an automobile crash. She was twenty-five years old. Her death on March 27, 1994, stunned and saddened everyone who knew her.

In the course of my research, David N. Cutler graciously endured lengthy face-to-face interviews, telephone conversations and electronic mail exchanges with me. He also gave me much information about his career and selected memos he wrote during the making of NT. (I obtained additional memos through other sources.) I am grateful for his help.

For help in arranging certain interviews and obtaining background material, Claire LaMotta, Cheri Johnson, Pam Edstrom and Jon Lazarus were invaluable.

Wendy Lustbader and Mark Kavanagh reviewed various drafts of this book, generously providing much advice and guidance. Their aid was greatly appreciated. Paul Saffo, Jack Prizmich, Dave Winer and David Readerman also helped at crucial stages in this project.

Charlotte Sheedy, my agent, offered intelligent counsel, as did my editors at The Free Press: Joyce Seltzer, Marion Maneker and the late Erwin Glikes.

My wife, Honorah, and son, Liam, brought joy, solace and many diversions as I researched and wrote this book. Words are only a poor payment on my debt to them.

G. P. Z.
June 1994

INDEX

295